ALSO BY JOHN S.D. EISENHOWER

Yanks: The Epic Story of the American Army in World War I
Agent of Destiny: The Life and Times of General Winfield Scott
Intervention: The United States and the Mexican Revolution, 1913–1917
So Far from God: The U.S. War with Mexico, 1846–1848
Allies: Pearl Harbor to D-Day
*The Bitter Woods: The Dramatic Story, Told at All Echelons, from Supreme
Command to Squad Leader, of the Crisis That Shook the Western
Coalition: Hitler's Surprise Ardennes Offensives*

*Dwight D. Eisenhower announces the end of World War II in Europe, May 7, 1945.
With him is his deputy, Air Chief Marshal Sir Arthur Tedder.*

GENERAL IKE

A Personal Reminiscence

❧

JOHN S.D. EISENHOWER

FREE PRESS

NEW YORK LONDON TORONTO SYDNEY SINGAPORE

fP

FREE PRESS

A Division of Simon & Schuster, Inc.
1230 Avenue of the Americas
New York, NY 10020

For information about special discounts for bulk purchases,
please contact Simon & Schuster Special Sales:
1-800-456-6798 or business@simonandschuster.com

Manufactured in the United States of America

10 9 8 7 6 5 4 3 2

Library of Congress Cataloging-in-Publication Data

Eisenhower, John S.D.
    General Ike : a personal reminiscence / John S.D. Eisenhower.
      p. cm.
    Includes bibliographical references and index.
    1. Eisenhower, Dwight D. (Dwight David), 1890–1969—Military
leadership. 2. Generals—United States—Biography. 3. United
States Army—Biography. 4. World War, 1939–1945—Biography.
5. Eisenhower, Dwight D. (Dwight David), 1890–1969—Friends
and associates.

E836.E425 2003
940.54/0092 B—dc21   2003041045

ISBN 0-7432-4474-5

To Joanne

CONTENTS

Author's Note

Dwight D. Eisenhower, Supreme Commander, General of the Army, and Thirty-fourth President of the United States, was one of the dynamic and influential men of the twentieth century. As his only son to survive early childhood, I was able to observe him in different circumstances, sometimes official and sometimes intimate. Though I have previously avoided writing a book devoted solely to him, I have, through the years, read enough misleading material, most of it written by people who have no idea of what he was really like, that I finally decided to record my own view of him. Some of my conclusions are based on what I observed, but much stems from what I have learned in the course of my own writings. No matter how biased in his favor my slant may be, it cannot add much to the confusion that already exists.

I never called my father "Ike" to his face. It was always "Dad." Still, in this book I'll always refer to him by his popular nickname, partly for convenience and even more because "Ike" was, to all intents and purposes, his real name. That short, pithy epithet that connotes "roughneck" in the Old West was his. It served him well as an icebreaker in the Army. It was even more useful in politics. Eisenhower was the only President out of forty-three as of this writing to be burdened with a last name of four syllables. Can you imagine the public chanting, "We like Eisenhower"? Or even "We like Dwight"? Ike was more than a name; it was his persona.

By no stretch of the imagination is this book a comprehensive biography of Ike, nor is it even a history of the battles he fought. Instead, my essays will deal almost exclusively with Ike's relations with his associates, for the simple reason that the facets of his personality appear differently depending on the individual he was dealing with at a given time. Ike was one man when assigning a mission to General George Patton, another when interacting with Field Marshal Bernard Montgomery, and yet another when working with Prime Minister Winston Churchill.

Admittedly, the structure I have chosen brings with it certain difficulties. One is the matter of chronology. More serious is the fact that various incidents in the Second World War appear in more than one chapter. To avoid dreary repetition, therefore, I have tried to avoid covering the details of a single incident in more than one place. Some overlap is, unfortunately, inevitable, and some incidents must be at least mentioned more than once in order for each chapter to stand on its own.

Ike had two separate careers, the military and the political. In my own mind, there were really two Ikes. The military Ike faded from the picture when he returned to the United States from Frankfurt in November of 1945, ending his occupation duties in Germany. The Ike of the next quarter century was the political Ike, or at least the politico-military Ike.

I have chosen to write about the military Ike, even though the consequences of his activities during the Second World War often carried over into his presidency. The main reason I have done so is that I know more about Ike's career as a soldier than I do his career as a civilian. I am also convinced that Ike's military career was far more important to him personally than his political life. Though I believe that he was an excellent President, especially in his role as commander-in-chief, he did not worry much about what his political opponents said about him in that position. When it came to his military judgments, however, he was vociferous in defending the validity of his decisions. As he contemplated his career at the end of his life, nearly all the men he considered "great" came from the war days, not the political era. To me, at least, Ike's place in history will hinge far more on his days in uniform than on his days in the White House.

With those limitations in mind I have given a son's view of a great military leader—highly intelligent, strong, forceful, kind, yet as human as the rest of us.

An Atlas of Turning Points in Ike's Command

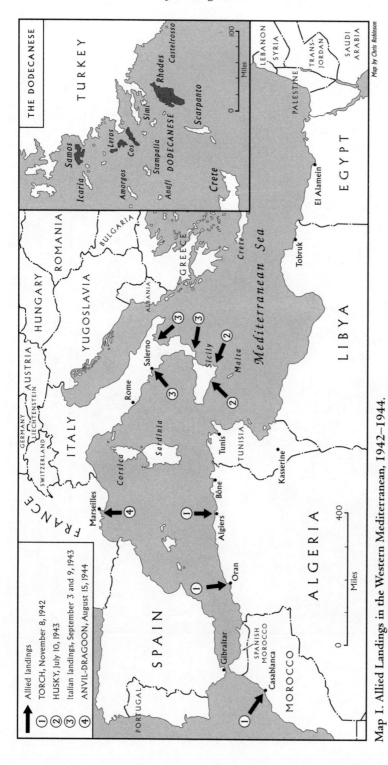

Map I. Allied Landings in the Western Mediterranean, 1942–1944.

Ike spent over a year in the Mediterranean, from November 7, 1942, to Christmas of 1943. This map shows the location of the TORCH landings (November 1942), the HUSKY landings (July 1943), the landings in Italy (September 1943), and ANVIL-DRAGOON, August 15, 1944. Insert shows the location of the Dodecanese, so important to Winston Churchill.

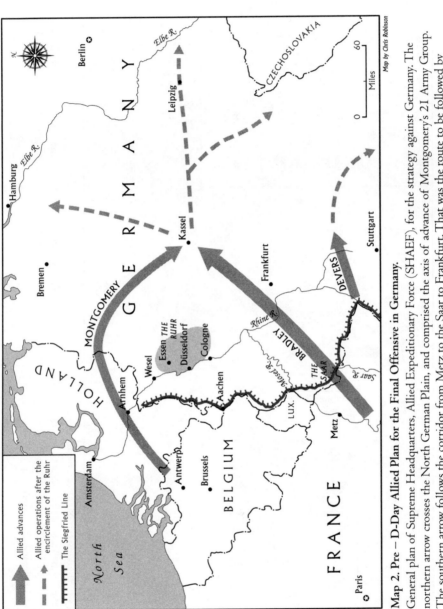

Map 2. Pre – D-Day Allied Plan for the Final Offensive in Germany.
General plan of Supreme Headquarters, Allied Expeditionary Force (SHAEF), for the strategy against Germany. The northern arrow crosses the North German Plain, and comprised the axis of advance of Montgomery's 2I Army Group. The southern arrow follows the corridor from Metz to the Saar to Frankfurt. That was the route to be followed by Patton's Third Army, under Bradley's 12 Army Group. The plan closely resembles the campaign as it later unfolded.

Map by Chris Robinson

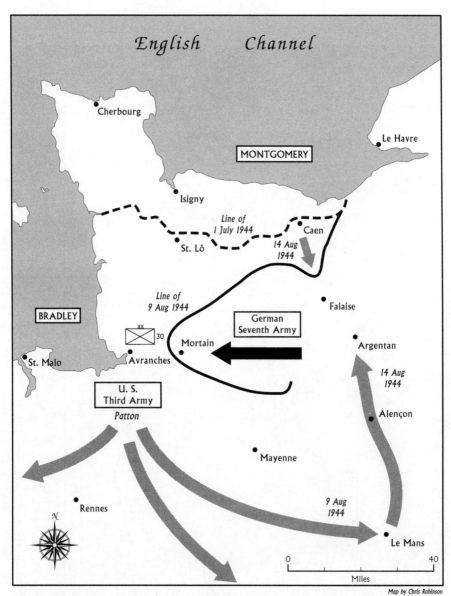

Map 3. Breakout in Normandy, August 1944.

The Avranches corridor risk, undertaken by Ike and Bradley, with Monty's concurrence, on August 8, 1944. Line of July 1 indicates the front when I returned from my visit with Ike.

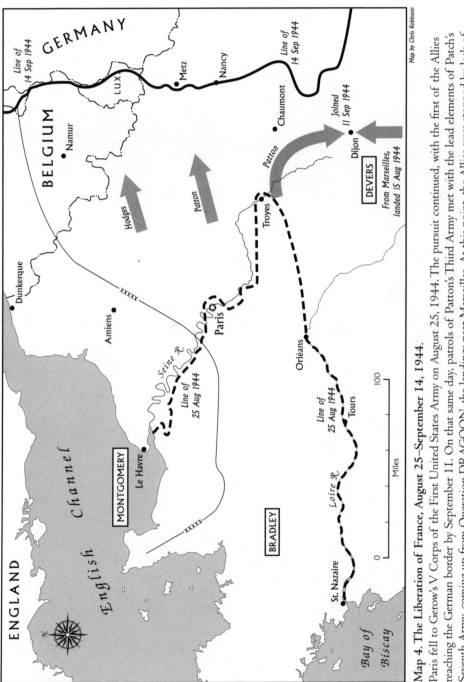

Map by Chris Robinson

Map 4. The Liberation of France, August 25–September 14, 1944.
Paris fell to Gerow's V Corps of the First United States Army on August 25, 1944. The pursuit continued, with the first of the Allies reaching the German border by September 11. On that same day, patrols of Patton's Third Army met with the lead elements of Patch's Seventh Army, coming up from Operation DRAGOON, the landings near Marseilles. At this point, the Allies were stopped by lack of supply. Performance had vastly exceeded the expectations of the logisticians.

Map by Chris Robinson

Map 5. Plans for the Liberation of Holland, September 1944.

With France liberated in early September 1944, Ike's attention centered on the north, in the sector of Montgomery's 21 Army Group. There were two important objectives, (1) the clearing of the Schelde Estuary of German forces, thus opening Antwerp for Allied shipping, and (2) MARKET-GARDEN, an effort to secure a bridgehead over the Rhine River, bypassing the Siegfried Line. Of the two, Ike was most anxious to clear the Schelde, but Monty assured Ike that both operations could be executed together. They could not. The Schelde was not cleared until nearly two months after the failure of MARKET-GARDEN.

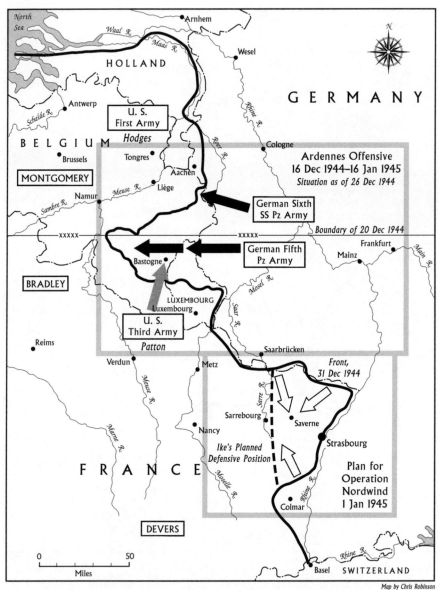

Map 6. Hitler's Counteroffensives, December 1944 and January 1945.

This map of the winter campaigns of 1944–1945 shows two operations, Hitler's Ardennes Campaign (Battle of the Bulge) and his subsequent campaign into Alsace, called Operation NORDWIND. The map of the Ardennes campaign shows the boundary that Ike drew between Montgomery and Bradley on December 20, 1944. It also shows Patton's drive northward to relieve Bastogne, the decision resulting from the Verdun meeting of December 23. The important point to note in the NORDWIND map is the defensive position that Ike planned in order to save divisions for the Ardennes campaign—and which would have given up Strasbourg. Fortunately, NORDWIND fizzled.

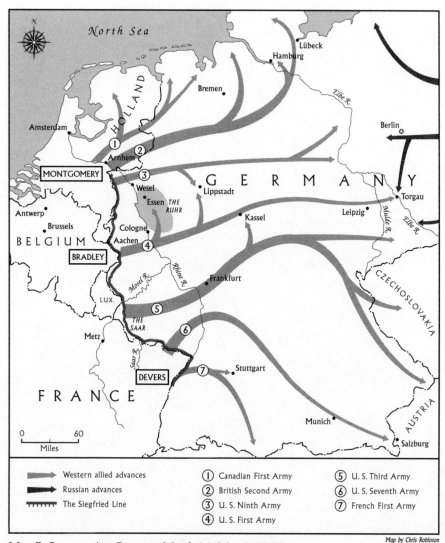

Map by Chris Robinson

Map 7. Overrunning Germany, March 24–May 8, 1945.
After the Western Allies crossed the Rhine River on March 23 and 24, 1945, the end of
the war was only six weeks away. This map shows how closely Ike's final plan followed the
original SHAEF plan, made back in London a year earlier. In the last week of the war,
however, Ike allowed political considerations to enter his planning. Since there had been
no previous agreement between the Allies and the Russians on occupation zones in
Denmark and Austria, he sent Montgomery northward to occupy Lübeck, thus
eliminating the possibility of a Russian occupation of Denmark. In the south he sent
Patton as far as possible into Austria.

GENERAL IKE

*Three early influences (left to right): Fox Conner, George S. Patton,
and John J. Pershing.*

I

EARLY INFLUENCES

George S. Patton, Fox Conner, and John J. Pershing

There are no "great men" as we understood that expression when we were
shavers. The man whose brain is so all-embracing in its grasp of events, so
infallible in its logic, and so swift in formulation of perfect decisions, is
only a figment of the imagination. [Yet] some men achieve goals for which
numbers have been striving—and it is interesting to look over those who
have attracted special attention in some field, to try to make an estimate of
their character, their abilities, and their weaknesses.

—DWIGHT D. EISENHOWER[1]

PATTON

One dark night in late 1919, a lone automobile crept slowly along
the few miles of unlit, two-lane blacktop road leading into Camp
Meade, Maryland. In the car were two young Army officers, each

grasping a Colt automatic pistol in his hand, both peering intently out in the blackness. Ike and his friend George Patton were expecting, at least hoping, to be accosted. As Ike told the story with a touch of swagger in later years, "We had been told that the road was full of highwaymen. We wanted to run into one so we could see the guy's face when he found himself looking down the barrels of two guns."

They were disappointed, so they later claimed, that the highwayman never appeared. It is fortunate that the intended victim had chosen to take the evening off, because the careers of Ike and George could never have profited from this caper; they might have wound up in a good deal of trouble. Whose idea it was to go bandit-hunting will never be known, but both men were bored with their lives as temporary bachelors in a camp that lacked family quarters, and they shared the emotional letdown that afflicted the whole Army following the exciting days of the First World War. This was Ike's and Patton's way of entertaining themselves.

Those were the days when Patton's influence on Ike was at its peak. In his brief period of military service, Ike had already made close, lifelong friends, especially when serving with the 19th Infantry on the Mexican border in 1916. Among them were Leonard T. Gerow, Wade H. Haislip, and Walton H. Walker. However, none of these men exerted the impact on Ike's development remotely comparable to that of George Patton.

Patton was already a noted man in the Army. Graduated from West Point in 1909 and commissioned in the Cavalry, he had received public accolades for his daring exploits as a member of General John J. Pershing's Punitive Expedition into Mexico in 1916. He enjoyed close personal ties with Pershing, based at least partly on Pershing's affection for Patton's comely sister, Nita. Patton made the most of that personal connection, using it to obtain a berth in Pershing's original entourage to France in June of 1917. Once in France, however, Patton had quickly perceived that the Army's fledgling Tank Corps promised shining personal opportunities, and he easily secured the general's blessing to leave his personal staff to join the tanks. As an energetic thirty-year-old major, he quickly rose to the command of the 1st Tank Brigade, the largest United States tank unit in France. His time in battle was short; the St. Mihiel campaign, in which he participated, lasted only two days, and he suffered a wound in the leg on the first day of the Meuse-Argonne campaign in September 1918. Nevertheless, his reputation had been made.

Adding to Patton's larger-than-life image in the Army was the fact that he was personally wealthy, and his wife was even wealthier. His consequent lack of need for his Army pay had exerted a considerable effect, no doubt, on his attitude. The Army was a hobby with Patton, though a mighty serious hobby.*

Ike had no such aura attached to his name, though he was also recognized as a promising young officer. He had been a successful organizer and trainer of troops during the First World War, and in that capacity had earned a prestigious Distinguished Service Medal for his energy, zeal, and leadership in commanding the Army's Heavy Tank Brigade at Camp Colt, Pennsylvania. But though DSMs were extremely rare among young officers—Ike was only three years out of West Point at the time—Ike's accomplishments were performed in the United States. Nothing achieved in stateside training could compete in prestige with a few days of combat service in France.

Nevertheless, despite the disparity between Ike's and Patton's positions in the Army "club," Ike was far from intimidated by Patton's éclat. Ike's admiration was based strictly on Patton's generous nature and soldierly qualities. And Patton, on his part, recognized leadership qualities in an officer six years his junior. In his effusive way, he predicted a future war in which Ike would be the Robert E. Lee and Patton would be Ike's Stonewall Jackson. Eventually Patton's prediction would prove at least partially correct; Ike would be Patton's superior— and have to use every bit of diplomacy in his makeup to keep Patton performing his role as a combat leader.

On duty, Patton and Ike were officially co-equals, both commanders of tank brigades under the Chief of the Tank Corps, Brigadier General Samuel Rockenbach. The entire tank strength of the Army consisted of those two brigades, one light and one heavy. Colonel Patton commanded the brigade of light tanks, equipped with the small French

---

*Patton owned a string of polo ponies, and during the 1930s an aristocratic and indulgent Army permitted him to take them with him when he was transferred from post to post. He and a friend were both excused from the course in equitation at the Command and General Staff School at Fort Leavenworth in order to exercise his stable.

Renault tanks, and Lieutenant Colonel Eisenhower commanded the heavy brigade, equipped with the American-built Mark VIII Liberties, designed as support for infantry. Though the two brigades were organized for different missions, all the tankers considered themselves to be members of one family, and they soon established an informal school that prevailed on Patton and others to share their wartime experiences in a series of lectures. Many members of the group contributed, and Ike, as a brigade commander, was one. He later recalled with pride that Patton habitually attended his lectures, "taking extensive notes."[2]

Together, Ike and Patton set out to develop a doctrine for the future use of the tank in warfare, which they believed had not been sufficiently exploited in the recent conflict. Running parallel with such other thinkers as the British J.F.C. Fuller and the German Heinz Guderian, they jointly concluded that the tank had a role in the wars of the future that transcended its traditional mission of supporting the infantry, no matter how vital that was. They visualized armored formations operating independently, attacking in masses and breaking through an enemy's line and tearing up his rear. They took a special interest in a new tank developed by an engineer named J. Walter Christie, a vehicle that could move at twenty miles per hour, in contrast to the three miles per hour previously considered sufficient to keep up with the infantry. In the blush of their enthusiasm, both Patton and Ike wrote articles for the *Infantry Journal* supporting their ideas.

Eisenhower's article was radical for an infantryman. It called for a new tank armed with a six-pounder main gun as well as its standard machine guns. To replace the clumsy, inefficient machines of St. Mihiel and the Meuse-Argonne, he advocated a "speedy, reliable, and efficient engine of destruction. . . . In the future," he went on, "tanks will be called upon to use their ability of swift movement and great fire power . . . against the flanks of attacking forces."[3]

Prescient though Ike's article may have been, it was not admired by certain authorities in Washington. Notable among those authorities was the Chief of Infantry, who was highly displeased with Ike's advocating a role for the tank beyond that of supporting the chief's own doughboys. He called the young upstart on the carpet and threatened him with court-martial if he expressed his views further in writing. The Chief of Cavalry did much the same with Patton. The Army soon went even further: it abolished the Tank Corps as an independent branch and incorporated it into the Infantry. Patton requested transfer back to the Cavalry, and Ike, already an Infantry officer, merely accepted reassignment.[4]

George and Ike parted ways, not to serve together for another twenty years. They remained friends, but on a far more casual basis. Nevertheless, Ike remembered Patton with admiration and affection as an outstanding officer who, despite his eccentricities, was a man who loved to fight, a valuable potential associate in the future war they all expected.

My first, brief exposure to Colonel Patton occurred in the early 1930s, probably about 1933. At that time Ike was a major, assigned to duty in the War Department, and our small family lived in the Wyoming Apartments, on Columbia Road, a few blocks north of the State-War-Navy Building. One Sunday afternoon my parents announced that the three of us were going to drive out to nearby Fort Myer, Virginia, to visit the Pattons. This was not a commonplace event, and the afternoon was memorable for an eleven-year-old boy.

The officers' quarters at Fort Myer are neither large nor elaborate—not even Quarters Number One, where the Army Chief of Staff lives. And Patton, as executive officer of the 3d Cavalry Regiment, was not at the top of the priority list for housing. But in whatever quarters were assigned to the Patton family, the interior was always embellished into something spectacular. One wall of the living room was covered by a great bookshelf full of gleaming silver cups, trophies won by various members of the Patton family in the horse shows that kept the Army entertained during peacetime.

During our short call, Colonel Patton occupied center stage in his glistening living room, holding forth on various subjects, always conscious of his captive and generally admiring audience. On such social occasions he confined his colorful language to mere blasphemy, saving his earthy, four-letter words for the troops. Nevertheless, the spectacle was a source of wonderment to a boy who was being raised in a strict household, a boy who had heard such words only from his friends in the schoolyard.

The Pattons had three children. The two daughters, Beatrice and Ruth Ellen, were a little older than their son George, and me, and they sat properly as part of the group of adults. But George, a lad of about ten, received special attention. Called into the room before the adults, he was asked a couple of leading questions, to which he responded with colorful, well-rehearsed swear words. Colonel Patton beamed.

It would be years later, in Britain during World War II, before I would see the elder Patton again, though young George and I were cadets at West Point together a decade after this visit.

FOX CONNER

George Patton's influence on Ike was significant, but his greatest contribution to Ike's development was indirect, his role in bringing his friend under the tutelage of his true mentor, Brigadier General (later Major General) Fox Conner.

The introduction appeared to happen largely by chance. One day in October of 1920, Patton and his wife Beatrice entertained a group of friends at a Sunday brunch, and both the Conners and the Eisenhowers were among the guests. I doubt that Ike had ever met Conner before, but he certainly knew something of the older man's outstanding military reputation. Conner had gone to France with General Pershing as a member of the Inspector General Section of AEF headquarters. His abilities as a planner soon attracted notice however, and by the time American troops went into action in 1918 he was Pershing's Operations Officer (G-3). Though only forty-four years of age at the end of the World War, Conner had attained the rank of brigadier general and had subsequently kept his rank despite the general cutback of the Army after the Armistice. At the time of his visit to Camp Meade, Conner was still a member of Pershing's phantom AEF Staff, which had been maintained on paper so that four-star General Pershing would not be forced to serve under two-star General Peyton C. March for the duration of March's term as Chief of Staff of the Army.

The brunch hosted by the Pattons far transcended a mere social gathering. Apparently the work that Patton and Ike were doing with their respective tank brigades had come to Conner's attention, and the general may have seized on this outing as an opportunity to take a look at what was going on. Whether planned on Conner's part or not, he wasted little time after the guests left the luncheon table in asking the two younger officers to conduct him around Camp Meade and to show him their tank training site. This they did enthusiastically—very few senior officers were giving them much by way of encouragement—and they spent the afternoon setting forth their thoughts and reporting on the status of their training. Conner, for his part, asked penetrating questions.

Ike's presentation must have impressed Conner, because within a few weeks the general sent him a message offering a plum of an assignment. General Pershing would soon become Army Chief of Staff, he advised, and the phantom AEF staff would go out of existence. Conner, on release, expected to be named to command a new infantry brigade being organized to defend Panama. He would like Ike to come along as his brigade chief of staff. Would Ike be willing? Ike seized on such an opportunity.

One compelling reason for Ike's desire to join Conner was personal. At Christmastime 1920, less than two months after the Conner visit, Ike and Mamie suffered the greatest tragedy of their lives, the death of their three-and-a-half-year-old son, Doud Dwight "Ickie" Eisenhower. Ickie had contracted scarlet fever just before the end of the year and had died the day after Christmas. The bereaved parents longed to leave a location so full of memories of their loss.

Another reason Ike wished to leave Fort Meade was professional. It was very shortly after the Conner visit that Ike wrote the article on tank employment for the *Infantry Journal* that angered the Chief of Infantry. Now aware of a lack of support for his work with tanks, Ike wished to return to straight duty with the infantry. At first he was unsuccessful. Brigadier General Samuel Rockenbach, the Chief of the Tank Corps, refused to release him. Ike was indispensable in his current position—not for his work with tanks but for his success in coaching winning football teams for the two previous seasons. As a result, Ike and Mamie were forced to remain another full year at Fort Meade. In late December of 1921, however, Ike received orders to report to Panama as Conner's chief of staff. The chance encounter at a Sunday luncheon had provided an opening to a new world for Ike.

Captain and Mrs. Dwight Eisenhower* arrived at Camp Gaillard, Panama, in early 1922. It was not an inviting place, especially for Mamie, a young woman who was used to comfortable, if not luxurious living, and who happened to be pregnant once again. Their home was perched on high ground over that portion of the Panama Canal known

---

*Ike's temporary grade of lieutenant colonel expired while he was at Fort Meade. He then reverted to his permanent rank of captain. He was soon promoted to the grade of major, where he remained for the next thirteen years.

as the Culebra (or Gaillard) Cut. Mud slides were frequent. Their living quarters were miserable. Ike later described them with more amusement than he must have felt at the time:

> The houses at our new station were old, flimsy survivals of Canal construction days. To keep vermin out was difficult. They were infested with bats, and Mamie hated bats with a passion. Frequent thundershowers penetrated roofs and walls and windows and made living there too damp for comfort—except for those black, winged unwelcome visitors who seemed to thrive in the Turkish bath our house became after every storm.[5]

Another version came from Virginia Conner, the general's wife, that was perhaps even more revealing. Mamie, she later wrote, "did not like Gaillard with its mouldy houses and she felt sick, as she was expecting another baby." Mamie, she continued, "made no bones" about her unhappiness over having been sent to such a horrid post. Nevertheless, Mrs. Conner gave Mamie credit for being "the most honest person" she had ever known and noted that after giving birth Mamie felt better. Though she described Mamie as being "callow" at first, Mrs. Conner was delighted to see her become a person to whom everyone turned. She developed a "sure and steady hand." Furthermore, with her gay laugh, she was able to "smooth out Ike's occasional irritability."[6]

But if domestic conditions were difficult, the tour for Ike was pleasant and highly rewarding professionally. The reason was the attentiveness and kindness of General Conner. Since Ike has written so thoroughly and eloquently of his days with Conner in his personal memoir, *At Ease*, it would be futile for me to attempt to repeat it. However, I can make some observations.

It seems to me that Conner did two things for Ike. First, he occupied the young officer's mind with thoughts other than the loss of his son and the daily routine of garrison life. Second, he aroused in Ike an appreciation of the study of military history and other subjects, including the classics.

As a boy, Ike had been an avid reader of history. His high school yearbook, in fact, predicted that Ike would become a history professor and his brother Edgar, who graduated in the same class, would be President of the United States. But Ike, only a slightly above average student at West Point, had been discouraged, even offended, by the manner in which military history was taught in that institution. "In the case of the Battle of Gettysburg," he wrote later, "each student was instructed to memorize the names of every brigadier in the opposing armies and to know exactly where his unit was stationed at every hour during the three days of the battle. Little attempt was made to explain the meaning of the battle, why it came about, what the commanders hoped to accomplish, and the real reason why Lee invaded the North a second time. If this was military history, I wanted no part of it."[7]

Conner understood Ike's negative attitude, but he did not refute it with long-winded arguments. First he gave his protégé a few historical novels to read. When Ike found them interesting, Conner went to his extensive library and drew out some books on military history that covered the same periods as the novels. He refused to accept Ike's word that he had read his assignment; he quizzed him. And then the two would discuss the books on the long horseback rides they would take together along the jungle paths of Panama, where they inspected preparations for defending the Canal Zone against a possible enemy attack.

Conner did not stop there. He broadened his student's outlook. Discussions around the campfire included Shakespeare, Plato, Tacitus, and even Nietzsche. The general also gave Ike permission to drop by his home at any time during the day or evening to borrow books. When Ike did so, Conner often suggested others. If Conner was unusual in his zeal to teach the younger man, he was rewarded; Ike was an apt and enthusiastic student. He appreciated every effort that Conner took to prepare him for future responsibilities.

Conner's concern for Ike's welfare and education did not end when Ike returned to Camp Meade after three years in the Canal Zone. He continued to look out for the young man's welfare. Ike was still out of favor with the Chief of Infantry, and all of his efforts to attend the Infantry Advanced Course at Fort Benning were thwarted;* it appeared that his career was stymied. An officer could attend the all-important Command and General Staff School at Fort Leavenworth only if he had already graduated from his branch school—and attendance at Benning had been denied him.

---

*The Infantry School was located at Fort Benning, near Columbus, Georgia. It remains there today.

Conner soon learned of Ike's predicament and immediately took action. He sent Ike a strange telegram advising him to make no protest, no matter what orders he received from the War Department. He must accept those orders without question. Ike was puzzled, and his perplexity increased a few days later when orders arrived transferring him from the Infantry to the Adjutant General's Corps. Had it not been for Ike's complete faith in Conner, he would have protested quickly, because transfer from a combat branch to a service branch would have been unthinkable. In due course, however, the mystery was cleared up. Conner had been behind Ike's transfer to the Adjutant General's Corps, because that action took him out of the jurisdiction of the Chief of Infantry. Vacancies to Leavenworth were available in the Adjutant General's Corps, and Ike's name was on the list.

Ike went on to stand number one in his class at Leavenworth, thanks not only to Conner's manipulation of the Army bureaucracy but to the training that Conner had given him in Panama. No wonder that Ike later wrote that "in a lifetime of association with great and good men, he is the one more or less invisible figure to whom I owe an incalculable debt."[8]

I never knew Fox Conner when I was growing up, since I was only two years old when my parents returned to Camp Meade from Panama. Nevertheless, Conner's aura was felt in the Eisenhower household for a long time. I still have in my possession a photograph of the General standing by his horse, inscribed to me (a two-year-old), and it was said around the house that I was foreordained to marry General Conner's granddaughter, Pauline Vida, a tot about my age. That was said lightly, of course, but for years I took it seriously.

After our family left Washington for the Philippines in 1935 and 1936, the name of Fox Conner seems to have disappeared. By that time, Ike had his hands full serving under Douglas MacArthur. Later, at Fort Lewis, Ike was too busy to think of anything but the job at hand. Conner, after a full career, retired from the Army in 1938 as a major general, twenty years after his brilliant contribution to the AEF in 1918.

I finally met "The General," as Conner was called in our household, when I was a cadet and my mother was living at the Wardman Park

Hotel in Washington, D.C. I believe that the visit occurred in December 1943, after Ike had been appointed as Supreme Commander for OVERLORD. My memory of the occasion is hazy, but I recall it as rather subdued. The General was only in his seventieth year at the time, but his health was failing from a series of strokes. In any case, Conner

General Fox Conner as he appeared in Panama, 1924. Photo is inscribed "My Pal Johnnie" to the author, age two.

Author's Collection

was very quiet, perhaps conscious that he was much on the shelf.

Only two letters written by Ike to Conner during the war are included in Ike's published papers, and those letters were spaced only six weeks apart, written just after he had arrived in London in 1942. The first one, dated July 4, seems to have been prompted by his efforts to get a feel for his position as the senior American commander in Europe.

> More and more in the last few days my mind has turned back to you and to the days when I was privileged to serve intimately under your wise counsel and leadership. I cannot tell you how much I would appreciate, at this moment, an opportunity for an hour's discussion with you on problems that constantly beset me.

The letter then goes on to discuss the matters of "chiefs of services" in a theater of operations. Ike was addressing mundane but important matters that had to be solved. He was still feeling his way.[9]

On August 21, 1942, Ike wrote a second letter, this one in answer to one the General had written a month earlier.[10] In it Ike agreed with Conner's contention that the greatest problem confronting the Western Allies was to keep Russia in the war. Presumably that meant that the British and Americans should launch an attack across the English Channel in 1942. Ike, as a member of George C. Marshall's staff, had advocated such a venture, but that cross-Channel operation had just been shelved in favor of landings in North Africa. In the meantime Ike had been elevated from his role as an American to that of an Allied commander. He makes no mention of his elevation in his letter to Conner, possibly because word had not yet been made public.

In any case, that exchange was all that passed between Ike and Conner for the rest of the war. Ike grew constantly more confident in his own judgment. Conner probably wished to avoid impinging on Ike's time. And, except for letters home to his family, Ike rarely initiated correspondence. Most of his letters are in answer to those of others.

I was happy to read, in Mrs. Conner's book, that the Eisenhowers and Conners got together for a visit after the war. (I was still in Europe and was unaware of the reunion.) One day in 1947 Mrs. Conner called Mamie and asked her and Ike, who was Chief of Staff of the Army, to dinner. She had an interesting Russian friend she wanted to introduce them to, she said. The only stipulation to the invitation was that they would have to meet in a restaurant; the apartment the Conners were occupying was too small for entertaining. Mamie could not accept the invitation as offered, however, because by that time she and Ike could no longer appear in public without being mobbed by well-wishers. She therefore countered with an invitation to Quarters Number One at Fort Myer. Mamie's parents were visiting at the time, and Mamie knew that they would also love to see the Conners again. They had an "old home week," and Mrs. Conner was especially intrigued to see Ike's decorations, including the "ruby and diamond star presented by the Russian government." At the end of the evening, Mrs. Doud, Mamie's mother, said, "This is the kind of evening the children [meaning Ike and Mamie] need so much."[11]

Though that incident appears to be the last time the old friends met, Ike never forgot Conner. In 1967, in his late years, Ike said in an interview that Conner was "the ablest man I ever knew."[12]

JOHN J. PERSHING

After Ike graduated from the Command and General Staff School in 1926, he was sent to Fort Benning to command a battalion and once more coach football. Since the post commander placed primary emphasis on a successful football team rather than a well-trained battalion, Ike was unhappy. The period did not last long, however, because Ike soon received orders to report to Washington, possibly to join the staff of John J. Pershing, who had retired as Chief of Staff and who now headed the American Battle Monuments Commission. I have no evidence for this conjecture, but I presume that Fox Conner gave Ike's name to Pershing, as Conner remained Pershing's warm friend in the years after Pershing's retirement.

On arrival at the War Department in 1927, Ike was given the choice of joining the General Staff or serving on the Battle Monuments Commission. Though service on the General Staff would normally have been preferable from a career standpoint, the commission offered the intriguing prospect of rewriting a rough draft of a guidebook of the American

Battle Monuments Commission, Paris, 1929. General Pershing is fifth from the left. Ike is second from the right. Third from the right is Ike's immediate boss, Major Xenophon H. Price.
Author's Collection

battlefields in France during the Great War, 1917–1918. With that opportunity beckoning, he chose the Battle Monuments Commission. His serious work was delayed briefly when the opportunity to attend the all-important Army War College cropped up. The course was apparently of short duration, however, and when it was finished, Ike's position at the Battle Monuments Commission still awaited him. In August 1928, our family of three left Hoboken, New Jersey, aboard the SS *America*, bound for Cherbourg. My most vivid memory of the trip was the immense birthday cake the ship provided. I had reached the age of six.

Many aspects of our life in Paris remain in my memory—our small apartment on the Quai d'Auteil, overlooking Pont Mirabeau, Ike's office at 20 rue Molitor, and especially tramping over the battlefields of the First World War with my parents. Though I have attained a different impression from some of my parents' correspondence, it seemed to me that Ike was richly enjoying his work rewriting the guidebook. My conclusion is that Ike enjoyed visiting the battlefields and studying them, but the atmosphere in the office left something to be desired.

Ike seems to have had little direct exposure to General Pershing, because his immediate boss was Major Xenophon Price, an Engineer officer who had decided to make the Battle Monuments Commission his career.[13] Another reason why Pershing and Ike never became better acquainted was Pershing's natural aloofness and his preference for association with officers who had been with him in the AEF. When Ike left Paris in late 1929, Pershing presented him with a copy of the current version of the *Guide to the American Battlefields in Europe* with an elaborate inscription acknowledging Ike's role, but there seems to have been little warmth between them.

It is difficult, as Pershing's name fades from memory, to realize the hold that the former Commander of the AEF still held on the U.S. Army after his retirement, indeed up to his death in 1948. When he was writing his memoirs, Pershing felt free to call on his former subordinates, some of whom were still on active duty in responsible positions, to submit reports of their activities of over a decade earlier. Pershing used these reports freely in writing his account. His deadlines for the contributions were sometimes remarkably short. For example he gave Fox Conner, commanding a corps area, only two weeks to check over his entire manuscript. Although some of the responses came in late, sometimes by weeks, his former subordinates still treated him as the Old Man. (In that regard he resembles Winfield Scott, who saw the young officers he had trained in the Mexican War wage the much greater Civil War. In both cases, the young, vigorous generals still revered the elderly Scott and Pershing as their mentors.)[14]

Ike was not one of those who held Pershing in awe, however. In his memoir, *At Ease*, his treatment of Pershing is reserved, correct, and brief. He notes Pershing's "cautious and slow" writing habits and his careful and precise editing. "In going over my work," Ike wrote, "if I had used the word 'exhaustively,' I would find it changed to 'thoroughly'; if I should use the word 'speedily,' he would change it to 'rapidly.'"[15] Ike once remarked to me that "Pershing was the most cautious man I ever served under." Those words made sense; Pershing spent the last thirty years of his life reliving and justifying those seventeen months that he had commanded the AEF.

One of Ike's stories about Pershing, which he told me and which he also included in *At Ease*, described the time when the general showed Ike the drafts of two chapters of his memoirs, which he was then in the process of writing. They had to do with the two greatest American campaigns of the Great War, St. Mihiel and Meuse-Argonne. Throughout the course of Pershing's informative but colorless account of his days with the AEF, he had followed his diary entries almost slavishly. Since many issues would be confronting the general at any given time, the result was a fairly thorough book but one very much lacking in direction. The general asked Ike's opinion.

Ike read the section over and concluded that Pershing should diverge from his diary format regarding those two chapters in order to give the reader a clear picture of what Pershing was trying to do during those all-important campaigns and how well his efforts had been rewarded. Pershing seemed to like the idea and assigned Ike the job of rewriting the chapters on St. Mihiel and the Meuse-Argonne. All this had to be done in off-duty time, of course.

Pershing liked Ike's version, but he refused to decide on the matter until he could consult a former aide, Colonel George C. Marshall, on whose judgment Pershing relied heavily. Marshall read Ike's chapters over, and though he said he liked them, he recommended that Pershing stick to his diary-form account. "I think [your chapters] are interesting," Marshall said to Ike. "Nevertheless, I've advised General Pershing to stick with his original idea. I think to break up the format right at the climax of the war would be a mistake."

Ike stood his ground, insisting that he thought the two battles should be "treated as a single narrative with the proper annotations to give it authenticity." Marshall, rather kindly, according to Ike, thought Ike's idea was a good one, but "he thought that General Pershing would be happier if he stayed with the original scheme."[16] That incident was the only time that Ike and George Marshall conversed before meeting at the beginning of America's entry into World War II.

I have often wondered about that episode. Insofar as one can make a judgment, I suspect that the challenge of describing the Meuse-Argonne campaign, a confused affair that defies any definite pattern, was a task that Pershing simply did not feel up to tackling. He was better off concentrating on his own activities, and Marshall knew his chief well enough to realize that fact.

But I also wonder if these two veterans of that campaign, Pershing and Marshall, were unwilling to accept the viewpoint of a younger officer who had not been part of the scene in France. Perhaps Ike, always frank, had found flaws in the conduct of the Meuse-Argonne campaign, the most flagrant of which was the Sedan fiasco at the close of the war.[17] To get a better understanding of what was involved, I have attempted to locate copies of Ike's rejected drafts, but my efforts have come to naught.

Pershing does not seem to have loomed large in Ike's life; as I have mentioned, Ike was never one of "Pershing's men"[18] as were Fox Conner, George Marshall, and George Patton. He did not admire Pershing very much. I remember asking my father how he thought Pershing had done in the Great War. He chuckled a little and said, "Well, he did a couple of good things. One was to hold the American Expeditionary Force together against the opposition of the French and British, who wanted to use American troops as replacements for their own units." He did not mention the other accomplishment.

Yet Ike realized that the name of John J. Pershing retained a special symbolic place among the officers who had been part of the campaigns in France in 1917 and 1918. On May 8, 1945—V-E Day—Ike sent the ailing old general a message recognizing the continuity between the American armies of the two wars. In particular, he expressed gratitude for the school system that Pershing had established:

For the second time in less than thirty years, American arms are celebrating, with their allies, victory in Europe. As the commander of this second American expeditionary force I should like to acknowledge to you, the leader of the first, our obligation for the part you have played in the present victory. . . . The tactical judgment and skill and the identical command and staff conceptions . . . have resulted directly from our magnificent military and educational system that was completely reorganized and expanded under your wise leadership. The stamp of Benning, Sill, Riley and Leavenworth is on every American battle in

Europe and Africa. The sons of the men you led in battle in 1918 have much for which to thank you.[19]

Pershing died on July 15, 1948, while Ike was visiting friends in Vermont. When the news arrived, he immediately left for Washington to attend the funeral. The route to be followed by the procession was a long one, from the Capitol in Washington down Pennsylvania and Constitution Avenues and across the Memorial Bridge to Arlington Cemetery. Despite the distance and the threatening weather, Ike refused to make the trip riding in a car. He carried a touch of sentiment, especially for Pershing, the symbol of past American military glories. So he and General Omar N. Bradley marched together for the entire distance in the rain. As Ike later wrote of the occasion:

I was certainly not going to give an example of the brass running from a rainstorm when all the marching men in the long column had to take things as they came. Not in the last walk for General Pershing of the AEF.[20]

Ike and MacArthur are honored by the National Football Hall of Fame in late 1958.

National Archives

2

IKE AND MACARTHUR

A Study in Contrasts

On a late afternoon during the summer of 1933, my mother and I drove down Connecticut Avenue from the Wyoming Apartments to pick my father up at his office in the State-War-Navy Building, next to the White House.[1] We were planning to eat dinner at our favorite restaurant, the Allies Inn, which was situated just across 17th Street from the formidable old edifice. Unable to find a parking place, Mother sent me in to try to find him.

I knew the right floor but when I reached what I thought was my father's office, he was nowhere to be found. I spotted a tall, balding, middle-aged gentleman and asked him if he could help me. He seemed delighted, and he entered several doors making inquiries. After he succeeded in locating the missing Major Eisenhower, I thanked him and gave the matter no further thought.

Once out in the car, Ike turned to me with a grin. "Do you know who you had running around the halls looking for me? It was General MacArthur." I was duly impressed.

Exactly when Ike began working directly for General MacArthur is difficult to pinpoint. In his informal memoir, *At Ease*, Ike says that during the administration of Herbert Hoover, he was working in the office of Assistant Secretary of War Frederick Payne. Payne, of course, departed the scene on March 4, 1933, on the inauguration of President Franklin D. Roosevelt, and MacArthur supposedly picked Ike up at that time. Ike's memory seems to have been hazy on the matter, because there is no doubt that he had accompanied MacArthur when the latter made his ill-advised appearance at the dispersion of the Bonus Marchers months earlier, in July 1932.[2] The answer to the conflict of dates may lie in the way the War Department operated. Since the offices of the Secretary and the Chief of Staff consisted of such a few number of officials, it functioned as a sort of family. Ike apparently did not move into MacArthur's office abruptly; he gravitated there. (According to *At Ease*, the previous Chief of Staff, Charles P. Summerall, forbade members of the General Staff from entering the office of the Assistant Secretary. MacArthur had put a quick end to that animosity when he took office in 1930.)

Ike and MacArthur were on cordial terms during their two years together in Washington. Ike greatly admired MacArthur's extraordinary mind, and he was impressed by MacArthur's moral courage in fighting for greater Army appropriations in Congress, at considerable risk to his own position.[3] Moreover, Ike was acutely conscious of MacArthur's value as a symbol of American military prowess, an almost tangible asset to Army standing and morale. The general, on the other hand, showed his regard for Ike largely by the amount of work he was willing to pile on the younger officer, and the respect with which he usually listened to Ike's advice.

Once every year, on the day late in November when the Army football team played that of the Navy, I got an inkling of the rapport

General Douglas MacArthur on the day he was sworn in as Army Chief of Staff, 1930.

National Archives

between MacArthur and Ike. In those days, before professional football took on such importance, and when college football players were
actually drawn from the student bodies of their institutions, the
Army-Navy football game was one of the big sporting events of the
season, to the academies and also to the public. Ike and MacArthur
were letter men at West Point, Ike in football and MacArthur, too
slight in build for that sport, in baseball. Both were fanatical Army
football fans.

Television was far in the future during the 1930s, so the only way
that fans could follow the progress of the game was by radio. Sometimes it was difficult to discern what was going on, because radio
announcers became so excited that they could hardly describe what was
happening. The suspense, therefore, was heavy, and Ike was invariably
frantic. When that annual ordeal rolled around, I habitually stretched
out on the floor to hear the radio better, and I always looked up in
wonderment and fear bordering on terror as Ike paced the floor,
roared, and cursed with either exultation or frustration.[4] On one occasion Ike burst out, "I'll bet the general fainted on that one." He then
picked up the phone and called MacArthur to exchange excited comments. MacArthur and Ike were not general and major on that one day
of the year; they were fellow West Pointers sharing an experience that
involved their hearts and souls.

MacArthur's four-year tour as Army Chief of Staff was completed
in 1934, but President Roosevelt requested that he stay on for an additional year. Fortuitously, it seemed at the time, the Tydings-McDuffie
Act, a measure of exceptional statesmanship, was enacted into law in
1935, declaring that the Philippine Islands, American possessions
since 1901, would be granted independence in 1946. To ensure the
new nation's ability to administer itself—the Philippines had been
under Spanish or American domination for nearly four centuries—the
new nation would serve an apprenticeship as the Philippine Commonwealth for ten years, during which time it would govern itself under
United States guidance and protection. At the end of the commonwealth period, the Philippine government would naturally assume
responsibility for its own military defense. To prepare for that day, the
commonwealth government would need to build an army of its own.
To assist him in that task, the Philippine President-elect, Manuel Que-

zon, specifically requested that MacArthur, who was about to retire as Army Chief of Staff, be assigned to advise him.

Douglas MacArthur was the obvious choice for that position. His father, General Arthur MacArthur, had been extremely popular among the Filipinos because of his sympathetic attitude toward the Filipinos once the so-called Philippine Insurrection had been put down.[5] Moreover, the son, Douglas, had enjoyed a similar popularity in his own right when he served there between the First World War and his appointment as Army Chief of Staff.

MacArthur was delighted with the opportunity. The alternatives would be to retire completely at age fifty-five or to continue on active duty under another Chief of Staff in a lesser role. Furthermore, going to a country for which he had a strong affinity as a sort of proconsul was an exceedingly attractive prospect. So MacArthur eagerly accepted Quezon's offer, and at the same time he asked—practically demanded—that Ike go with him as chief of staff of the Military Mission.

That development brought on a crisis between my parents, and I was an occasional eavesdropper to their discussions. My mother, though she had become more cheerful in the latter days of their tour in the Panama Canal Zone, had never come to like the place; she wanted no part of another tour in the tropics. Ike had a different reason for wishing to avoid the Philippine assignment: he longed to get back to field duty, with troops. He had been behind a desk in Washington and Paris for some eight years, much too long. Unlike Mamie, however, Ike felt that he had an obligation to accept MacArthur's offer. Legally, he might have been able to defy MacArthur's wishes, but MacArthur was still Army Chief of Staff at the time for decision, and Ike sensed that a thwarted MacArthur might be petty enough, if sufficiently angered, to ruin Ike's career. Ike decided to go.

My unhappy parents finally agreed on a compromise. Since I had been fortunate enough to attend the nearby John Quincy Adams School throughout the first seven years of school, they decided that it would be best for me to stay on for the final year and graduate from the eighth grade. Mother and I would therefore remain in Washington for one more year and then, in 1936, we would join Ike in Manila. Mother may have been hoping that Ike's tour in the

Philippines might end within the first year and he would return home.

Ike accompanied MacArthur and his small entourage as it crossed the United States by rail, bound for San Francisco, where they would begin the month-long sea voyage to the Philippines. The party included the general's ailing eighty-two-year-old mother, Mrs. Arthur MacArthur, and his sister Mary. Ike and Captain Thomas Jefferson "T. J." Davis, the general's aide, were the only officers along. Major James B. Ord, a West Point classmate of Ike's, was also going to Manila on Ike's request, but he would travel separately, taking his wife and two children.[6]

The MacArthur argosy began on an ominous note. MacArthur believed, perhaps erroneously, that President Roosevelt had promised to defer naming his successor as Chief of Staff until a month after MacArthur had arrived in Manila wearing four stars on his uniform. Along the way, however, word reached the train on which they were traveling that General Malin Craig had just been named as the Army Chief of Staff, thus automatically reducing MacArthur to the grade of two-star general. According to Ike, MacArthur expressed himself with

an explosive denunciation of bad politics, bad manners, bad judgment, broken promises, arrogance, unconstitutionality, insensitivity, and the way the world had gone to hell. Then he sent an eloquent telegram of congratulations to his successor.[7]

As if this humiliation were not enough to beset the sensitive retiring Chief of Staff, tragedy struck. The general's mother, whom he affectionately called "Pinkie," took violently ill while their ship, the *President Harding*, was in the mid-Pacific. (She died within a month after the *Harding* docked in Manila.) Despite MacArthur's éclat in public and the physical courage he displayed on the battlefield, he was unusually dependent upon this very strong woman. His introduction during the voyage to a comely, petite brunette from Tennessee, Miss Jean Faircloth, whom he married eighteen months later, only partially alleviated his distress.

The living arrangements of the MacArthurs and the Eisenhowers in Manila kept them apart from the rest of the American Army stationed in or near the city. The officers assigned to the Headquarters, Philippine Department, lived in a community in the city of Manila; those assigned to troop units lived on such posts as Fort McKinley, Fort Stotsenburg (later absorbed into Clark Air Force Base), and Corregidor. Most of the members of the MacArthur Mission, however, lived in the sumptuous Manila Hotel.

When my mother and I arrived in Manila in October of 1936, Ike was occupying a two-room suite on the third floor of the main part of the hotel. Though luxurious by Philippine standards, the rooms were hot. Everyone slept with mosquito netting, and small lizards scurried

General Douglas MacArthur at a ceremony in Manila, probably in 1935. Behind him in straw hat is Major Eisenhower. Next to Ike, partially hidden by MacArthur, is Major James B. Ord.

National Archives

about the ceilings, much to my mother's horror. The humidity was high, and most people, especially if overweight, accepted with little complaint the streams of sweat that continuously trickled off their chins. I have no idea how General MacArthur managed during the first few months of his tenure, but by early 1937, when he married Jean Faircloth, he had been provided with a seven-room, air-conditioned penthouse in the newer section of the hotel. Some time thereafter Ike and Mamie were given a much more modest suite on a lower floor in the air-conditioned part of the building. I have heard that MacArthur was miffed at this luxury provided to an underling, but I never knew it at the time.

The members of the MacArthur Mission never wore uniform, and their offices were located in a modest building inside the nearby Walled City, in a section called the Cuartel d'España. On rare occasions, Ike and MacArthur rode back and forth to work in the general's official car. Usually, however, the two men kept different schedules. Because of the low domestic pay scale in Manila—and the laws that made it risky for an American to drive—Ike found it prudent and affordable to employ a Filipino driver to take him around in his small Plymouth.

Ike's schedule was a strange one, geared to the tropics. He arose very early and left the Manila Hotel at something like 6:30 A.M. every day, bound for Camp Murphy, a Philippine Army post located just outside the environs of the city. There, after the Philippine government had established a small air force of about five Stearman trainers and one Stinson Reliant, he took daily flying instruction for an hour or so before going into the Cuartel d'España to work.[8] The normal workday was only about five or six hours, and Ike, along with the rest of the staff, called it quits at 1:00 P.M. After lunch and a short siesta at the Manila Hotel, he habitually joined a group of Manila businessmen in an attractive room just off the hotel lobby for an afternoon of bridge. He and Mamie dined in the spacious and pleasant downstairs dining room every evening. Then an early bedtime to prepare for the next day's flying instruction.

MacArthur, on the other hand, went to the office fairly late in the morning. During this period of his life he was practically a recluse. He returned to the hotel at about the same time Ike did, and that seems to have been his only appearance during the day. It was a strange, unnatural life for both men. I hate to think how difficult the bird-in-a-gilded-cage life was for their wives.

Not long after the Military Mission was established—in fact, even before MacArthur and Ike left Washington—it became apparent that almost irresistible forces were working to make the creation of a Philippine army a frustrating, even hopeless experience. The principal obstacle was budgetary. The fledgling Philippine government, while needing an army for prestige purposes and for internal security, was unwilling to pay for it. Assumptions that Ike and Jimmy Ord had used as the bases for planning while still in Washington were continually being torpedoed. The original figure of $25 million a year was soon cut in half. MacArthur and his staff attempted to cope with that reduction by equipping the Philippine Army with obsolete American rifles and practically no artillery. They also cut the pay of the Philippine conscripts to what Ike described as "cigarette money."[9]

At the end of the first year of the mission, Ike and Ord prepared what they considered a factual report for submission to President Manuel Quezon. MacArthur, however, rejected what he deemed a pessimistic exposé and in its place substituted a new, more cheerful picture. Claiming that the progress had "exceeded original anticipation," he went on to predict that his defense system would "present to any potential invader such difficult problems as to give pause even to the most ruthless and powerful."[10] Ike could only shrug. His relations with his chief were now beginning to fray.

A far more personal problem cropped up at about the same time. President Quezon, pleased with MacArthur's initial report, proposed to give four of the American officers exalted rank in the new Philippine Army. He would make Ike and Ord general officers and raise MacArthur to the rank of field marshal. Ike reacted negatively, arguing that their acceptance of high rank in the Philippine Army would make them look ridiculous in the eyes of their fellow Americans. Furthermore, Philippine rank would put a price tag on them when they were dealing with higher-ranking generals of the Philippine Army. T. J. Davis and Jimmy Ord agreed, though Ike noted in his diary that Ord was a little less vehement about it than he.[11]

MacArthur, however, seemed delighted with the prospect, and Ike's violent disagreement began a heated argument. Ike told the general

that the name of "MacArthur" was magic in the American Army, and
for him to accept rank in the Philippine Army would degrade it.
MacArthur, in harsh terms, refused to take Ike's advice. In a rage, Ike
turned to leave the room, only to find his way blocked. Putting his
hand on Ike's shoulder, the general said, "Ike, it's worthwhile to argue
with you sometimes just to see that Dutch temper of yours." Ike,
charmed, melted. But he did not change his views.[12]

MacArthur later claimed to have second thoughts on the matter of
accepting Philippine rank, and he announced that he was accepting the
rank only to avoid giving offense to Quezon. Ike wrote disgustedly in
his diary that MacArthur was "tickled pink."[13]

Progressively the relations between Ike and MacArthur continued
to deteriorate. Ike's future was perhaps saved by the fact that the general, sometime in 1937, voluntarily retired from the United States
Army, presumably to avoid being reassigned elsewhere. That development left Ike as the senior active-duty American officer in the mission,
and MacArthur no longer made out efficiency reports on him. At the
same time, however, Ike concluded that he would be well advised to
keep a record of events as he saw them on a day-to-day basis. He therefore began keeping a detailed diary in which he recorded every happening of importance every day.

That diary has led to exaggerated stories of the rift between the two
men. Often, in exasperation, Ike used vituperative terms. In some ways
the diary is useful for researchers, but on the whole I wish that the staff
had followed Ike's orders and destroyed it. Ike was articulate, especially
with the written word, and he suffered from a violent temper. Forced
to suppress that temper in his dealings with others, he committed his
frustrations to paper. I do not believe that everything he said in those
pages represents his lifetime views of Douglas MacArthur.

The most serious confrontation between these two strong-willed
men grew out of the budgetary problem, at least indirectly.
MacArthur, according to Ike, conceived the idea that it would be ben-
eficial to Philippine morale if an impressive parade of Philippine
Army troops were to be conducted on the streets of Manila. He issued
orders to Ike and Ord to make arrangements to bring units from all
over the 7,000 islands and concentrate them at Manila, presumably
Camp Murphy. The younger officers protested against the cost, but

they obeyed, confident (still according to Ike) that the concept of the parade carried the approval of Philippine President Manuel Quezon.

When Quezon learned of the projected parade, however, he became furious, and he telephoned MacArthur demanding an explanation. MacArthur thereupon claimed that he had issued no such orders; he had merely instructed his staff to "begin planning" for such an event. Whatever the facts of the case, both Ike and Ord felt betrayed, and Ike later wrote that "This misunderstanding caused considerable resentment—and never again were [MacArthur and I] on the same warm and cordial terms."[14]

That period, from 1935 to 1939, represents the low point of the two men's careers. It is impossible, when one stops to consider the situation, not to have a great deal of sympathy for both of them. MacArthur, flawed though he may have been, was going through an extraordinarily difficult period of his life. He had once been the darling of the American Army, the man who became Chief of Staff at the age of fifty, one of the most highly decorated soldiers in John J. Pershing's AEF. Now he was out of power, hamstrung by a Philippine defense budget that was less than adequate. Furthermore, his position gave his active mind little challenge. Apparently without hobbies and too aloof to develop friends, he was confined for some six years to an elaborate penthouse atop a hotel, where he whiled away much of the time pacing up and down on his spacious balcony. MacArthur was a difficult boss to Ike, but his career by no means can be judged by his performance during those years of the late 1930s.

Ike, for his part, was also unhappy. He wanted to be with troops in the United States, and he had lost the warm feeling he had once felt for MacArthur. On the other hand, he appreciated the additional remuneration that all the members of the American party received from the Philippine government, and he enjoyed learning to fly. He also learned a good deal about the forming of an army from scratch. But he, too, was underchallenged. Mamie was unhappy, and dramatic events were beginning to unfold back home in the United States. To add to his discontent, Jimmy Ord, his principal source of solace in the increasingly difficult situation, was killed in a plane crash near Baguio, in the mountains north of Manila, in early 1938. Following that tragedy, nearly all of Ike's interest in his job evaporated.

Nevertheless, contrary to popular mythology, no open rift ever occurred between Ike and MacArthur, even while Ike was still in the Philippines. On one occasion, during the height of the tensions, I rode from the Cuartel d'España to the Manila Hotel with them. From the front seat of the car I could of course hear their conversation. MacArthur talked a great deal—pontificated might be a better way to put it—but the tone was friendly. And when I left Manila for Brent School in Baguio in September of 1939, Mrs. MacArthur insisted that I say goodbye to the general. When I approached the solitary figure pacing on his penthouse balcony, he shook hands at length and turned on the charm, sending me off feeling elated. His knowledge of my school activities gave evidence that he had been listening to Ike, not always simply talking to him.

Ike's departure from the Philippines became inevitable on September 3, 1939, when war broke out in Europe. The evening that war became official remains as one of my life's memorable moments. Warned of what was coming, my parents and I went to the apartment of friends who owned a shortwave radio, capable of picking up signals from Europe. There we hovered over the radio, straining to hear the words of British Prime Minister Neville Chamberlain as he announced, "Now Great Britain is at war with Germany."[15]

Ike was convinced that Fox Conner's prediction of America's involvement in another European war was now coming to pass, and he wanted to be on the scene for the Army's response to this event. Further, his normal four-year tour of duty was up. Granted, an extension of a year might have been legally possible, but Ike turned a deaf ear when President Quezon offered him in effect a blank check to dramatically raise the pay augmentation he had been enjoying.[16] MacArthur also went through the motions of attempting to dissuade him from departing, but I have the feeling that the general was quite satisfied to replace Ike with Major Richard K. Sutherland, who had come down from Tientsin to act as Ike's assistant after the death of Jimmy Ord.

In any event, General MacArthur also went out of his way to give Ike a warm send-off. When our family boarded the *President Cleveland* at Pier Seven, General and Mrs. MacArthur appeared at the dock, the general carrying a going-away present, a bottle of scotch whisky. Ike and Mamie seemed to leave Manila with feelings of satisfaction. Or so it appeared to me, who admittedly was watching my parents' reactions no more closely than does any other seventeen-year-old.

Ike and MacArthur continued to correspond on rare occasions even after my parents returned to the United States. At Fort Lewis one day, according to my recollection, Ike showed me a letter he had received from General MacArthur in which the general quoted President Roosevelt as having assured him that he, MacArthur, would be the next John J. Pershing in the event of United States involvement in the current European war. The last sentence of the letter read, "Of course this pleases me very much."[17]

As time went on, however, MacArthur reportedly developed an animosity toward Ike that the latter did not reciprocate. It probably began when, in mid-December of 1941, Ike was summoned to the War Plans Division of the War Department. With the battleships of the United States Pacific Fleet sitting on the bottom at Pearl Harbor, it was impossible for the Americans to send reinforcements to relieve the Philippines, then under Japanese attack. MacArthur can readily be excused for wishing that his countrymen could do more to help his beleaguered force, even to feel resentment over their inability to do so. But I have had the impression that the general also believed that Ike, and possibly even Chief of Staff George C. Marshall, were personally conspiring against him.[18]

As time went on, Ike became more and more prominent in the public mind, and even though MacArthur had been glorified out of reasonable proportions during the dark days of the war in early 1942, his Southwest Pacific Theater was progressively becoming recognized in nearly all quarters as a secondary arena. The final blow, from MacArthur's viewpoint, came when Ike was named to command OVERLORD, the invasion of northwest Europe in the summer of 1944.

The careers of the two men were no longer even remotely related. MacArthur, after the end of the war in the Pacific, went on to perform stellar service as Allied Supreme Commander for the Japanese occupation. His role in writing the Japanese Constitution, still in use a half century later, stands as evidence of his remarkable intellectual breadth. His performance in Korea exhibited audacity when he landed at Inchon in September of 1950 and virtually destroyed the North Korean army. On October 28, MacArthur's forces were pursuing the beaten North Koreans. It looked as if MacArthur's career would end with another brilliant victory. On that date, Ike sent him a message of congratulations:

> I have not wanted to bother you with correspondence during the more active phases of your recent campaign, but I cannot longer stay the impulse to express the conviction that you have again given us a brilliant example of professional leadership. . . . My most sincere congratulations, as well, of course, as my very best wishes to you and your family. With warm personal regard.[19]

MacArthur's reply, equally warm, said that Ike's note had "brought back so vividly the memories of our intimate relationships over so many hard years of effort and travail."[20]

The axe, however, was about to fall. Even as the two generals were exchanging greetings, Chinese forces, which had already crossed the Yalu and had hidden in the mountains of North Korea, were poised for the counterattack. Four days later, on November 2, they emerged into view and decimated a regiment of the American 1st Cavalry Division driving northward up the west coast of the peninsula. MacArthur, suffering from inexplicable hubris, made a colossal blunder in ignoring them. Three weeks later the Chinese struck in even greater force on both coasts, causing the Eighth Army to retreat southward and the separate X Corps to be evacuated from North Korea by sea. That disaster would have brought about the relief from command of any lesser figure than MacArthur, but for the moment his great prestige saved him.

In April of 1951, however, MacArthur finally overstepped himself. Frustrated by the tactical restrictions that President Harry S. Truman and the Joint Chiefs of Staff placed upon him in order to keep the war limited to the Korean Peninsula, he publicly denounced the government's policies. The President, exasperated, had no choice but to relieve him. Ike may have felt that Truman had emboldened MacArthur by being too lenient on him in the past, but given MacArthur's conduct, he sided unequivocally with President Truman. When asked his views of the episode, he said, "When you don a uniform, there are certain inhibitions that you assume."

President Truman's relief of MacArthur caused a nearly unprecedented furor in the United States. The general returned home as a
hero, to be given a spectacular public reception. He appeared before
Congress to deliver an impassioned but eloquent attack on President
Truman's conduct of the Korean War. It appeared for a while that,
despite his seventy-one years, MacArthur might be nominated by the
Republicans for President in 1952. Again it was his former subordinate, Ike, who was selected. Though MacArthur said little in public,
his private utterances were reportedly bitter.[21] When Ike and
MacArthur were photographed together at the home of Bernard
Baruch in December of 1952, MacArthur, puffing on a cigar, was a
picture of disdain.

Yet Ike continued to treat his old boss with courtesy. In 1954, as
President, Ike hosted a White House luncheon in MacArthur's honor,
at which the guest list included many prominent members of the
Defense Department. Four years later the two old soldiers appeared
together to receive gold medals from the National Football Hall of
Fame. I am not aware of any meetings after Ike left the presidency;
MacArthur died in 1964, three years later.

I have often thought about how difficult MacArthur must have
found the last thirteen years of his life, living as he did in retirement in
a penthouse atop the Waldorf-Astoria hotel in New York. He was not
a total recluse; in fact he held a titular executive position in some large
company. But the challenges were gone. That period covered a longer
time span than all of MacArthur's glory days from the beginning of
the Second World War through his command in Korea. The thought is
nearly inconceivable.

MacArthur, assisted by Ike, did important work during the 1930s both
in Washington and Manila. The matter of primary interest to me, however, is the effect that service under MacArthur had on Ike's attitudes
later as a Supreme Commander and President. Ike was critical of
MacArthur's public habit of claiming the lion's share of the credit for
favorable developments. Indeed, he is often said to have remarked, "I
studied dramatics under [MacArthur] for seven years."[22] Whether Ike
spoke those actual words or not, I know they represent his views. In any

case, once he became a world figure, Ike adopted a conscious policy of accepting blame for failure and giving credit for success to others.

By no means do I think that Ike was totally correct in what might have been overreacting to MacArthur's histrionics. His modest manner doubtless served him well as a Supreme Commander, when the morale and performance of his subordinates was all-important and public relations was secondary. I sometimes wonder, however, if that policy served him equally well as President. There is much showmanship in the job of President, and I wonder if Ike's abhorrence of theatrics contributed to his being viewed for a while by those not in the know as a "do-nothing" President. I am inclined to think so. Ike may have learned an unfortunate lesson during his service under MacArthur.

On the Plain at West Point there stand two large statues that, with Sylvanus Thayer, dominate the scene. The statues are of the two West Pointers who rose to positions of greatest prominence in the Second World War, Douglas MacArthur and Dwight Eisenhower. These two men were closely associated for a time but went their separate ways. In some respects they were rivals, as each commanded American forces in competing areas of the globe.

Yet both filled their roles admirably. Ike Eisenhower could never have played the role of Emperor of Japan as well as did MacArthur, and MacArthur could never have contended with Winston Churchill and Bernard Montgomery, men he did not control, so well as Ike. Thanks to Providence or just plain chance, each man was in his right place. The country was well served by both of them.

Lieutenant Colonel Eisenhower, 15th Infantry, Camp Ord, California, 1940.

Photo by the Author

3

A GENERAL
IN THE WINGS

(Or, An Exercise in Nostalgia, 1940–1941)

Janie, you've always wanted to see what a general looks like before he becomes a general. Well, just take a look at Colonel Eisenhower.

—MAJOR EDWIN B. HOWARD[1]

The SS *President Coolidge*, of the old American President Lines, docked in San Francisco in early January 1940 after a three-week voyage from Manila. Among the passengers were Ike, Mamie, and me, all looking forward eagerly to our new life. After a short delay, during which Ike performed some special chore at the Presidio of San Francisco, we settled in at Fort Lewis, near Tacoma, Washington, in mid-February.

Ike's reporting in at Fort Lewis was a happy moment. For the first time, after many years behind a desk, he would be back with troops. His command would be the 1st Battalion, 15th Infantry Regiment, 3d Infantry Division. For some reason, perhaps a shortage of qualified officers, he also doubled in brass as the regimental executive officer, and that duty, it seemed to me, occupied most of his attention. But no matter: Ike was finally back in uniform.

Life at Fort Lewis brought a significant change in the Eisenhower domestic life. Having been away at boarding school during almost all of my high school years, I would now be living at home again. As a result, I regarded my parents, especially Ike, with a degree of curious detachment. Because of Ike's very novelty, I observed his activities with keener interest than would usually be the case.

My most vivid memory of Ike at this time involved a trivial incident, which occurred shortly after our furniture had arrived from storage and my parents had finished settling the house. The 3d Division was about to undergo summer training at Camp Ord, California, and in preparation Ike had to get his personal field gear ready. With the weather becoming pleasant, and the rain and drizzle that besets the Puget Sound region in winter abating, he summoned his orderly one evening and had him spread his field gear out on the ground behind our house. With it all laid out to view, Ike could check and ensure that no items were missing. I can still see him as he stood, hands on hips, bareheaded in his olive drab shirt and light tie, totally engrossed. He stood erect but at ease, reviewing in his mind what he would need during the weeks ahead—quiet, contemplative, and strangely at peace.

Ike's orderly was also notable in his own way. He was a slow-moving Southern boy who bore the contradictory name of Blizzard. He was a handsome lad, only a couple years older than I, slim with light blue eyes. He was probably straight off the farm, and also, like so many of the soldiers of that day, a fugitive from the Great Depression. I liked him.[2]

Having been away from the Army for so long, I was interested to observe Ike's attitude toward Blizzard. Though Ike always respected every man and woman as an individual, some people attracted his notice and others did not. Blizzard fell into the second category—only a name, totally interchangeable with any other Army private. None of us ever asked Blizzard's first name—nobody used them in the old Regular Army—and I doubt that Ike even saw him that evening. His mind was focused entirely on the equipment he was preparing to take with him to Camp Ord.

Although moving an entire 15,000-man division several hundred miles by motor convoy was an unusual event for the still sedentary peacetime Army, life at Fort Lewis, in garrison, remained geared to the relatively slow pace of peacetime. Ike always worked hard, but his schedule was not frantic. Thanks to President Franklin D. Roosevelt's Public Works Administration (PWA)[3] during the 1930s, the brick quarters that Ike and Mamie occupied at Fort Lewis were comfortable. A lieutenant colonel was assigned a two-storied house, with three bedrooms and one and a half baths, a far cry from the small apartment my parents had occupied in the Manila Hotel. Ike was always a farmer at heart, and here he was able to dig up a few square feet of lawn to make a small vegetable garden. He grew corn, tomatoes, and radishes, made easier by the cheap labor I provided when I was at home. Life at Lewis was sociable enough, but far from the glitter of either Washington or Manila.

Unconscious of how important troop duty was to any Army officer, and especially to Ike, I found myself a bit puzzled at the zeal with which my father plunged into this relatively modest assignment. During the ten years before arriving at Fort Lewis, he had functioned at the seats of power in positions that had involved him in high-level matters, concerned with the organization and maintenance of national armies. Here, as executive officer of the 15th Infantry, he was no longer serving under a four-star general, but under a colonel, practically a contemporary. Yet Ike performed his duties with all the energy he had exerted under men of more august positions.

Fortunately, Colonel Jesse A. Ladd, Class of 1912 at West Point, was an excellent regimental commander. He was a man of impeccable character, pleasant, his position enhanced by a wife who was loved by everyone. Florence Ladd was an ideal "mother of the regiment." She was warm and friendly, at the same time conscious of the "von" in her maiden name of von Kanel. Heavyset, she was no beauty, but her dignity and dark, aristocratic features set her off from any crowd. She was also fun. When she showed up at a regimental party wearing a flapper gown from the 1920s, everyone laughed and applauded. But nobody ever forgot that she was the Colonel's Lady.

Jesse Ladd allowed Ike a great deal of latitude as executive officer of the regiment, and Ike made full use of it. Certainly he would never take any step that Ladd would disapprove of, but his own personality was very much felt. I was able to see him in action for a few days in April 1940, when Mrs. Ladd, her son Jim, and I drove down from Fort Lewis to Camp Ord. In those days the Army still allowed the sons of officers to visit their fathers in camp, sharing their tents if space so allowed.

We all realized, I think, that we were witnessing the last of the peacetime Army, even though the dramatic events of the summer of 1940 in Europe still lay ahead. Hitler's panzers had not yet overrun France, forcing the French to surrender and the British Expeditionary Force to make a close-run escape across the English Channel from Dunkirk. The first draft of American manpower was still months away.

Concrete vestiges of the Old Army were still in evidence. The encampment of the 15th Infantry, for example, was laid out in old, "regular" fashion, a veritable tent city. Ike, as regimental executive officer, was authorized a wall tent all to himself. Inside the tent were two cots, two camp chairs, and a large folding camp desk. On the desk stood a couple of kerosene lamps that threw bright light and eerie shadows on the tent walls. Between the individual tents, the streets of the camp were immaculately laid out, the sidewalks lined with uniform whitewashed rocks.[4] In retrospect my memories of Camp Ord recall the impression described by an Ohio volunteer, Luther Giddings, when in 1846 he first laid eyes on Zachary Taylor's camp in Mexico. Its organization, Giddings had noted, was impeccable. Infantry, artillery, and cavalry were each in its place, their "appointments and discipline perfect."[5] Nearly a century later, Giddings would have felt at home surveying the 15th Infantry encampment at Ord.

One of the remarkable aspects of the old 15th Infantry was its high state of morale. It had not been one of the regiments of the famed 3d Division in the First World War,[6] but it carried its own style of mystique; it was the regiment of the "Old China Hands" of Tientsin, a token unit stationed in that city to show the American flag during the days when the Western Powers held sway in the disorganized region known as China. There it had performed garrison, spit-and-polish duties until it was withdrawn under Japanese pressure in 1937.

Service with the 15th in China carried with it a sort of cachet. Its alumni included distinguished men such as George Marshall, Matthew B. Ridgway, "Vinegar Joe" Stilwell, and others, and much of the spirit remained.[7] Its motto was "Can Do," the watchword of the regiment long before that admirable profession of confidence was preempted by the Navy's Seabees[8] during the Second World War. Its crest bears a Chinese dragon. Before I arrived at Camp Ord, the 15th had suffered through a period of intensive rains. To commemorate the ordeal in a humorous way, some amateur artist had drawn a large poster cartoon of the regimental crest, substituting a rain-drenched Donald Duck for the dragon and changing the motto from "Can Do" to "Did Do." The poster hung proudly in the officers' mess.

Military morale is often built on things that seem trivial to a civilian. In early 1940 the lilting tune "Beer Barrel Polka" was immensely popular on the American scene and nobody enjoyed the tune more than did Ike, who declared the "Beer Barrel Polka" to be the official marching song of the 15th. He so designated it to someone at 3d Division headquarters. When the division staged a review, therefore, the band would invariably suspend whatever march it had been playing and swing into "The Polka," as it was unofficially called, when the 15th arrived at the reviewing stand. When the last man of the 15th had passed by, the band would revert to whatever other march it had previously been playing. It was said that the rank and file of the 15th would refuse to march to any other tune. I doubt that everyone in the regiment felt that strongly about the matter, but Ike insisted that they did. Men liked to joke about it. The device was effective.

Novelty, if not a sense of urgency, prevailed at Camp Ord in early 1940. Not only the soldiers involved but also the civilian guests from around the area were all intrigued to witness, at a public field day, the accuracy of the new 81mm mortar, of antiquated light tanks plunging into deep holes and coming out the other side. We gasped at the spectacle of machine guns spewing tracers at night. We were impressed with the accuracy of the new 37mm antitank gun. Many of the weapons in use at Camp Ord would be obsolete within a year, but a sleepy army was learning new techniques, with the prospect of great new adventures lying ahead.

In the summer of 1940, I left Fort Lewis to enter Millard Preparatory School at 1918 "N" Street, NW, Washington, D.C., there to begin intensive cramming to pass the very rigorous West Point entrance examinations. "Beanie" Millard's was a demanding but interesting place, sometimes made amusing by the antics of its eccentric owner. So effective was its methodology that I easily won the competition for Senator Arthur Capper's West Point appointment from Kansas. Once that had happened, with no reason to stay, I left Beanie's on my own volition and crossed the continent in a railroad coach. I arrived home at Fort Lewis by Christmastime, somewhat to my parents' surprise.

By early 1941 Ike was no longer with his beloved 15th Infantry. Major General Charles F. Thompson, commanding the 3d Division, had brought him up from the 15th Infantry to be division chief of staff. Ike was bitterly disappointed by the move. He liked and respected General Thompson, but he was apparently working with less latitude than he had enjoyed with the 15th. "General Thompson doesn't think he's commanding this division," Ike growled one evening, "unless he knows every little thing that happens." Since the ability to delegate authority would later turn out to be one of Ike's greatest strong points, I have since regarded that remark as significant.

One evening during the winter I accompanied Ike on a visit to 3d Division headquarters, which was located in a small wooden building a mile from our quarters. The place was nearly empty, and almost the only officer present was Major Edwin Howard, the division intelligence officer (G-2).[9] Something came to Ike's attention that made him think that division headquarters was getting a bit high-handed. "I think we're developing a little self-importance around here," he remarked. "We're forgetting to read Gray's 'Elegy' every now and then."[10]

By early spring of 1941, the atmosphere at Fort Lewis had changed.

"Business as usual" had given way to an atmosphere of preparation for war. Some of the first draftees were beginning to arrive on the post, and at first their appearance caused some chuckles. Apparently more men had been called up than the Army had modern uniforms for, so some of the new recruits were clad in ill-fitting uniforms taken out of mothballs from the First World War. The blouses were high-necked; the overseas caps were squashed down on their heads; the men still wore wrap leggings. Even more jolting, in a way, was the sight of fresh-faced, newly commissioned lieutenants, in their blouses and riding breeches, being instructed in the rudiments of close order drill on the parade ground by tough old sergeants. Who could have guessed at the time that these men, during the next five years, would be leading the vast and competent armies that would help spell the doom of Hitler, Mussolini, and the Japanese dictator Tojo?

With those conditions prevailing, Ike's personal preferences could no longer be considered, and his assignment at 3d Division headquarters came to an end. Major General Kenyon A. Joyce, commanding IX Corps, reached down and pulled Ike up to be his own chief of staff. Fortunately, all three headquarters—15th Infantry, 3d Division, and IX Corps—were within a mile of each other at Fort Lewis, so none of these transfers entailed any physical move of the family. And Ike's elevation to IX Corps at least brought with it a promotion to temporary colonel. I remember the date well: March 4, 1941.

None of the three commanders that Ike served under at Fort Lewis ever became noted to the general public. Jesse Ladd attained the grade of temporary brigadier general, and Charles Thompson briefly commanded I Corps in the Pacific. Kenyon Joyce commanded a corps in the Pacific and later joined the Allied Control Commission in Italy.

Joyce was a fine soldier, but at that time he was still suffering from a strange preoccupation with military punctilio. With the Army awakening into the realities of American involvement in war, Joyce retained his penchant for formalities. Even on duty he wore Class A uniform: formal blouse and riding breeches.[11] While the general admired Ike's abilities, he found his chief of staff wanting in proper respect for military niceties.

Ike customarily went to the office ready for work wearing a regular olive drab shirt. General Joyce could tolerate that informality, but one day he called Ike's attention to the fact that his belt buckle was tarnished. Ike made a quick survey of the situation and discovered the heartening fact that web belts with shiny buckles were selling for fifteen cents in the post exchange. He thereupon sent a sergeant from his office to buy ten such belts, for a total cost of $1.50. From then on that sergeant was charged with inspecting Ike's belt every morning and informing him if it needed replacement. When a belt buckle failed to pass muster, Ike would throw it in the wastebasket and replace it with a new one. To the best of my knowledge the original supply was never used up.

During the early spring of 1941 my mornings were filled with study and the afternoons with tennis. In the evenings, however, I was sometimes privileged to accompany Ike on inspection tours that involved the two divisions attached to IX Corps, the Regular 3d Division and the National Guard 41st Division.

The inspection that sticks out most in my mind occurred on the evening I received word that I had passed all the requirements to enter West Point. I was ordered to report with the class that was then designated as the Class of 1945.[12] Ike and I went out to the training area where both divisions were conducting an evening exercise. Though the rain was coming down hard, Ike and I were feeling elated.

What Ike saw in the 41st Division, however, did not please him. Like many other newly mobilized National Guard units, the division was still in a relatively untrained state. He stopped at several places to visit with officers and men, intent on ascertaining how much they knew of their mission, where the surrounding units were, and matters of that sort. I never inquired after the specific reasons for Ike's displeasure, but I suspect that he found a certain confusion and lethargy among officers not yet masters of their duties. "When I think of putting one of these National Guard units up against a German panzer division," he mused after leaving one tent, "I just shudder."[13]

Toward the end of the evening, around midnight, we arrived at a large squad tent. We made our way through the driving rain and passed through the tent flaps into the tactical command post of IX Corps headquarters. It was a gloomy place, illuminated only by dim, naked light bulbs hanging by long wires. It was barely furnished with camp chairs, tables, and map stands. In the middle of the tent stood a solitary figure disconsolately studying a situation map, its shiny acetate cover smeared with grease pencil markings showing the locations of the various units.

Ike strode up to this rather strange-looking man and quickly engaged him in serious conversation. As I studied Ike's companion, I was struck by how gaunt and drawn he appeared. His face was arresting, with an aquiline nose and bulging eyes. He wore a band around his head and spoke only in a whisper, as if suffering from a chronic case of laryngitis. That officer, the IX Corps G-3 (Operations), was Lieutenant Colonel Lucian K. Truscott, Jr., one of the Army's champion polo players and a man Ike thought highly of.[14] Little did Colonel Truscott give the impression that he would later become one of the greatest combat leaders of World War II as commander of the 3d Division, VI Corps, and eventually, after V-E Day, Third Army.

Somewhere in early June 1941, Ike received orders that would take him away from Fort Lewis. He had been requested by General Walter Krueger, at San Antonio, to be Third Army chief of staff. The new position almost assuredly meant promotion to the grade of brigadier general, but Ike was still let down. (I was unaware, of course, that he had been angling to join Major General George Patton's 2d Armored division at Fort Benning, and this assignment would put an end to any such hopes.) He would now remain with a staff, farther than ever from the combat troops.

As the date for departure approached, I watched with casual interest as Ike and Mamie, working together, packed up their belongings, wrapping each cup, each dish, each piece of silver in newspapers. Then in late June they drove me out to a small railroad stop called Nisqually Station on the edge of the Fort Lewis Military Reservation. I boarded the train for the trip back east, to report to West Point on July 1, 1941. By coincidence, Ike was to report to Fort Sam Houston on the same day.

Ike's tour of duty at Fort Lewis had been short, only about sixteen months. During the time that Ike and Mamie were there, however, the whole world had undergone change. Hitler's juggernaut had overrun France; Britain had defied Hitler in defeat and had miraculously survived. Hitler had invaded the Balkans. At about the time we left Fort Lewis the German dictator crossed into the Soviet Union in Operation BARBAROSSA.

Yet during that time, so tumultuous to the outside world, my parents' lives had been relatively serene. The glare of publicity had not yet gobbled them up. At Fort Lewis they were happier, in my observation, than at any other time of their lives.

Ike and Patton at a football game, Frankfurt, Germany, in October 1945. This occurred only a few days after Ike had removed Patton from command of Third Army.

Author's Collection

4

IKE AND PATTON

The Master and His Pit Bull

In the late summer of 1940, while Ike was still enjoying his service with the 15th Infantry at Fort Lewis, the name of his old friend George Patton emerged in the public print. In July Patton had left the 3d Cavalry at Fort Myer, Virginia, and had taken over the 2d Armored Brigade of the newly organized 2d Armored Division, stationed at Fort Benning, Georgia. Soon to be promoted to the grade of brigadier general, Patton was now at the center of the vast mobilization program that was just getting under way.

Back with tanks after an absence of twenty years, Patton performed his new duties with his usual panache. I recall seeing a photo that appeared in a newspaper, probably the *Seattle Post-Intelligencer*, showing Patton wearing the new tanker's uniform he had personally designed, which included a gold helmet and dark tunic with brass buttons up one side. Along with his dashing costume, Patton was wearing his fiercest "war face." His old Army friends compared him to "Flash Gordon," a character in a popular science fiction comic strip, or to the "Green Hornet," the hero of a popular radio series. It was exactly what his friends expected Patton to do; he was in character.

But they laughed with Patton, not at him. Despite his short-lived comic opera uniform, he was instilling a strong esprit de corps in the new Armored Force, adding excitement to the somewhat somber national mobilization. Though subordinate to others on the organizational charts, Patton was commanding the sole tank brigade of our only armored division and was popularly seen as Mr. Armored Force himself.

Patton had no intention of remaining a brigadier general, however, nor did his friend George Marshall, Chief of Staff, intend that he do so. By September of 1940, Patton was daily expecting to take command of the entire 2d Armored Division, not just a single brigade. In the process of finding officers to staff his new command, he wrote to Ike, his old friend from twenty years earlier, suggesting that the latter request transfer from the Infantry to the Armored Corps, specifically to Patton's 2d Armored Division.

Ike was pleased and flattered. At that time his sights were set only on commanding a regiment in the coming war, and an armored regiment sounded even more exciting than the 15th Infantry. He responded immediately and enthusiastically. "I suppose it's too much to hope that I could have a regiment in your division," he wrote, "because I'm still almost three years away from my colonelcy. But I *think* I could do a damn good job of commanding a regiment."[1]

Two weeks later Patton followed up with word that he would request Ike as chief of staff (which Patton would prefer) or as a regimental commander. He finished his letter with a typical flourish: "Hoping we are together in a long and BLOODY war."[2]

The exchange, of course, came to nothing, because Ike's services were considered too important at other, higher echelons—successively as chief of staff at 3d Infantry Division, IX Corps, and Third Army. When he was summoned to the Army General Staff in Washington a week after the Japanese raid on Pearl Harbor in December 1941, he knew that he had lost all contact with troops. Patton, on his part, was elevated from the command of the 2d Armored Division to that of the I Armored Corps at Indio, California. Both men were working overtime but in their respective spheres.

At this point Patton's previously assumed status as Ike's senior began to fade. In February of 1942 Patton visited Washington and could see that Ike, though still a brigadier general, was now located at the seat of power. After leaving, Patton wrote an ingratiating letter:

My dear Ike: Of all the many talks I had in Washington, none gave me so much pleasure as that with you. There were two reasons for this. In the first place, you are about my oldest friend. In the second place, your self-assurance and to me, at least, demonstrated ability, gave me a great feeling of confidence in the future. I am very glad that you hold your present position and have the utmost confidence that through your efforts we will eventually beat the hell out of those bastards—"You name them; I'll shoot them." Devotedly yours.[3]

Ike promptly replied, "I don't have the slightest trouble naming the hellions I'd like to have you shoot; my problem is to figure out some way of getting you to the place you can do it."[4]

Two months later Patton visited Washington once more. Again Ike wrote a note of encouragement: "Maybe I'll finally get out of this slave seat, so I can let loose a little lead with you. By that time you'll be the 'Black Jack' [Pershing] of the dam [*sic*] war."[5]

Unlikely as Ike's statement sounds, it had a basis. He had just undergone a face-off with Army Chief of Staff George Marshall, and he thought he might be removed as head of Operations Division. In that event, he might realize his dream and be available to join Patton. Instead of firing Ike, however, Marshall promoted him to the rank of major general. Ike now carried the same rank as Patton.

Yet Ike was serious in his offhand suggestion that Patton would be

the leader of any expeditionary force that America might send overseas. In June of 1942, when the Army staff was thinking of dispatch-
ing an armored division to assist the British in the Eastern Sahara, Ike's
mind "turned instantly . . . to Major General George S. Patton, Jr.,
who was not only a tank expert but an outstanding leader of troops."
Such an assignment would entail a technical demotion for Patton,
because it would mean stepping down from a corps command to that
of a division. Such a consideration, however, was secondary to Patton
if it offered an opportunity for battle. When Ike sent for him, he
reacted as expected; he immediately and enthusiastically accepted the
opportunity. Circumstances stepped in to cancel the War Department's
plans to deploy the armored division, but the incident reinforced Ike's
confidence in Patton's fighting instincts.[6]

As time went on, the relations between Patton and Ike changed even
further. Patton, ever sensitive to nuances of Army politics, received the
impression on a visit to Washington that he was being supplanted in
Marshall's favor not only by Ike but by Ike's friend and associate,
Major General Mark W. Clark. "From the rumors I heard," Patton
wrote to a friend, "it now seems that Eisenhower and Clark will have
the big jobs."[7] Events would soon prove Patton's conjecture to be well
taken.

In late June 1942, Major General Dwight Eisenhower departed Washington, bound for London, where he was soon promoted to the grade
of lieutenant general and named as the Commanding General, United
States Army in Europe. Along with him went the young (forty-six)
Major General Mark Clark, whose prospective assignment was the
command of II Corps, the senior American Army headquarters in
Europe. Ike came from Marshall's staff; Clark came from Army
Ground Forces. The two, however, were a team. Clark has, in fact, been
given much credit for Eisenhower's summons to Washington to head
War Plans the previous December.

When Ike and Clark went to London, it was presumed, at least in
Washington, that they were going to participate in an Allied attack
across the English Channel against Nazi-held northern France that
year. Soon after they arrived in London, however, plans were changed

because Prime Minister Winston Churchill rightly considered that the risks were too great. President Roosevelt accepted Churchill's veto of the operation but insisted that American troops must be fighting the Axis powers somewhere by the end of 1942. He and Churchill then decided that the Americans and British should invade North Africa, a region controlled by the Vichy French government of the aged Marshal Henri Pétain.

In view of the eventual consequence of that decision, which committed the Allies to long campaigns in the Mediterranean, we must remember the two political leaders did not originally visualize it as a major undertaking. French forces, it was assumed, would offer only token resistance to the Anglo-American landings and then the forces of all three nations would quickly occupy all of French North Africa, including Tunisia. The Germans and Italians, who were still fighting the British Eighth Army in eastern Libya, would therefore be cut off from any supply and reinforcements being sent to them from Europe through Tunisia. It looked easy, given the assumptions.

By odd circumstance, Ike was chosen to command TORCH, as the operation was code-named. His appointment over the heads of experienced British generals, as well as many Americans, was political. The French military were bitterly resentful of the British at that time, so Roosevelt and Churchill agreed that the operation should present an American complexion.

If an American were to command the operation, who would it be? There was some discussion, but in a remarkably short time Ike was selected. During the few weeks he had been in London, he had earned the confidence of the British, a confidence he already enjoyed on the part of Marshall. So a relatively young officer, who had been a lieutenant colonel of Infantry only fourteen months earlier, found himself in command of a great Allied force about to launch a very high risk operation.[8]

The change in Ike's role meant a shuffle in the American command structure. In order to ensure that the Allied command would remain in American hands if Ike were killed or incapacitated, Mark Clark was elevated from the command of II Corps to be Ike's deputy. To replace Clark as senior American ground commander, Ike's first thought was Patton. There is no indication that he even considered anyone else.

Yet even the self-confident Ike was reticent to request as his subordinate an officer who throughout the years had been his senior. That initiative would have to come from General Marshall. On July 29, 1942, therefore, Ike wrote to Marshall saying that "anyone you name to important commands . . . will be completely acceptable to me." But then he offered his own suggestions. Patton's name was one of four candidates for the position of Commanding General of the American Force. If someone else were selected for that position, Ike submitted Patton's name as one of four qualified to command the armored corps.[9]

Plans for an overall American tactical commander were soon abandoned, however, because the vast distances between the prospective landings on the North African coast made it impossible for a single commander to control all three. It was over 600 miles airline between the easternmost landing (Algiers) and Casablanca, and much more by sea. The three task forces would therefore report directly to Ike's headquarters, which in early November would be moved from London to Gibraltar, to arrive just before the landings were made. That being the case, Ike asked Marshall for Patton to command the Western Task Force, which would sail directly from the United States and land on the Atlantic coast of Morocco.[10] He was delighted when Marshall agreed.[11]

All this happened very rapidly. Patton was summoned from his I Armored Corps headquarters in the California desert, and by August 5, 1942, was flying to London to help Ike in the latter planning phases for TORCH.[12]

Ike was delighted to renew direct contact with Patton. The two old friends sat up late over drinks one evening, and talked very freely. They confidentially agreed, so Patton recorded, that Operation TORCH was "bad and mostly political." However, having been told to execute it, they would "succeed or die in the attempt."[13] Ike happily reported back to Marshall when Patton left London that

> General Patton has shown a definite capacity to absorb the essentials of his problem and has approached all his work in a very businesslike, sane, but enthusiastic attitude. I am delighted that you fixed upon him as your choice for leading the American venture.[14]

Those were strange words being passed between two men who both knew Patton intimately. Between the lines Ike was implying that "Georgie" had set aside, if not overcome, his impetuous ways.

Despite Ike's elation, Patton was less enchanted. He readily accepted serving under Ike, whom he respected, but he could not abide the fact that Ike's deputy for TORCH was Mark Clark, eleven years his own junior. Of Ike, Patton wrote, "It is very noticeable that most of the American officers here are pro-British, even Ike. I am not, repeat not, pro-British." And of Clark, he wrote, "I do not trust [him] yet."[15]

From that time on, Patton made frequent comments critical of Ike in letters to his wife and in his diary. Very often he would make derogatory remarks about Ike and Clark together. Ike, he wrote, was getting "megalomania," was not "as rugged mentally" as he had thought.[16] If Ike was aware of Patton's feelings, however, he did not show it. He continued to write frank, confidential letters to Patton long after the latter's departure from London for the United States to organize his task forces. He was delighted to have Patton with him.

On November 8, 1942, Patton's Western Task Force landed at three locations in Morocco: Fedala, Casablanca, and Port Lyautey. For some reason he lost communication with Allied Force Headquarters (now at Gibraltar) and some anxiety resulted. The surf at Casablanca was known to be dangerous, and rumors began flying around Ike's headquarters that Patton had "given up." Ike discounted such ideas. Knowing Patton as he did, he was sure that they could never be true. He was not certain whether the communications breakdown between Casablanca and Gibraltar had occurred totally by accident, but he never pursued the matter.

Events moved rapidly. After a brief resistance, the formerly Vichy French forces joined the Americans and British in fighting the Germans and Italians. Ike tried desperately to seize Tunisia quickly but was defeated by long supply lines, miserable weather, and stiff German resistance. Then set in a long winter of fighting in Tunisia, in which the commander of British and American troops was British General Kenneth Anderson, whose command was designated as the First British

Army. The American component of that army was the II Corps, commanded by Major General Lloyd R. Fredendall, an officer who could boast few admirers among his contemporaries.

During December and January, Patton was assigned to planning and training duties in Morocco. His opportunity to fight eventually arrived, however, when the Americans suffered a sharp defeat at Kasserine Pass in late February 1943. As a result of that debacle, the American II Corps was badly demoralized and needed a boost. So Ike called Patton from Morocco and sent him to take charge of the battle. Patton did not disappoint him. He soon instilled fighting spirit into the American troops on the south end of the Tunisian line, even devising some limited objectives, such as El Guettar, to assist it. His performance has been extolled by his admirers and damned with faint praise by his critics, but he did what Ike wanted. He then returned to Morocco, where he was charged with planning the landings of Seventh Army in the invasion of Sicily the following July. Major General Omar Bradley replaced him in command of II Corps.

From that time on, there would always be an echelon of command sandwiched between Ike and Patton. In Tunisia Patton's II Corps was at first part of Anderson's British First Army, as mentioned. In the latter phases of the Tunisian battle and in Sicily the de facto commander of the Allied ground troops was British General Sir Harold Alexander, now deputy to Eisenhower.* Nevertheless, Patton, always the highest ranking American in Sicily, held an attitude that bordered on the chauvinistic. When he detected any evidence of a pro-British attitude on Ike's part, he became resentful, apparently unable to accept the fact that Ike, as a coalition commander, had to make concessions to the British viewpoint. Patton recorded his feelings in his letters and his diary. He was not bashful about expressing them in the presence of his staff. In public he was always correct.

The invasion of Sicily in July 1943, code-named HUSKY, has often been criticized, primarily because the two German divisions, including

---

*Mark Clark had left Allied Force Headquarters to assume command of the U.S. Fifth Army, training in Morocco.

the vaunted Hermann Göring Panzer Division, escaped across the Strait of Messina into Italy during the closing days of the campaign. However, in the elation that resulted from the liberation of the island—and since the successful culmination of the operation triggered the fall of the Italian dictator Benito Mussolini—any criticisms

Ike pins the third star, for lieutenant general, on his friend in North Africa in spring of 1943. Nothing gave Patton more pleasure than obtaining an additional star. Notably, George had already sewn his new rank on his jacket before the ceremony.

Library of Congress

of the operation were muted at the time. With the benefit of hindsight, however, it appears that General Sir Harold Alexander (commonly called "Alex") still viewed the Americans as second-class troops. Recalling their poor performance at Kasserine Pass, he gave Patton only a minor role, that of protecting the left flank of General Bernard L. Montgomery's British Eighth Army as it drove up the east coast of Sicily toward Messina. In practical terms, Alexander gave Monty an inordinate preference by giving Eighth Army the important Vizzini–Caltagirone highway, though it was essential to Patton's northward advance. Now Monty was to attack on both sides of Mt. Etna, and Patton was deprived of the road running south to north along its western slope.

Patton was furious but not defeated. Resolved to overcome the obstacle that Alex had placed in his path, he sideslipped Bradley's II Corps westward and then sent it northwestward to Palermo, on the island's northern coast. Turning eastward along the northern shore of the island, he reached—and took—the ultimate goal of Messina before Montgomery. Patton covered himself with glory, and if he was unmerciful in the way he drove his men, he saved lives by so doing. The enemy never got a chance to dig in on Patton's front.

Then came a stunning blow, an act on Patton's part that overshadowed his stellar performance on the battlefields of Sicily. That, of course, was the notorious "soldier-slapping incident."

On August 3, 1943, Patton stopped off at an evacuation hospital to visit the newly arrived wounded. Among them he encountered a soldier who showed no visible wounds, and he asked the man why he was in the hospital. "I guess I just can't take it," was the answer. Patton swore, called the soldier a coward, and ordered him out of the tent. When the man failed to move, Patton slapped him in the face with a glove, picked him up by the collar of his shirt, and shoved him out of the tent with a kick. That night he issued a memorandum to all the officers of the Seventh Army instructing them to "see that such cases are not sent to the hospital but . . . tried by court-martial for cowardice in the face of the enemy."[17]

A week later Patton repeated the scene, this time behaving even worse. Encountering a man who had been hospitalized for combat fatigue, he called the soldier a "yellow son of a bitch" and berated him for crying. He reportedly drew a pistol from his holster and waved it under the man's nose. Later investigation pointed up Patton's injustice, because the man had been with II Corps since March; he had actually resisted being evacuated to the hospital and had been sent there against his will.[18]

In a way Patton's conduct is not surprising, considering that he had acted in somewhat the same fashion at previous times. At the beginning of the Meuse-Argonne campaign in September 1918, he had hit a skulking soldier on the head with a shovel, afterward presuming he had killed him.[19] And at the Casablanca landing of November 8, 1942, Patton "kicked [a man] in the arse with all my might and he jumped right up and went to work."[20] Those acts, performed in the heat of battle, apparently caused Patton to assume that corporal punishment and humiliation were proper means of enforcing discipline under all circumstances.

Word of Patton's acts spread like wildfire throughout Seventh Army. Ike first learned of them on August 17, 1943, when he received the news from Brigadier General Frederick Blessé, the Chief Surgeon, one of whose medical officers had reported the incidents. Three days later a newspaper reporter, Demaree Bess, came to Ike's headquarters with the unwelcome word that the story had been picked up by the press. The general opinion among Bess's colleagues was that Patton had "subjected himself to court-martial by striking an enlisted man under his command."[21]

Bess, a responsible correspondent, had not yet filed a story on the subject, so Ike met with him and two other reporters to assure them that he would take appropriate action. He asked them to bury the story in light of Patton's value as a combat leader. The Army, he said, could ill afford to lose Patton's "driving power" for the rest of the war. The correspondents agreed.[22]

Ike saw Patton's actions as inexcusable. Had his transgressions been committed in the heat of battle, Ike later wrote, they might have gone unnoticed. But Patton's conduct in abusing a man in a hospital, in the presence of others, was "nothing less than brutal."[23] Nevertheless, Ike's own task was to try to minimize what damage had been done—if indeed such were possible. First he sent three emissaries from Algiers to Sicily. One went to see Patton himself; another went to visit the hospitals. The third visited the various divisions of the Seventh Army to determine the reaction of the troops. As a result of the reports, he determined to retain Patton but to exact a heavy price by way of retribution:

> I first wrote him a sharp letter of reprimand in which I informed him that repetition of such an offense would be cause for his instant relief. I informed him also that his retention as a commander in my theater would be contingent on his offering an apology to the two men whom he had insulted. I demanded also that he apologize to all the personnel of the hospital present at the time of the incident. Finally I required that he appear before the officers and representative groups of each of his divisions to assure them that he had given way to impulse and respected their positions as fighting soldiers of a democratic nation.[24]

Not every officer would have accepted such a draconian set of conditions in order to stay in battle, but Patton immediately agreed. When he received Ike's "very nasty letter" on August 20, he reflected, "Evidently I acted precipitately and on insufficient knowledge. My motive was correct because one cannot permit skulking to exist. . . . My method was wrong but I shall make what amends I can." But he still called the men cowards in private, and when he learned fully of Ike's attitude, he described his feelings as "very low."[25] Yet he was unrepentant. Forced to shake hands with one of the men he had abused, Patton commented in his diary, "It is rather a commentary on justice when an Army commander has to soft-soap a skulker to placate the timidity of those above."[26]

Ike may have been timid in Patton's eyes, but in fact the opposite was true. He was, in fact, being unrealistically optimistic in hoping that the two incidents could ever be kept from general knowledge. As it turned out, the correspondents were amazingly cooperative; all but one kept the secret. Finally, however, the inevitable happened. A prominent reporter named Drew Pearson, who for years had written a Washington gossip column, revealed the story in the American newspapers, and the result was an instant explosion. People who were already irritated by Patton's personality fell upon the incident with relish. Even the average American was taken aback. The public was unaware of the humiliations that Patton had been forced to endure as punishment for his acts.

I happen to remember that moment vividly. I was a cadet at West Point at the time, and my mother was on the post for a visit. While there she was admitted into the station hospital with some malady, and during a visit one evening we received the news. Reports claimed that Ike was under fire for standing by Patton, and for a while it appeared that the careers of both men might well be equally jeopardized. I have no idea whether Ike realized the extent of the risk he had taken in retaining Patton. In any case, General Marshall, and consequently President Roosevelt, eventually supported Ike. In less than a month after that news broke, Ike was appointed to be Supreme Commander for OVERLORD, the invasion of northwest Europe.

At that point, Ike's name filled the headlines, but Patton mysteriously disappeared from public view. After the furor over the slapping incident had blown over, however, he reappeared in Britain, though his assignment was not revealed. In the meantime Ike had announced that Lieutenant General Omar N. Bradley was to be the senior American ground commander for the invasion, reporting directly to Ike's own headquarters.[27] If Patton were to participate, therefore, he would have to serve under his former subordinate, Bradley. Patton accepted that dictum philosophically, at least outwardly.

Once Patton's presence in Britain became known, Ike made use of his reputation by making him part of Operation FORTITUDE, an elaborate scheme designed to keep the enemy guessing as to Allied intentions. There was only so much that the Allies could hide; the fact that they intended to invade France from the United Kingdom could never be kept secret. The American troop buildup, the tons of supplies that lined all the country roads, and the presence of the former Mediterranean command team made the imminence of OVERLORD obvious. Allied intelligence, therefore, had to settle for keeping the Germans guessing on only two matters, the timing and the place of the invasion.

Patton's role in FORTITUDE actually began after D-Day, June 6, when the Americans and British landed on the beaches of Normandy. His role was to keep Hitler and his generals in doubt as to whether the

Normandy landing was truly the main Allied effort, or a mere feint to distract attention from a later, stronger crossing at the Pas de Calais. The Germans did not necessarily believe Ike's announcement of Bradley's seniority; further, there was much to be said for the Pas de Calais as the place for the gigantic effort they expected.[28] The English Channel is only twenty miles wide at that point, and Calais is 300 miles closer to Germany than Cherbourg.

Many devices were used to keep German intelligence expecting a second landing. Dummy encampments, sprinkled with rubber models of tanks and artillery, were established in East Anglia, where Patton's fictitious First Army Group headquarters was supposed to be located. More important was the bombardment of the airwaves with fake radio traffic. But the absence of Patton on the Normandy front was probably the most important means of creating doubt in the enemy's mind. When Allied agents began spreading the rumor that Patton was slated to command the later, true invasion, Hitler and his generals were at least partially taken in. They feared Patton more than they feared any other Allied officer.

There was no mistaking Patton's presence, because in late spring of 1944 his conduct again threatened his future. Despite the lavish promises he had given Ike that he would keep a low profile, he burst into the headlines with another indiscretion. Asked to speak at the opening of a welcome center at the small town of Knutsford, in northern England, he expounded on the need for Britain and America to remain allies. After the war, he declaimed, the two together were destined to "rule the world." Patton was always good copy, so his remarks received a great deal of attention, particularly in the United States.

Patton's simplistic and foolish prediction of Anglo-American world hegemony was not the cause of the furor; it was his failure to include our Russian allies. Sensitive to the immense amount of suffering the Soviet Union had undergone during the war, many people at home were overly fearful of offending Joseph Stalin and the other Russian leaders. The depth of feeling at home became so serious that some Republican leaders in the Senate informed General Marshall that they would never approve the pending promotion list of general officers if Patton's name was on it.[29] Worse, the public (as well as Ike) were beginning to wonder if Patton had any sense of responsibility at all.

Once again Ike had to decide whether to retain Patton or not. And once again Ike decided that success in battle was the overriding consideration: he gave Patton one more chance to weather the storm and once again Marshall supported him. As Ike later described it,

> . . . George came to see me and in his typically generous and impulsive fashion offered to resign his commission so as to relieve me of any embarrassment. When I finally announced to him my determination to retain him as the prospective commander of the Third Army, he was stirred to the point of tears. At such moments General Patton revealed a side of his make-up that was difficult for anyone except his intimate friends to understand. His remorse was very great, not only for the trouble he had caused me, but, he said, for the fact that he had vehemently criticized me to his associates when he thought I might relieve him. His emotional range was very great, and he lived at either one end or the other of it.[30]

It was shortly after D-Day, in late June 1944, that I saw Ike and Patton together. I found the episode both instructive and amusing.

On General Marshall's orders, I was spending my West Point graduation leave with Ike, who was undergoing an exasperating period of inactivity. The troops in France were organized into a single army group, commanded directly by General Montgomery, and until such time as Ike would assume personal command of all the Allied ground forces, he had little to do. Accustomed to intense activity, he fretted like a caged lion. So during that period of forced inactivity, we did various things together. We made two trips to Normandy, visited Portsmouth, where the D-Day decision had been made, played a little bridge, and even visited Prime Minister Churchill in his Whitehall office.

On June 28, 1944, Ike decided to visit the 35th Division, which was camped on the Salisbury Plain, awaiting commitment in Normandy. Since the Salisbury Plain was within a couple of hours' distance from London, it was possible for Ike to board his private train, visit a division, and return to London that same evening. On the day I accompanied him, General Patton, likewise undergoing enforced idleness, went along.

Ike's train, as I recall it, had a small, private area, but it also had a larger living room, where a conversation between a reasonable number of people could be carried on. There the small group sat, with Ike and Patton on one side, and with me and a couple of others across.

From the outset it was obvious that the irrepressible Patton had recovered completely from the hiding he had received in recent weeks from Ike. In fact, such unpleasant episodes seemed to have little or no lasting effect on him, provided that he found the outcome satisfactory to his interests. In any case, Patton was in high spirits that June day.

Ike was the senior officer present, and military custom practically dictates that the senior holds center stage in any such gathering. Not so that day. Patton, a large man, shining with fifteen stars* and wearing all his authorized decorations, sat up in his chair and held forth as if surrounded by his own staff. "Ike," he said, "when we finish licking these bastards, I want you to make me the Heinrich Himmler for the occupation." Then rubbing his hands together, his eyes gleaming, his face in a half-grimace, half-grin, he declared, "I'll show them a reign of terror like they have never imagined."

From across the center aisle, I glanced at Ike's face. He seemed exceedingly glum. Saddled with an annoying but by no means unfamiliar situation, he acted like a host whose guests had brought along unwelcome children who were a cause for embarrassment but not direct action. Throughout the whole trip down to Salisbury, Ike simply seemed resigned.

When we arrived at the encampment of the 35th Division, Ike and his party were whisked to a field where the troops were drawn up for inspection. At that point Ike did his stuff. He did it well, having practiced it time and again. He moved from soldier to soldier, asking brisk questions to ascertain each man's alertness. With the 35th, he was particularly comfortable, because it came partially from his own home state of Kansas. He prided himself on his "farm boy" background, so when he found a soldier who came from a farm, which many of them did, he grilled the man on the type of cattle he raised, how many bushels of wheat the farm produced per acre, and questions of that nature. Once satisfied, he would say a sharp "Good!" and move on to

---

*Three on each shoulder, three on each shirt lapel, and three on the front of his helmet liner.

the next. Finally he called for the troops to break ranks and gather around him for an informal talk.[31] He did this as much for show as for his own information, on the premise that once the word of his presence got around, every man in the division would soon be convinced that he had seen Ike in person. At the end of the inspection, Ike and his party retired to the top of a hillock to watch a tactical demonstration of a rifle company in the attack.

During the inspection, Patton, lacking a role, bided his time properly. When the tactical demonstration began, however, he became excited. Something hit him as very wrong. What agitated him was the sight of a squad of men running along the bottom of a deep swale, crouched over as if to present as low a profile as possible. Since the banks of the swale exceeded more than ten feet, such protection made it unnecessary for men to seek safety by running at a crouch. Losing his head, Patton burst away from Ike's reviewing party and ran down to the field, where the troops had reached the crest and were properly stretched out in firing position, flat on their bellies.

Patton selected one of the soldiers—why that particular man, I don't know. He rushed up and stood above the boy, who was lying prone. Shaking his fist to the sky, Patton roared out, "You have no need to stoop when you are under cover! Save your energy!" Then, as a clincher, he shouted out, "You show you have no knowledge of the art of war!"

The spectacle will stay with me as long as I live. Goodness knows what that young Kansan, peering up with a bewildered look, thought of this star-bestudded man in the shiny helmet liner who hovered over him, but I presume that the lad had little interest in demonstrating his knowledge of the art of war; all he wanted was to get away. While the outburst was going on, Ike's reviewing group simply waited until Patton swaggered back to join them.

The trip back to London on the train was uneventful, at least not memorable. If Ike spoke to Patton about his bizarre outburst, I never heard of it. My guess is that he did not. Certainly he would never have criticized Patton in front of others. I cite the incident simply to illustrate the type of annoyance Ike was willing to undergo in order to save this man for what he was best at, fighting.

☙

Because of my relationship to Ike, I was privileged, by the age of thirty, to have met a remarkable number of very accomplished men. From that I have come to realize what a mistake it is to judge an individual by his foibles. I apply that conclusion in particular to General George Patton, for in only a little over a month after I was secretly amused by his antics on Salisbury Plain, Patton's Third U.S. Army was committed at Avranches, on the northern corner of the Brittany Peninsula, and he was about to make history.

Third Army became operational on August 1, 1944, and even before it went into action, its mission had been changed. Originally, the OVERLORD planners had visualized turning Patton westward with three corps to seize and consolidate the Brittany Peninsula, thus providing seaports for a methodical buildup in the so-called Continental Lodgment Area between the Seine and the Loire Rivers.* But after the spectacular American success at St. Lô on July 25, Ike advised General Marshall informally that if all went as hoped, he would "consider it unnecessary to detach any large forces for the conquest of Brittany and would devote the bulk of the forces to the task of completing the destruction of the German Army, at least that portion west of the Orne, and exploiting beyond that as far as we possibly could."[32] That was where Patton came in: he would take the bulk of Third Army, three of his four corps, and drive eastward to complete the occupation of the lodgment area.

He did it brilliantly. Sending the XXX Corps southward, he drove the other, Wade H. Haislip's XV Corps, eastward. By noon of August 5, he had taken the town of Mayenne and four days later had taken Le Mans. In five days he had gone seventy-five miles, his army stretching for 200 miles between his eastward spearhead and the advance elements of his VIII Corps, taking the Brittany Peninsula. When his spearheads were a hundred miles from the Paris–Orléans gap, he turned one corps northward to Argentan, there to form the southern shoulder of the

---

*The Seine and Loire Rivers, both unfordable, constituted formidable obstacles to any attacker. Between Paris, on the Seine, and Orléans, on the Loire, the distance is only about sixty miles. Thus the northwest corner of France, between those two rivers and including the Brittany Peninsula, made a near-island. Originally that area was to be occupied by D+90 days, that is, by September 6. After a major supply buildup in that lodgment area, the Allies planned to cross the Seine in the direction of Germany The Seine and Loire Rivers are shown on Map 4.

"Falaise Gap," so murderous to the German army. By August 25 he had bypassed Paris on the south, and by September 11 his tanks and infantry had reached the city of Dijon, where they joined up with the spearheads of the Seventh U.S. Army, coming up from Marseilles.[33]

Perhaps another officer could have driven the Third Army eastward with all the energy as that exhibited by Patton, but I don't believe so. Far more importantly, neither did Ike. His risky retention of Patton in command had paid off handsomely.

The public at home, incidentally, was kept in the dark as to who was making these long advances, because Ike had kept Patton's command of the Third Army secret. When Supreme Headquarters announced to the world that it was Patton who had commanded the spectacular dash, Old Blood and Guts was once more a national hero. Characteristically, he basked in the adulation.

The war looked as if it might end in the early fall of 1944, but it was not to be. The front line troops of the Western Allies—the United States, Britain, and now France—simply ran out of supplies, especially gasoline. Despite the gargantuan efforts of the Communications Zone and such extraordinary measures as the famed one-way truck circuit called the Red Ball Express, it was impossible to end the war in one blow. A frustrating and deadly set of battles followed, fought under miserable conditions, to set up a solid base from which the war could be won in the spring.

At this point, the national feelings between the Americans and British began to erupt into mutual criticism. Ike was not exempt from British attacks, especially from Montgomery in private and British Chief of the Imperial General Staff Sir Alan Brooke more openly. Churchill's complaints against the apparent stalemate were muffled but real. It was then that the controversy over the "single thrust" versus the "broad front" strategic concepts came to a head. The viewpoints fell largely along national lines.

The so-called Broad Front, a term invented by and sniffed at by many of the British hierarchy, was made to sound like a timid strategy, a compromise forced on Ike by pressure from the United States. In the mind's eye, one pictures a "broad front" as millions of men, spread evenly across the front, all joining hands and moving forward in a line. Such, if that had been the case, would of course have been ridiculous. It was far from the actual idea.

Historically there have been two main avenues of approach between France and Germany, one or the other being used from time immemorial. During the twentieth century, the most touted of these avenues has been the wide area of Belgium known as the North German Plain, north of the Ardennes. The more traditional avenue is the east-west route, which runs south of the Ardennes from Frankfurt in Germany westward through the Saar Basin, Metz, Verdun, Châlons (where Attila the Hun was stopped in A.D. 451), thence along the Marne westward to Paris. Because of the attention given to the famous Schlieffen Plan of the First World War, the North German Plain has been emphasized to the point that in the popular mind there exists no other. For many reasons, geography had dictated that General Montgomery's 21 Army Group was deployed on the left as the Allies drove eastward toward Germany. He was therefore on the North German Plain.

The Single Thrust concept advocated by Montgomery and many other British officers called for a virtual halt along the rest of the Allied line in order to provide a superabundance of supplies to Monty's 21 Army Group. That strategy would force the bulk of the Americans to remain inactive; the rest would come under the command of Montgomery.

The Broad Front strategy, on the other hand, called for using both corridors, one north of the Ardennes (and the Ruhr beyond) and the other south of that supposedly impenetrable obstacle. Along the Metz–Saar corridor, in late 1944, Patton's Third Army was to constitute the main American effort. Such was the American plan and, since the Americans were coming daily into a position of preponderant strength and influence, that was the strategy followed by Ike, with the backing of the American Joint Chiefs of Staff.

On December 16, 1944, Adolf Hitler's forces, in a last desperate bid to achieve at least a stalemate with the Allies, launched a gigantic counterattack through the rough, partially wooded Ardennes, an area whose road net was generally considered inadequate to support major offensive operations.[34] For a few days it appeared, at least to the British and American publics, that Allied defeat was very possible, that the German General Staff had "done it again." That situation called forth perhaps the most significant, certainly the most dramatic, exchange between Ike and Patton of the entire European War.

Patton, when the attack had begun, was slow to sense what was going on, largely because the intelligence available to his Third Army headquarters was far narrower than that available to Ike. He was also probably influenced because the blow had not hit his Third Army position.

By chance, Ike and Omar Bradley were together at Eisenhower's Versailles headquarters on the evening of the attack. The subject foremost in their minds was not the tactical situation on the 12 Army Group front but the need for further infantry replacements. The heavy fighting on the frontiers of Germany was causing manpower shortages in the American front-line units. Both Ike and Bradley were concerned that the authorities in Washington considered the European War already won, and they also feared that pressure was mounting to send more resources to the Pacific at the expense of Europe.

In the course of the early evening conversation, a message came in from the SHAEF* intelligence officer, British General Kenneth Strong. The Germans, the message said, had made five penetrations through First Army positions in the Ardennes, the so-called quiet zone, where tired or new divisions were sent either for rest or for their initial combat indoctrination. Those divisions were spread out: there were only four to cover a seventy-mile front.

Ike and Bradley had previously discussed the risk of holding the Ardennes with such a thin line. Together they had agreed that the Germans could attack in that area—Bradley halfway hoped they would. To make any normal "spoiling" attack fruitless, they had agreed to keep all major supply depots behind the Meuse River, thus denying the enemy any remunerative long-term objectives in the Ardennes area. An attack there would have to be a major effort, designed to cross the Meuse.

When five penetrations were reported that evening, therefore, Ike became suspicious almost immediately that the attack must have some purpose behind it other than local annoyance. Bradley, on considera-

---

*Supreme Headquarters, Allied Expeditionary Force.

tion, agreed. Ike then sent for a situation map and found that two armored divisions were out of the line at the moment. One was the 7th, assigned to General William Simpson's Ninth U.S. Army in the north, and the other was the 10th, assigned to Patton's Third Army, which was scheduled to attack into the Saar region on December 19. Ike directed Bradley to send both of those divisions to Courtney Hodges, Commander of the First Army, whose front had been hit.[35]

Securing the 7th Armored from Simpson would not be difficult, for Simpson was the soul of cooperation. But taking the 10th Armored from Patton would be something else. Ike therefore handed Bradley that unpleasant task. As predicted, Patton screamed over the phone that this was not a serious attack; the Germans had launched it merely to distract attention from his own effort into the Saar. But the order stood. "Tell him," Ike growled to Bradley, "that Ike is running this damned war." But he let Bradley convey the message. He spared himself that ordeal.

Circumstances bore Ike's decision out. The major Ardennes counteroffensive was certainly no mere spoiling attack. Furthermore, the two armored divisions in question both played key roles in delaying Hitler's offensive, the 7th at St. Vith and the 10th at Bastogne.

By December 19, the day that Patton had originally been slated to begin his drive to the Saar, Ike met with his commanders at Bradley's main headquarters in Verdun. The conference was held in a small, chilly barracks, the room heated by just a single potbellied stove. Since it was only the Americans who had been hit, all the attendees at the meeting, with the exception of Deputy Supreme Commander Sir Arthur Tedder and Kenneth Strong, were American.[36] As they filed into the room, the atmosphere was somber.

There was plenty of reason for gloom. On that very morning, the position of the 7th Armored Division at St. Vith was becoming precarious. Two of the three regiments of the 106th Infantry Division on the Schnee Eifel, east of St. Vith, had been captured almost without a fight. The group did not know whether Bastogne, a critical crossroads town in the southern portion of the Ardennes region, was yet surrounded.

Ike would tolerate no pessimism, however. "The present situation," he announced at the outset, "is to be regarded as one of opportunity for us and not disaster. There will be only cheerful faces at this conference table." He had already decided what he intended to do. He would hold Bastogne and would change the direction of Patton's attack from the east toward the Saar to the north toward Bastogne. Turning an army ninety degrees to attack in a new direction would be no mean task, but he knew that Patton would be capable of doing it. Having adjusted the boundary between Third Army and Alexander Patch's Seventh Army, Ike turned to Patton and asked how quickly Patton could begin a movement of six divisions northward.

"The morning of the twenty-first," said Patton. "With three divisions."

Ike bristled. "Don't be fatuous, George," he said. "If you try to go that early, you won't have all three divisions ready and you'll go piecemeal. You will start on the twenty-second and I want your initial blow to be a strong one! I'd even settle for the twenty-third if it takes that long to get three full divisions."

The effect of this exchange was electrifying to the assembled group. Relieving three divisions from the line, turning them northward, and moving them over icy roads to the current line of contact, near Arlon, ready to fight a major action in less than seventy-two hours, was an astonishing undertaking. But those were the orders that Ike gave. The Third Army was to jump off no earlier than December 22 and no later than the 23d with a strength of three divisions to relieve the garrison at Bastogne. Ike would provide ample air support.

If the rest of the group were taken aback, Patton was not. Before leaving his headquarters in Nancy that morning, he had left his household in order. He had held a staff meeting in which he had anticipated three possible orders he could receive at Verdun. For each contingency he had left a code word. Once he received Ike's order, he needed only to telephone his chief of staff, General Hobart Gay, and issue a single code word. That he did and then asked permission to leave the meeting. Ike walked with him to the door.

At that point, a glimmer of the old personal friendship shone through. Nearly two years before, Ike had just received his fourth star, to the rank of general, when his forces in Tunisia were hit at Kasserine Pass. Now, only a few days before the Verdun meeting, Ike had been promoted to the new rank of General of the Army and the same thing had happened, this time on a larger scale. Conscious of the coinci-dence, he said, "Funny thing, George. Every time I get another star I get attacked."

"And every time you get attacked," Patton replied with his impish grin, "I have to bail you out."[37]

It was a remarkable episode, an illustration of the confidence Ike had in Patton. Normally, as Supreme Commander, Ike did not interfere in tactical matters, but this crisis was so important that he attended to it himself, dealing directly with the army commander involved. To be sure, Ike made a nod to Omar Bradley's 12 Army Group, and on Ike's departure, supervision of Patton's attack would then fall to Bradley. But this exchange was between Ike and George.

The vignette recalls to mind Patton's prediction, made when he and Ike were young officers, that in the next war Ike would be the Robert E. Lee and Patton would be the Stonewall Jackson, Lee's "right arm." That was a flattering forecast, especially because Patton made it when he was the senior of the two. It has become a mischievous prediction, however. Most students agree that Patton was a "Stonewall Jackson," but was Ike to be compared directly with Lee? Ike was not, and he should not have been. Lee was commanding a single army of some 45,000 men at the Battle of Chancellorsville, the climax of his part-nership with Jackson. Ike was commanding five million men by the time the war ended, and he was two echelons, not one, above Patton. Omar Bradley, not Patton, had become Ike's standard "right arm"; Pat-ton was a valued instrument. But in crisis, the mutual confidence between the two old friends took over.

Patton turned northward, as ordered, and executed a hard-driving campaign to relieve Bastogne, which had been surrounded late on December 20. After six days, his lead division, the 4th Armored, entered Bastogne from the south, eliciting from General Anthony C. McAuliffe, in command, a relieved, "I'm mighty glad to see you."*

From then on to the end of the war, Patton operated as a compo-

---

*McAuliffe's terse reply to the German demand for surrender, "Nuts!" has become promi-nent in the lore of the campaign. There is no question of its authenticity.

nent of 12 Army Group, performing the kind of operation he loved: hot pursuit of the enemy. His Third Army drove down through Austria, ending up at Linz, the town of Adolf Hitler's birth.

May 8, 1945—V-E Day—found me assigned to the G-3 (operations) section of the 1st Infantry Division, located at Cheb (Eger), Czechoslovakia. Aware that my contributions to the war in Europe had been minimal, and also aware that the 1st Division was slated for occupation duty in Europe, I asked General Clarence Huebner, who

Ike and Patton meet in Bastogne in March of 1945. In the background is Lieutenant General (later General of the Army) Omar N. Bradley.

National Archives

was awaiting orders to go to the Far East, if I might accompany him. He readily agreed to my request, but we would have to wait until his turn came to head for Asia. In the meantime, Ike called me for temporary duty at Supreme Headquarters, now moved to Frankfurt, Germany. There we prepared for a trip to Moscow, scheduled for early August.

One day Ike said casually, "As long as you are marking time in the Secretariat, why don't you go down to visit George Patton? You might as well see Bavaria before you leave for the Far East." The idea sounded good, and I took a small liaison plane and hopped down to Bad Tolz, where General Patton had plenty of room in his sumptuous villa.

The visit was memorable, and I have described it in my memoir.[38] Patton, as might be expected, was a lively host. In a couple of days I saw him in a rage (over his young aide's picking up a suitcase, the job of an enlisted man), hitting a punching bag in the basement of the villa, berating some soldiers who had failed to salute, and acting as an attentive host. One evening, as we were retiring from dinner, Patton walked me to the door. Pointing to the four stars on his shoulder, he began to weep and said, "These are all the stars I ever wanted. I owe them all to your father." Then the evening was over. On the morning that I took my leave at breakfast, he stood up to shake hands, chat a moment, and say goodbye as if I had been a high-ranking officer.[39] The noteworthy aspect of the visit, however, is the fact that Ike felt free to send me on a purely social visit to Patton's headquarters.

My reassignment to the Far East never came to pass. On August 15, 1945, Japan surrendered, and all previous plans for individual transfers were canceled. As a young Regular who had arrived in Europe late in the war, I was slated for extended occupation duty. I was assigned, much to my delight, to the headquarters of General L. T. Gerow's Fifteenth Army, located at Bad Nauheim, north of Frankfurt. It promised to be heady work. Fifteenth Army, a headquarters without troops, was designated as the "Theater General Board," charged with studying the recent European campaign and making recommendations for how things could be done better in the future.

I arrived at Army headquarters in early September, and during the following two-month period, Ike and I were close companions, the closest in our lives. The excitement of the war was over, and we were both feeling a bit of loneliness. Since Bad Nauheim was only about a half-hour's drive up the Autobahn from Ike's home at Bad Homburg, I went down to have dinner with him at least twice a week. Sometimes he would ride back in the car and drop me off at the Westsanatorium, my billet. That period remains my most treasured memory.

One evening in October 1945, Ike seemed to be in a particularly pensive mood as we speeded along the Autobahn. "I had to fire George Patton today," he said. He went on to tell of a press conference that Patton had held in Bad Tolz complaining about his difficulties in try-ing to administer his occupation area. Under the late Nazi regime, Pat-ton claimed, anyone in a responsible position had been automatically forced to join the Nazi party. The Allied policy of forbidding the Army to hire anyone who had ever been a Nazi had therefore made it impossible to run power plants, utilities, and even railroad trains. Pat-ton, in complaining to the press of this restriction, had quipped that Nazis and non-Nazis were "just like Republicans and Democrats." A predictable uproar had followed, one that made Patton's retention as commander of his beloved Third Army well-nigh impossible. Conceiv-ably Ike might have saved Patton's command one more time, but no overriding justification now presented itself for doing so. Patton's tal-ents as a combat commander were no longer so critical. "Besides," Ike mused, "what after this? I'm not firing George for what he has done; I'm firing him for what he'll do next."

Naturally, I was sad, sad for Ike and sad for Patton. But I realized the inevitability of Ike's action. I was personally a bit apprehensive, moreover, to learn that Patton was taking over command of the Fif-teenth Army, where I was assigned. I had no idea of what Patton's atti-tude would be toward me.

Patton's public reaction to his dismissal was a class act. At the changeover of command ceremony at Third Army, he graciously expressed admiration for his successor, Lieutenant General Lucian K. Truscott, Jr., and then left immediately for Bad Nauheim. Soon after taking command, he held a reception. As I went through the receiving line, he pulled me out for a few moments of pleasantries. He lauded the assembled staff for the excellence of their work and then set about to rewrite all their reports to promote the achievements of his Third Army beyond all reason.

A few days after Ike had removed Patton from Third Army, the two of them attended a football game together at Frankfurt. In the famous picture taken that day, both were smiling but pensive. I took great pleasure in seeing that photo, thinking that the feelings on Patton's part were not hard. In fact, he was devastated, and the friendship of a lifetime was over.

That was the last time, to the best of my knowledge, that Ike and Patton ever saw each other. In early November 1945, Ike returned to the United States, presumably for a short visit, but he never returned to the command of the American zone in Germany.

In early December 1945, Patton was in a catastrophic automobile accident near Darmstadt, Germany, on the way to a hunting trip. He lingered between life and death in the Army hospital at Heidelberg, paralyzed from his neck down, while his wife Beatrice sat at his bedside. Daily we at Fifteenth Army headquarters received reports of his condition, and for a while there seemed to be hope of recovery. But it was not to be. He died a week after entering the hospital. With a friend, I drove down to Heidelberg to attend his funeral services. On my return to Bad Nauheim, I was ordered to report to Mrs. Patton in the late general's office. She was checking up on all the Army brats she knew, so that she could report to our mothers how we were faring. That act represented the family nature of the Regular Army at its best.

Ike and Patton were truly an odd couple, the realistic, analytic Ike and the flamboyant, whimsical Patton. Despite the frustrations each felt toward the other during the war, they shared a mutual respect for each other's professional ability and also feelings of personal warmth. Ike seemed to think of Patton as two different people. One was the instrument of war, which had to be treated with objectivity for the sake of the cause. The other was the old friend.

Ike outlived George by nearly a quarter century, and during that time the Patton-as-instrument-of-war faded in Ike's mind, while the memories of the friendship remained. Ike liked to tell Patton stories. A favorite involved a visit of the two with Britain's King George VI.

The King, according to Ike, was always solicitous toward Americans and as a matter of casual conversation he asked Patton one time how many men he had killed with his two ivory-handled revolvers.

Patton's answer was instantaneous. "About twenty, sir!"

Ike reacted. He turned on his heel and nearly shouted, "George!"

"Oh, about six," said Patton without a sign of remorse. Ike was sure the revolvers had never been shot.

I think that Ike treasured George's memory as a bit of nostalgia for simpler times, a simpler Army. In December of 1957, when he was speaking, as President, to an informal military audience, he referred to "George Patton's old sergeant, who was so disgusted with the men in his squad that he declared them 'not even fittin' to be civilians.'"

Patton did not live to indulge in nostalgia. He died, I presume, still thinking of Ike only as his military superior and tormentor. The personal relationship between Ike and George, however, is unimportant compared to their contributions to the war in Europe. As the result of an earlier friendship the two men made a formidable team. The war against Hitler was furthered immeasurably by the days when Ike and George were young together.

Ike and Marshall hold a joint press conference in Algiers, June 1943.

National Archives

5

MARSHALL AND IKE

A Winning Combination

It seems odd, in retrospect, that the name of George C. Marshall, a man destined to become so important in Ike's life, was never mentioned, at least in my presence, during all the years our family lived in Washington and Manila. The reason, I presume, is that Ike was involved in the War Department and Marshall was not part of the Washington scene at that time. I suppose that Marshall's absence from the center of power stemmed from the well-known animosity that Army Chief of Staff Douglas MacArthur held against all the members of General Pershing's entourage in the First World War—the "Chaumont crowd"—of whom Marshall was one.

I first heard of General Marshall in late 1939, and not from either of my parents. It was during my senior year at Brent School, Baguio, Philippines, that an American Army officer who occasionally invited me for Sunday lunch at his home made mention of him. One day when he was driving me home my host declared, "I got great news today. A man named George Marshall has just been named Army Chief of Staff, jumped over many others. He is absolutely tops. Very much like your father. We're lucky to have him."

I was interested but not startled. Major Hill—I never knew his first name—was an ebullient man, always open in his admiration for my father, but he was no sycophant, and he was obviously sincere. So I appreciated the compliment to Ike and took a casual interest in the name of the new Chief of Staff.

My father had met Marshall only twice in the course of a quarter century of commissioned service. One meeting had consisted only of a handshake. The other time was the incident I have described in the chapter on Ike's service with General Pershing at the American Battle Monuments Commission, when Ike and Marshall had disagreed on the question of how General Pershing should handle the St. Mihiel and Meuse-Argonne campaigns in his memoirs. Nevertheless, I understand that General Marshall kept a little book through the years in which he listed the names of officers who showed promise for important positions in the event of another war. For some reason, perhaps because of Marshall's close friendship with Fox Conner, Ike's name occupied a place on his list, obviously without Ike's knowledge.

When Ike reported to General Walter Krueger at Fort Sam Houston on July 1, 1941, the timing was fortuitous. He was taking over as Third Army Chief of Staff in time to play a leading role in organizing the army for the Louisiana Maneuvers. It was an exercise the magnitude and importance of which remain in the memories of veterans to this day. It involved over a million men, and took the form of a sham battle with two full armies pitted against each other. Walter Krueger's Third Army was one, and Ben Lear's Second Army was the other.

Third Army achieved a spectacular success, routing the Second, and Ike was given much credit for its performance, especially by a generous General Krueger. Ike also came to the public notice for the first time. Krueger, who still retained a touch of his native German accent, was a reticent man, and he delegated to Ike the job of keeping the press informed.[1] I doubt that Ike's press notices impressed General Marshall much, but General Krueger's favorable comments probably did.

A few months after the Louisiana Maneuvers, on December 7, 1941, the Japanese Imperial Navy attacked the United States Pacific Fleet at Pearl Harbor and the Army air base at Hickam Field, Hawaii. The United States was in the war against Japan, and within days against Germany and Italy also.

As a plebe at West Point, I felt the shock and experienced the strange elation that swept the Corps of Cadets. The news hit home, however. Many of my fellow cadets were Army brats, and we all felt much concern for our friends whose parents were stationed in Hawaii. I did not, of course, share the experience with my parents, but my mother later described my father's reaction in detail. On receiving a phone call telling him what had occurred, Ike went immediately to the office. Then, having ensured that Third Army was taking every step possible to alert the troops, he returned to his kitchen and began to make vegetable soup. Like Lucy Manette's father in Dickens's *A Tale of Two Cities*, who went back to cobbling when under excessive stress, Ike always tended to make vegetable soup. Perhaps going through an established ritual allowed him to pull his thoughts together.

With the United States now at war, the emergency affected everyone, including, or maybe I should say especially, Ike. Only a few days after the news of Pearl Harbor, he received orders to leave San Antonio and report to the War Department in Washington. He had been called to join the War Plans Division, at that time headed by his closest lifetime friend, Brigadier General Leonard T. "Gee" Gerow.[2] Ike always believed that he was called to the War Department, not so much for his excellent performance at Third Army but because Gerow, and possibly Mark Clark, had suggested the move to Marshall. Ike was known to be the one available officer who was familiar with MacArthur's plans for the defense of the Philippines.

Once Ike had reported in, Gerow took him into the office of the Chief of Staff, General Marshall. At that point a firm relationship began that sustained both men throughout the war. Ike came close to awe in meeting Marshall, and he never lost a touch of veneration for him.

❧

General (later General of the Army) George C. Marshall, Chief of Staff, U.S. Army.

Library of Congress

George Marshall was born in 1880, ten years before Ike. Like Douglas MacArthur, who was the same age, he had made a stellar record with Pershing's AEF in the Great War. The contributions the two men had made were very different, however. MacArthur was the flamboyant hero, the daredevil who voluntarily, some say unnecessarily, accompanied combat patrols into enemy lines. Marshall, on the other hand, was denied the privilege of commanding troops, being confined to staff duty. He went to France as the operations officer of the 1st Division, but after a year was brought up to Pershing's AEF Headquarters. When First U.S. Army was formally organized in August of 1918, Marshall was given the all-important position of operations officer at that echelon. Almost single-handedly he moved the First Army from St. Mihiel, the scene of its first battle, to the Meuse-Argonne, sixty-five miles away, in the incredibly short time of two weeks. MacArthur had attained the glory, but Marshall had attained the valuable experience.

When Ike reported to Marshall early on Sunday, December 14, the Chief of Staff indulged in no amenities. He wasted no time in outlining the situation in the Pacific. First of all, he said, the Navy planners had declared that losses sustained in the Pearl Harbor attack had rendered any offensive naval action impossible for the foreseeable future. The carrier force was relatively intact, but the battleship fleet was out of action. The Navy would therefore be forced to concentrate on defending Hawaii and the West Coast of the continental United States for the immediate future. Marshall's naval counterparts could give no estimate as to when offensive naval action could begin.

The immediate crisis involved the Philippines, where Japanese forces had already made minor landings at Aparri, on the northern part of Luzon, as early as December 10, and the main landing, on the Lingayan Gulf, was expected any day. General MacArthur had been recalled to active command of American troops earlier that year, but his prospects were not bright in this campaign. Even with recent reinforcements, his polyglot, understrength army came to only 30,000 men. Of these, 10,000 were continental American ground troops, consisting of the 31st Infantry Regiment and some artillery units. The native Philippine Scout contingent came to some 12,000, and the Army Air Corps strength was 8,000. MacArthur's air force at the outset had consisted of only thirty-five B-17 bombers and 220 fighter planes, and Marshall knew that MacArthur had suffered dramatic losses when the Japanese had raided Clark Field and Nichols Field on December 10. The extent of the damage to MacArthur's air arm was still unknown.[3]

Having gone over this situation for about twenty minutes, Marshall turned to Ike and asked, "What should be our line of action?"

Ike gulped. "Give me a few hours." Marshall agreed, and Ike began poring over situation maps and the latest reports. His intensive study completed, he returned to Marshall's office. First of all, he said, a relief of the Philippines by substantial naval forces was out of the question. Some resupply by submarine and blockade runners might be possible, but not in sufficient amounts to enable the garrison to hold out indefinitely against a major Japanese attack. The Allies would have to rely on Australia to provide their major base for communications with the Philippines. Australia must therefore be defended at all costs, along with its line of communications to the United States. So Hawaii, Fiji, New Zealand, and New Caledonia must be held in order to ensure the safety of that defense line. In the meantime, for the sake of morale in the Allied countries such as China, the Philippines, and the Dutch East Indies, every effort must be made to assist them. "[Those countries] may excuse failure," Ike said, "but they will not excuse abandonment."

"I agree with you," was General Marshall's reply. "Do your best to save them."[4]

Ike could not perform his task alone. His responsibilities for the conduct of operations could never be met unless his plans could be supported logistically. He therefore sought out General Brehon Somervell, his counterpart in the Supply and Procurement Division, and together the two officers struggled to find means of reinforcing the Philippines. It was a frustrating effort, because supplies were so short that they could not even start to meet the competing requirements of the Far East, the training base in the United States, and the beginning of a buildup in Europe. Years later Ike found a paragraph from a note he had written on New Year's Day 1942:

I've been insisting that the Far East is critical—and no sideshows should be undertaken until air and ground there are in a satisfactory state. At last we're getting some things on the road to Australia. The air plan includes four pursuit groups, and two heavy, two medium and one light bombardment groups. But we've got to have ships—and we need them now! Tempers are short. There are lots of amateur strategists on the job. I'd give anything to be back in the field![5]

Ike was not, however, destined to return to troops. Instead he was promoted to head the War Plans Division. General Marshall had concluded that "Gee" Gerow was out of place in heading War Plans; he was by nature too meticulous to cope with the ever-changing, high-pressure situation. On February 16, 1942, therefore, Marshall reluctantly sent his fellow VMI graduate,* without prejudice, to command the 29th Infantry Division. It was awkward for Ike to replace his closest friend, but Gerow felt no rancor. He was glad, in fact, to leave; his new command meant promotion to the grade of major general. Ike was actually envious.

It could be said that Ike was now running the war, at least from the Army side. In such circumstances, he was deskbound in his office in the old Munitions Building on Constitution Avenue. During that winter he arrived at the office so early and left so late that he never saw the light of day. The pressures on him were such that his going to Kansas to attend his father's funeral was out of the question. At Easter, however, he found a day and came up to visit me at West Point for a few hours.

The visiting facilities for families at West Point were limited in those days, but the Thayer Hotel, down next to the South Gate, provided some guest space. For our brief visit, therefore, my parents and I huddled together in a corner of the hotel balcony that overlooked the main lobby.

From the outset, I could see that Ike was in a somber mood; he had something he wanted to tell me. Finally, he came out with it: he had undergone a confrontation with General Marshall a few days before,

---

*Virginia Military Institute, Lexington, Virginia.

and he was preparing me for the shock that he was going to remain a brigadier general for the rest of the war.

He did not stop there; he felt he had to go into detail. One day recently, he said, General Marshall had seemed to make a point of expounding his philosophy on the matter of officer promotions. Harking back to his experiences in France during 1917 and 1918, he said he had strongly disapproved of the favoritism that Pershing's hierarchy had showered on itself and other members of higher headquarters in matters of promotions and decorations. Marshall was determined that in this, the Second World War, priority in promotions and decorations would go to the officers serving in the field.

But then, still according to Ike, General Marshall got personal. "Take your case," Marshall said. "I know that you were recommended by one general for division command and by another for corps command. That's all very well. I'm glad they have that opinion of you, but you are going to stay right here and fill your position, and that's that."

Ike, so he told me, was deeply offended, especially because Marshall seemed to assume that he enjoyed serving in the rarefied atmosphere of the Army General Staff. His exact reply to Marshall has more than one version, but in his memoir he quoted himself as saying, "General, I'm interested in what you say, but I want you to know that I don't give a damn about your promotion plans as far as I'm concerned. I came into this office from the field and I am trying to do my duty. I expect to do so as long as you want me here. If that locks me to a desk for the rest of the war, so be it."*

With that, Ike arose from his chair and strode to the door. But suddenly he felt a strong twinge of remorse, a sense that he was adding unnecessarily to the burdens the Chief of Staff was already carrying. With his hand on the knob, he turned around and grinned. In response, he thought he detected a look of some amusement on Marshall's face. That was where matters stood during our brief West Point visit; Ike had informed me that he would never rise above the grade of brigadier general.

---

*At Ease, pp. 248–250. In telling me about the incident, Ike quoted himself more strongly as saying, in essence, "I don't care what you do. You broke my heart when you pulled me away from troops and brought me to Washington. You can't do anything more to me."

I was perplexed by my father's concern. From the viewpoint of a West Point plebe, than which there is nothing lower, I thought it completely unnecessary for him to apologize for remaining a brigadier general. After all, had he not told me time and again throughout my youth that he expected to retire from the Army in the grade of colonel? Brigadier general, as I saw it, was a grade higher than his expectations. I gave the matter little further thought.

I had overlooked one caveat. Ike had always tempered his warnings about retirement as a colonel by adding, "Of course in case of war they'll make me a general right away." Underneath his mask of indifference to his personal future, Ike was highly ambitious.

A few days after our visit at West Point, I read in the newspaper that General Marshall was reorganizing the War Department. The War Plans Division was now being incorporated into a new command post to be called the Operations Division (OPD), headed by Major General Dwight D. Eisenhower. The new organization was more than a staff section of the War Department; it was to be considered a command that reported directly to the Chief of Staff himself. I was elated for Ike, of course, but I was also amused. Whether Marshall had been planning this move for some time, or whether the confrontation that Ike had so sadly reported had raised his stock, I shall never know. Ike never mentioned this new position to me. It was left to *Time* magazine to note Ike's promotion under the flattering headline, "Two Stars on Schedule." The caption under his photo read, "The Army said 'Amen.'"

The latitude that Marshall gave Ike as head of OPD was remarkable. One incident serves as a case in point. As part of the buildup of American forces in Northern Australia, Ike decided one day to send the transatlantic liner *Queen Mary*, temporarily converted to a troopship, from a port on the eastern coast of the United States to Australia. It was to travel without escort protection against submarines because her high speed would make it "only bad luck of the worst kind if a submarine had got close enough to attack her successfully."

Reasonable risk or not, the remotest chance of losing the pride of the British merchant fleet, with 14,000 American soldiers aboard, was frightening. Ike and his colleagues, in his own words, "lived in terror" until she was reported safely around Cape Horn and in the wide Pacific. In his memoir of the war Ike claims not to remember if he had told General Marshall of this action,[6] but in person he told me that he had not, reasoning that the Chief of Staff's burdens were already heavy enough without his adding to them. Marshall later approved his actions wholeheartedly. Not only did he think Ike correct in sending the division; he also appreciated his OPD chief's taking the responsibility on his own shoulders.

Despite the series of stunning defeats in the Far East, General Marshall refused to be dissuaded from his determination to carry the war offensively against the German-Italian-Japanese Axis at the earliest possible moment. Even before the fall of the Philippine stronghold of Corregidor in May 1942, Marshall and his staff were searching every means possible to take the pressure off the Russians, who were then sustaining the full onslaught of Hitler's Wehrmacht. Though the Red Army had succeeded in stopping the Nazi drive at the gates of Moscow during the previous December, it was now reeling from further attacks in the Caucasus. The obvious way to assist the Russians, aside from sending resupply convoys northward around Norway to Archangel and Murmansk, was to launch an Anglo-American invasion of northern France in order to draw German divisions away from the Russian front.

Current plans called for the invasion of northern France to be executed in two phases. The first step was called BOLERO, the code name for a buildup of American troops in the United Kingdom in preparation for the second step, ROUNDUP, the code name for a major invasion of France. The target date for ROUNDUP had been set for the summer of 1943. In early 1942, BOLERO was becoming a reality, and ROUNDUP was considered to be agreed upon.

ROUNDUP, the final offensive to put an end to Hitler and the Nazi regime, suffered from one major weakness: it could not be executed if the Russians succumbed to the German Wehrmacht during 1942 or even early 1943. To help ensure that the Western Allies gave every support to the Russians during the current year, therefore, OPD came up with Operation SLEDGEHAMMER, a cross-Channel invasion to be launched that very same year, 1942, to seize a limited bridgehead in France. Admittedly a high-risk enterprise, Marshall and

Ike considered SLEDGEHAMMER absolutely necessary to relieve the Russians by forcing Hitler to concentrate a large army in France.

Since British approval of SLEDGEHAMMER was critical, President Roosevelt sent Marshall and Harry Hopkins, Roosevelt's trusted emissary, on a visit to London to sell the idea to Churchill. For a while during that spring of 1942, it appeared that SLEDGEHAMMER would actually be executed; the Prime Minister seemed to be enthusiastically supportive.[7] But Churchill very quickly began to show signs of cooling toward the idea. The Americans, unaware of Churchill's sometimes indirect methods, seemed to ignore these signs. They should have been alerted, but they were not, when Churchill gave Soviet Foreign Minister Vyacheslav Molotov a note to Stalin saying that he could "give no promise"[8] on SLEDGEHAMMER. American planning continued to assume that the operation would be executed.

During Marshall's trip to London, he had been unable, because of time restraints, to inspect the American troops and installations in Great Britain. On his return to Washington, therefore, he sent Ike over to the United Kingdom to evaluate the condition of American troops. On Ike's request, Mark Clark, representing the newly established Army Ground Forces, was detailed to go with him.*

Ike and Clark left Washington in early May 1942, and made a ten-day tour of United States forces in Britain. On their return they submitted a drastic report. The officers on the spot, they said, through no fault of their own, were "in a back eddy, from which they could scarcely emerge except for a return to the United States."[9] Put more bluntly, Ike meant that the officers should be replaced by someone from the United States, probably from Marshall's staff. Ike's recommendation for the man to take over command in London was General Joseph McNarney, an Army Air Corps officer and a West Point classmate of Ike's. Marshall said nothing at the time but told Ike to draw up a directive for the new Commanding General, United States Theater of Operations.

Ike submitted his directive on June 8, 1942, and asked if Marshall

---

*The new reorganization had done away with the chiefs of branches and had organized the Army into three main branches: Army Ground Forces, Army Air Forces, and Services of Supply.

wanted to read it. The Chief was direct as always. "I certainly do want to read it. You may be the man who executes it."[10]

By that time, I had finished plebe year at West Point, and my class had made the traditional move from the barracks across the Plain to spend the summer at Camp Clinton. One day I received an exciting letter:

June 13, 1942

Dear Johnnie:

Confidentially, I am soon to leave the United States for an indefinite stay. Naturally, I am anxious to have a few hours with you just to say goodbye and to have a good talk. Today, I telephoned to the Adjutant at West Point, and he informed me that any day I could come to West Point next week, you could be excused from normal duties in order to have a few hours with me. He assured me that this would occasion no embarrassment to you, to the authorities there, or to anyone else. . . . Mamie intends to return to the Wardman Park Hotel where she will take a small apartment. She will have room for you when you come down next fall. Should there be no room in her particular apartment, she can always get an extra one for you. She is looking forward to your visit.

Best of luck. I hope to be seeing you very soon, probably about Wednesday or Thursday. Affectionately, DAD

P.S. The bosses are certainly giving me a tough job this time. I will tell you about it when I see you.

Naturally, I was thrilled until I received word that Dad's schedule would not allow him to make the visit after all. Without hesitation, therefore, I went down the company street to the tent to see the officer of the day. When I asked for an unheard-of weekend leave, Major George E. Keeler was a little taken aback at such a novel idea but submitted the request.* The request was approved, thus setting a precedent for other cadets whose fathers were being assigned overseas.

---

*After promising to submit the request, Major Keeler rather diffidently asked what direction Ike was going in, to Europe or the Far East. I was unable to say.

When I arrived at my parents' quarters at Fort Myer, I found the atmosphere sober but not the least dramatic. Ike and Mamie had been separated before, though not for an indefinite time, and we accepted that the future of millions of Americans, not just of our family, was uncertain. Mamie harbored no doubt of her ability to move the household furniture from Fort Myer to her future apartment in the Wardman Park Hotel, because she was a very capable executive. But I was intensely curious about the mysterious postscript to Dad's letter, so on stepping in the door, I immediately asked him what his job would be in Europe. "Oh, I'm to be the commanding general," he answered. I was astonished, for the assignment exceeded my wildest imagination.

Apparently Ike had requested only a day or so to be with his family, because we had only a few hours to visit. There was not much to say, and Ike and I spent most of our time discussing the one experience we now had in common, that of being a cadet at West Point. (We found that it had hardly changed during the thirty years between our attendances there.) The short visit over, I returned to West Point. I would not see Ike again for a year and a half, until January of 1944.

While Ike was preparing to leave Washington, Prime Minister Churchill, with key members of his staff, was in Washington to confer with the Americans on future plans. When Ike went to the White House to take his leave of Churchill and the President, he may have been aware that Churchill had come to argue against the execution of SLEDGEHAMMER. That issue, however, was no longer Ike's immediate concern. Marshall was sending him strictly in the capacity of an American theater commander, to serve as a subordinate to a British overall commander of SLEDGEHAMMER.

Marshall, as a key figure in the discussions, fought a valiant but losing battle to save SLEDGEHAMMER in 1942. After Churchill's return to London, Marshall and Harry Hopkins flew over once again to debate the issue. The Americans' efforts were futile, however; by now Churchill was fully aware that the Americans could provide no adequately trained troops, so the force would be almost exclusively British—and most likely doomed to fail. The Prime Minister's convictions were reinforced by the fact that the British War Cabinet voted SLEDGEHAMMER down unanimously.

Once Marshall finally accepted the fact that an invasion of France in 1942 was out of the question, he informed Roosevelt, who did not seem to be the least bit downcast. Instead the President instructed Marshall and Hopkins to consult with Churchill to find "some other way" to get Americans fighting against the Germans in 1942.[11] Marshall and Hopkins also seemed to accept the outcome in good humor, once the decision had been made. When they dined with Sir Alan Brooke on the evening of the decision, their host reported them to be in good spirits. By strange contrast, Ike was furious. "July 22, 1942," he confided to his aide, "could well go down as the blackest day in history."[12]

Ironically, the decision that Ike deplored with his typical intensity was responsible for his future prominence, including his election to the American presidency ten years later.

Marshall and Hopkins knew what Roosevelt had in mind as a substitute for SLEDGEHAMMER. It was to revive Operation GYMNAST, a previously rejected joint invasion of French North Africa, a region that was administered by President Henri Pétain's puppet Vichy French government. For reasons to be described in the chapter on Ike and Churchill, political considerations dictated that an American rather than a Briton be placed in command of the Allied forces for GYMNAST, now rechristened TORCH.

The agreement that an American would have to command TORCH did not, of course, mean that the Allied Commander would necessarily have to be Ike. To decide the issue, a special meeting of the Anglo-American Combined Chiefs of Staff (CCS) was convened in Washington. By then, however, Marshall and Admiral King had privately settled on Ike, so that body offered no objections. Skipping over so many senior officers represented a mark of supreme confidence on Marshall's part, because by the Army's reckoning Ike was young. Never mind that, at fifty-one, he was five years older than either Napoleon or Wellington had been at Waterloo. In modern war Ike was thought of as the "kid general."[13]

With Ike's appointment as Allied Commander, his relationship with Marshall automatically underwent a change. For administrative matters pertaining to American forces, he remained as always Marshall's subordinate. But in strategic matters, Ike was now an Allied, not merely an American commander. In that capacity he reported to the Combined Chiefs of Staff—not to Marshall, not to Roosevelt, not to Churchill. The channel of command to the Combined Chiefs would prove to be a buffer because it protected Ike from excessive meddling on the part of either Roosevelt or Churchill, a habit to which the latter was particularly addicted.

And yet, even Ike's messages to the Combined Chiefs of Staff went through Marshall. To facilitate communications, that body had set up a procedure whereby theater commanders such as Ike and MacArthur would send their communications through an "executive agent." Logically, Marshall was named as the executive agent for the European and North African theaters.[14] As a result, in the voluminous messages that Ike sent to Marshall during the three years that he was overseas, it is not always clear as to whether Ike was addressing Marshall as Army Chief of Staff or as the executive agent of the CCS. He made little effort to draw the line.

Ike's appointment as Allied Commander for TORCH did not at first carry the authority that the title implies. During the planning stage, while Ike remained in London, the volumes of correspondence that went back and forth between Whitehall and the War Department, particularly with regard to the landing sites in French North Africa, treated Ike very much as only one officer expressing his own views rather than as the commander of the expedition. His full responsibilities, in effect, began on November 8, 1942, when the three task forces had landed: Patton at the three locations in Morocco, Lloyd Fredendall at Oran, and Charles Ryder at Algiers. Though the bulk of the forces in North Africa would eventually be British, it had been decided at the highest levels that the troops making the original assault landings should be American.

Once he had arrived in his temporary command post in the Rock of Gibraltar, and after that in Algiers, Ike could not possibly have asked for a more supportive backup than Marshall, especially in the early days of the Tunisian campaign. Marshall was able to represent Ike's viewpoint in Washington far better than he could himself. Very little time went by before Ike needed Marshall's immediate support.

The first crisis, which arose within hours of the landings on November 7 and November 8, 1942, involved French politics. When the Anglo-Americans went ashore in Morocco and Algeria, their most immediate need was to induce the local French commanders to stop resistance against the Allies and join them in driving the German forces out of North Africa. These legalistic French officers, subject to the authority of the Vichy French government, needed a proper authority to justify their honor.

In order to bring that about, Ike made a bargain with Admiral Jean François Darlan, the head of the Vichy armed forces, who happened to be in Algiers when the Allies landed. Ike would recognize Darlan as the French commander in North Africa if the French commanders would obey his orders to stop fighting the Allies. Though the arrangement was successful, Darlan's reputation as a member of Marshal Pétain's despised Vichy government caused an uproar in both Britain and the United States.

Ike had done what he judged to be a military necessity on his own responsibility, without cabling back to Washington for permission. In so doing, he knew that he was sticking his own neck out, well aware that his action would be unpopular at home. He reported his line of reasoning in a letter to Marshall, who took it, as written, to the White House. President Roosevelt, after reading it, stood by the Allied Commander. My guess is that without the Chief of Staff's backing, Ike's career might have ended within days of the North African landing.*

Marshall went even further. Recognizing that Ike was in command of British officers who outranked him, the Chief of Staff urged the President to promote Ike to the grade of full general—four stars, the same rank that he bore himself. Roosevelt resisted for a time. He did not know Ike well, and he was prone to favor people of his own choosing. He therefore told Marshall that he would hold off promoting Ike until there was some "damn good reason."[15] Marshall could not induce Roosevelt to take such action until February 1943, three months after the North African landings.

---

*See chapter on de Gaulle for the details of this episode.

In January of 1943, Roosevelt and Churchill met at Casablanca, Morocco. Ike took little part in these discussions, even though they affected his own theater of war, because he was busy with events in Algiers and Tunisia, many miles away.[16] He was not at Marshall's side, therefore, when Marshall suffered one of his worst disappointments of the war, the decision of the political leaders to invade Sicily after the end of the Tunisian campaign. It was at this point that Ike's views began to diverge from Marshall's, even though only to a small degree.

Marshall was a very determined man, and from the beginning of the war until the launching of OVERLORD in June 1944, he focused all his efforts on promoting the invasion of northern France and resisting any side shows that might detract from that enterprise. To him, therefore, any further operations conducted in the Mediterranean after the fall of Tunisia were to be resisted. He was rightfully suspicious of Winston Churchill, whose proclivities toward creating a "ring" around Western Europe and making stabs into what he called the "soft underbelly"[17] were well known. Ike agreed with Marshall in principle, and out of personal loyalty probably supported the Chief beyond his own feelings. However, Ike commanded hundreds of thousands of troops in the Mediterranean who could not remain idle. The invasion of the Continent could not begin until the next year at the earliest. He was therefore more amenable to the British arguments about other possible objectives than was Marshall. In any event, despite Marshall's resistance, the political leaders decided that Sicily should be invaded after the expected fall of Tunisia.

The trend continued. Even before the launching of HUSKY, the invasion of Sicily, the Allied governments were engaged in debating the Allied move to follow it. Marshall, as always, advocated stopping any further operations in the Mediterranean in order to get on with the buildup for the invasion of northern France, which had been suspended with the beginning of TORCH. A visit by Churchill to Washington produced an impasse. Finally, a persistent Churchill prevailed on Roosevelt to send Marshall with him to Algiers, there to consult with Ike. The weary President was doubtless glad to see the British bulldog leave Washington. A similarly weary Marshall was directed to go with him.

Ike and his staff were on hand at the Maison Blanche Airport to meet Churchill and Marshall when they arrived late on May 28, 1943, only a couple of weeks after the fall of Tunisia. From the outset, it was obvious that Churchill intended to enlist Ike in support of an invasion of Italy. He was far from subtle in his methods. Ike had planned to ride in a car with Marshall from the airport, but Churchill preempted him. Churchill continued to make it impossible, in fact, for Ike to meet with Marshall that whole day. Immediately on arrival at their respective villas, the Prime Minister walked across to Ike's quarters and spent the rest of the time before dinner expounding the virtues of continuing operations into Italy after the fall of Sicily.

No issues were decided that evening, of course, but the next day Churchill and all the generals held a serious conference on the porch of the St. George Hotel. Marshall was noticeably quiet and noncommittal; he later revealed that he was simply tired of talking about the subject. Churchill attained his ends by sheer persistence. If the capture of Sicily should prove relatively easy, as was expected, Allied forces should then be launched across the Strait of Messina and elsewhere in southern Italy without delay. In exchange for consenting to these landings in Italy, Churchill gave Marshall a solemn guarantee that twenty-nine United States and British divisions would be in the United Kingdom by May 1944, and would be launched across the English Channel at that time.

Marshall by now was resigned, and in truth Churchill's points were well taken. ROUNDUP, still the code name for the cross-Channel invasion, was manifestly impossible for 1943, so there was little loss in continuing on to Italy that year. But the Algiers meeting illustrated a new relationship between Marshall and Ike. Ike was now being consulted as an entity separate from Marshall. He had been unwittingly used in Churchill's effort to force British strategy, rather than Marshall's, into operations for 1943.

The invasion of Sicily was launched by the Allies on July 10, 1943. Though under Ike's overall command, it was managed tactically by his deputy, British General Sir Harold Alexander, who maintained a separate headquarters designated as 15 Army Group. The campaign lasted thirty-eight days and ended on August 17, when the last of the Axis forces, protected by the two elite German divisions, crossed the Strait of Messina into the toe of the boot of Italy. Tactically, the campaign may have been disappointing to the extent that the two German divisions escaped, but strategically it was a resounding success. Among other benefits, as mentioned, it triggered the downfall of the Italian dictator, Benito Mussolini.

In late August, Ike was a busy man indeed. First he negotiated the surrender of Italian forces, which occurred on September 6. In the meantime, on September 3, he launched Montgomery's Eighth Army in Operation BAYTOWN, in which Monty sent two divisions across the Strait of Messina. He was also planning the landing of Mark Clark's Fifth United States Army* in Operation AVALANCHE, a series of landings on beaches near Salerno, scheduled for September 9. In the course of that planning, Ike and Marshall developed a disagreement of importance, the conflict of a global commander in Washington as opposed to the views of a field commander on the spot.[18]

Ike always viewed AVALANCHE, Clark's Salerno landing, as a risky operation in view of German ground strength in southern Italy. Ike would consent to making the landing only if provided with overpowering airpower. He was always willing—as in OVERLORD the next year—to fight with inferior ground strength provided that he enjoyed air supremacy. To ensure that the landing at Salerno would be successful, he set about to secure what he needed in the way of that airpower.

On July 27 and 28 Ike conferred with his air commanders, Air Marshal Sir Arthur Tedder and Lieutenant General Carl Spaatz, USAAF, and what he learned was disturbing. At that time American strength in heavy bombers consisted of only six groups of heavy bombers—about half the number that he and his deputies considered adequate. Ike therefore cabled to the Combined Chiefs, through General Marshall, requesting the temporary loan of four additional groups of B-17s from the United Kingdom, to remain in the Mediterranean until September 15, at which time Ike thought that the landings should be safe.

A copy of Ike's request to Marshall was sent to Lieutenant General Jacob L. Devers, the American Commanding General in London, who

---

*Despite its designation, Fifth Army was never completely American. The Salerno landing was made by one British and one American division.

then consulted with General Ira Eaker, commanding the strategic Eighth Air Force. Together the two men protested to Marshall against even a temporary loan. Operation POINTBLANK, the Allied effort to complete the destruction of the German air force, was just now beginning to show results, and they insisted that the loss of the four heavy groups from the U.K. would make a large difference.[19]

Marshall had a decision to make between two legitimate viewpoints, and he came down on the side of Devers and Eaker; Ike would have to take the chances of operating in Italy with fewer planes than he desired. Marshall hinted that he might send four groups of medium bombers but later backed down, again in light of protests from Devers. On August 17, therefore, the day that the Sicily campaign ended, Ike warned Marshall that if he were not allowed to keep three heavy groups currently in the theater, he would be "skating on very thin ice in AVALANCHE." He pleaded that the hostile bomber strength had been steadily building up for some days, and he asked to keep some bomber groups that had recently been assigned temporarily for a special raid but were scheduled for return to Britain.[20] Once again he was turned down.

There things stood on September 9, 1943, when the U.S. Fifth Army landed at Salerno. At first Clark's force was opposed only by the German 16th Panzer Division. Progress was considered fairly successful at the end of the day, but optimism was premature. German Field Marshal Albert Kesselring had seven other divisions in southern Italy, and those facing Montgomery in the south were easily able to break off contact and begin moving toward Salerno. By September 12, three days after Clark's landing, the four Allied divisions ashore were being ringed by six German panzer or panzer grenadier divisions.[21]

At this point, the emergency was becoming frightening. Ike secured the use of eighteen landing ships (LSTs) bound for India, capable of delivering further reinforcements to the beachhead. Admiral Sir Andrew Cunningham supplied two battleships to provide extremely effective naval gunfire. General Spaatz committed heavy bombers in direct support of ground troops, an unprecedented role for these aircraft.

By September 15 the beachhead was secure, but Ike did not know it. On that day he wrote the Combined Chiefs of Staff that the situation was "precarious." Asserting that he could affect the battle only by the use of airpower, he suggested:

If the long range air forces from the UK could operate against the lines into northern Italy it would tend to immobilize the hostile units in that area and have a morale effect throughout Italy. Second, if the CCS could find it possible to send back the three B-24 bomber groups that had considerable experience in this area we could use them daily on the basis of disrupting communications between the southern and northern enemy concentrations. Even if these three groups could operate here for a period of two weeks only it would have a most marked effect on our present critical problem.[22]

That message attained results. The American Joint Chiefs approved and so notified the British Chiefs. General Devers was ordered to prepare three B-24 groups for movement to the Mediterranean. The British, on their part, were more than cooperative. British bombers, in consultation with Ike's staff, hit targets in northern Italy from the U.K.[23] The Salerno bridgehead survived, but for a time it had been a close call.

The episode carried long-term effects. It was an ordeal for Ike that he never forgot, and as a result of it he was adamant, as commander of OVERLORD some months later, that the Strategic Air Forces based in Britain and the Mediterranean be placed under his control. He would never again tolerate the need to negotiate for the forces necessary to fight his battles.*

Salerno secure, Marshall and Ike became concerned with the question of how far to advance up the boot of Italy. Marshall visualized taking a line north of Rome and stopping there. Impatient to take Rome in a hurry, he hinted that Ike might have done so earlier. He disagreed with Ike's insistence that any amphibious landing had to be conducted within the range of fighter aircraft.

On September 22, 1943, Ike received two messages that were dramatic in their contrast. Churchill, elated over Ike's success in attaining a foothold in Italy, sent a message of congratulations. Comparing the Salerno landing with the Battle of Waterloo, the Prime Minister wrote, "As the Duke

---

*See chapter on Churchill.

of Wellington said of the Battle of Waterloo, 'It was a damned close-run thing,' but your policy of running risks has been vindicated." Churchill sent a similar message of congratulations to Mark Clark.[24]

Marshall, however, sent Ike a message with a different tone, expressing disappointment that Rome had not fallen. Perhaps Ike's landing at Salerno should have been launched even before Montgomery's landing in the toe of Italy, he wrote. In that case the Germans might have been caught unprepared. Marshall also remarked that the representatives Ike had sent to the recent Quebec Conference had advised that operations against Rome could have been speeded up. "At long range," Marshall concluded, "it would seem that you give the enemy too much time to prepare and eventually find yourself up against a very stiff resistance."[25]

This stung Ike to the quick. His naval aide, Harry Butcher, recorded that Ike hardly ate any breakfast or lunch until his message of self-justification had been sent. After a long defense of his strategy, he ended by saying,

> As a matter of interest to you I received this morning from the Prime Minister a telegram congratulating me on the success of my "policy of running risks." I feel certain that some of his correspondents in this look upon me as a gambler.[26]

Ike was now an established world figure, better known outside Washington and London than was Marshall himself. Nevertheless, he still considered himself a lesser cog in the machinery of war—which he was—and, in the best sense, Marshall's man. He was therefore alarmed when, in November of 1943, talk began circulating that he was Marshall's rival for the command of the forthcoming invasion of northwest Europe. He had never before allowed such a thought to enter his mind.

Up until mid-August 1943, it had generally been assumed that the invasion of Europe, now designated as OVERLORD, would be commanded by a British officer. The armada would be launched from Britain; the British had been in the war over two years longer than the Americans; and her generals, particularly Sir Alan Brooke, were presumed to be more experienced. By the time the Quebec Conference opened on August 15, 1943, however, President Roosevelt, with the prodding of Secretary of War Henry L. Stimson, insisted to Churchill that the commander had to be an American. By the time the war came to an end, Stimson and Roosevelt pointed out, the vast bulk of the men and resources would be American. The public in the United States would insist that one of theirs be in charge.

Churchill having agreed, there was little doubt in anyone's mind that General George Marshall would be the commander of OVERLORD. Not only was Marshall the highest ranking officer in the Army and the most prestigious; he had also been the most insistent and vociferous advocate of the operations in northwest Europe, BOLERO and ROUND-UP/OVERLORD. And President Roosevelt thought it only just that the Chief of Staff be given the most important command of the war. So certain was everyone that Marshall would soon leave for London that Mrs. Marshall began moving some of the family furniture from Fort Myer, the Chief of Staff's residence, to their own home in Leesburg, Virginia.

Ike, along with all the others, assumed that this would be the arrangement. But rather than go back to Washington as "acting Chief of Staff," which was also assumed, he personally desired to stay overseas. Since he carried four stars on his shoulders, he was not being presumptuous to hope for the command of an army group under Marshall. That was his preference.

Not everyone was enthusiastic about Marshall's leaving Washington, however. In late October 1943, Ambassador Averell Harriman, administrator of Lend-Lease in Britain, arrived in Algiers on the way to Cairo, where Roosevelt and Churchill were to meet at the end of the month. Ike was away at the time, and Harry Butcher, Ike's naval aide and a Washington radio executive in civilian life, pumped Harriman for any light he could shed on the matter. Harriman cast doubt as to the finality of that decision.

The problem, it turned out, was that the Chief of Staff was now considered so indispensable in Washington that many officials, including Roosevelt himself, would feel uncomfortable with him out of touch across the Atlantic. One such official, Harriman reported, was the Chief of Naval Operations, Admiral Ernest J. King. King, though a Navy man through and through, had an extraordinary admiration for his Army colleague, and, in Butcher's words, "strongly protested the loss of Marshall, who, he emphasized, was a great teammate." King was seeking to influence both Secretary of War Henry Stimson and President Roosevelt to keep Marshall in Washington. Marshall had remained aloof from any such discussions.[27]

On Saturday morning, November 20, 1943, Ike met President Roosevelt and his party at Oran, Algeria, when they debarked from the battleship *Iowa* after a seven-day Atlantic crossing. From there the party flew to Ike's forward headquarters at Carthage so that the members could enjoy a couple of days of relaxation. That evening the President invited Ike to dinner alone, but on the way to Roosevelt's villa Ike dropped in for a short visit with Marshall and King. Almost as Ike stepped in the door, King brought up the question of the future command, saying that he considered Marshall's leaving Washington a mistake. Only because Ike would come to Washington in Marshall's place, King added courteously, could he "view the plan with anything less than consternation." Nevertheless, he protested against "shifting the key members of a winning team." He declared that he was going to renew his arguments with the President.[28] There the matter rested for the moment.

The next day, Roosevelt and Ike went out for an informal tour of the recent Tunisian battlefields, enjoying a speculation on the unknown site of the historic Battle of Zama, in 202 B.C., where Scipio Africanus decisively defeated Hannibal. Though Ike did not realize it, he was being interviewed. Ike recalled the meeting later:

> The President spoke briefly to me about the future OVERLORD command and I came to realize, finally, that it was a point of intense official and public interest back home. He did not give me a hint as to his final decision except to say that he dreaded the thought of losing Marshall from Washington. But he added, "You and I know the name of the Chief of Staff in the Civil War, but few Americans outside the professional services do." He then added, as if thinking aloud, "But it is dangerous to monkey with a winning team." I answered nothing except to state that I would do my best wherever the government would find use for me.[29]

After staying over an extra day at Carthage, the President and his group went on to Cairo to join Churchill and his party. Ike joined the conference for only a single day in order to give a report on the Italian campaign. Then, at Marshall's insistence, he took a few days off to take a trip up the Nile to visit Luxor while the rest of the party continued on to Tehran for their critical meeting with Joseph Stalin.

Many things were discussed at Tehran during the last days of November and the early days of December 1943, but the issue that most affected Ike—and Marshall too, for that matter—was the command of OVERLORD. Soviet Marshal Joseph Stalin had had enough of what he considered Western delay in launching a "second front" against Nazi Germany in the west, and he stated bluntly that until Roosevelt named a commander for that operation, he could not take it seriously. Roosevelt, though his feet were to the fire, would not be stampeded. He promised to notify Stalin of his choice very shortly after he returned to Cairo and consulted with his staff.

The story of Roosevelt's decision has been often told. On December 4, 1943, back at Cairo, the President decided that he could delay no longer. Essentially he desired to retain Marshall in Washington, but to ease his own conscience he wanted Marshall to volunteer to stay. Like Ike, however, Marshall refused to express a preference as to his future assignment. Roosevelt persisted. The next day he sent his alter ego, Harry Hopkins, to try to elicit an expression of preference from Marshall (meanwhile expressing the President's concern over Marshall's leaving Washington). The hint was clear that Roosevelt was asking Marshall to volunteer to remain in his present position, but the Chief of Staff refused to make it easy. The decision had to be Roosevelt's.

The next day, around lunchtime, Roosevelt asked Marshall to come by his villa to settle the matter. In Marshall's words:

> [Mr. Roosevelt] asked me after a great deal of beating about the bush just what I wanted to do. Evidently it was left up to me. Well, having in mind all this business that had occurred in Washington and what Hopkins had told me, I just repeated again in as convincing language as I could that I wanted him to feel free to act in whatever way he felt was to the best interest of the country and to his satisfaction and not in any way to consider my feelings. I would cheerfully go whatever way he wanted me to go and I didn't express any desire one way or another. Then he evidently assumed that concluded the affair and that I would

not command in Europe. Because he said, "Well, I didn't feel I could sleep at ease if you were out of Washington."[30]

The decision had been made, but it was not formalized until the next day, when Roosevelt directed Marshall to draft a note to Stalin. Marshall scribbled the following words on a yellow pad: "The immediate appointment of General Eisenhower to command of Overlord Operation has been decided upon." After the President had signed the document and it had been sent to the telegraph room for transmittal, Marshall retrieved it. At the bottom, he wrote his own note to Ike:

Dear Eisenhower. I thought you might like to have this as a memento. It was written very hurriedly by me as the final meeting broke up yesterday, the President signing it immediately. G.C.M.[31]

Marshall returned to the United States from Cairo by way of Australia and New Guinea, there to meet with General Douglas MacArthur. Little is known about what went on between the two. Marshall recorded nothing; MacArthur recalled their meetings only by writing, "We had a long and frank discussion."[32] The meeting seems to have benefited MacArthur, however, for from that time on Marshall seems to have given more of his attention to the Southwest Pacific Theater. Perhaps he simply considered the situation in Europe taken care of satisfactorily.

On his return to Washington on December 22, Marshall sent Ike a message that was half-plea and half-order:

Come on home and see your wife and trust somebody else for twenty minutes in England. Things have been going ahead in the UK for a long time under a wise and aggressive man* and [General Walter Bedell] Smith has already been there. You will be under terrific strain from now on. I am not interested in the usual rejoinder that you can

---

*Presumably, Lieutenant General Sir Frederick Morgan, the British general who had been put in charge of planning OVERLORD the previous August.

take it. It is of vast importance that you be fresh mentally and you certainly will not be if you go from one great problem to another.[33]

Ike received that message on Christmas 1943, and he was not elated. He was anxious to get to London. After a brief exchange, however, he gave in, though he insisted that he was not required to do so.[34] In the meantime, President Roosevelt had announced Ike's appointment to command OVERLORD on December 24, 1943. Churchill was Ike's guest at Carthage at that time, recovering from a dangerous case of pneumonia. The Prime Minister soon left Algiers for further recuperation at Marrakech, and Ike visited him there while on the way back to the United States.

True to his intentions, Ike spent only a minimal amount of time back in the United States, though he was able to visit me at West Point and also to make a quick trip to see his mother in Kansas.* During our short visit in the railroad yards below West Point, I could see that Ike had changed during the year and a half since our last visit. He was heavier and definitely more authoritative. He was also anxious to get on with his next challenge, and it was with a sense of relief that he left on January 14, 1944, for London. He arrived to assume his new duties the next day.

In London, Ike set to work with gusto. He held a press conference and in a short time he had (a) organized his personal staff at headquarters, (b) made a drastic change in the OVERLORD plan, expanding the landing from a three-division to a five-division assault, and (c) opened a hard but successful battle to secure for himself temporary control over the heavy bombers—B-17s, B-24s, and British Lancasters—that he had been forced to beg for during the Salerno campaign. These were busy but confident times.

It soon began to appear, at least in Ike's mind, that the entire Com-

---

*Ike's presence in the United States was a closely held secret, not released until his return to London. One morning, at the Wardman Park Hotel, where Mamie was staying for the duration, Ike unexpectedly encountered a janitor. He said nothing. "I just left it to Mamie to explain what a man was doing in her bedroom," he later remarked with a laugh.

bined Chiefs of Staff, not just Marshall, were turning their attention to the war in the Pacific, apparently considering OVERLORD as a project now taken care of. Eight days after arriving in London, Ike sent a message to Washington that carries a bit of admonition:

> I have now had the opportunity of discussing the OVERLORD plan with my commanders-in-chief. We are convinced that in all discussions full weight must be given to the fact that this operation marks the crisis of the European war. Every obstacle must be overcome, every inconvenience suffered and every risk run to ensure that our blow is decisive. We cannot afford to fail.[35]

Perhaps that admonition was unnecessary, but it reflected Ike's frame of mind at the time. Evidence to confirm Ike's concern that the Combined Chiefs—therefore Marshall—were taking OVERLORD for granted was their delegating to Ike the responsibility of negotiating the timing and even the execution of the landing in southern France with Prime Minister Churchill. (See the chapter on Churchill.)

Throughout the next year and a half, while Ike served as Supreme Commander, Allied Expeditionary Force, he continued his practice of writing voluminous letters to Marshall, as always making little effort to distinguish between his business as Supreme Commander and his administration of the United States forces in Europe. When he did so, Marshall rarely if ever made a suggestion as to tactics and strategy. A prime example of the Chief of Staff's policy manifested itself on December 17, 1944, the day after Hitler had launched his final, desperate offensive through the Ardennes (the Battle of the Bulge). Though the situation in Europe looked serious, Marshall realized that the battle would be over before the War Department could do anything to help. "We can't help Eisenhower in any way other than not bothering him," Marshall told his staff. "No messages will go from here to the ETO [European Theater of Operations] unless approved by me."[36]

The Battle of the Bulge ending successfully, the European campaign came to an end three months later. In the early morning hours of May 7, 1945, Ike sent a message to the CCS:

The mission of this Allied force was fulfilled at 0241, local time, May 7th, 1945.[37]

A German delegation headed by Colonel General Alfred Jodl had signed the instrument of surrender in a red schoolhouse in Reims, France.

Marshall received the news with unaccustomed emotion. During the war, both to Ike's amusement and concern, the closest thing Marshall had come to commendation was a grudging, "Well, you haven't done so bad thus far."[38] But now Marshall was lavish in his words of praise:

> You have completed your mission with the greatest victory in the history of warfare.
>
> You have commanded with outstanding success the most powerful military force that has ever been assembled. . . .
>
> You have made history, great history for the good of all mankind and you have stood for all we hope for and admire in an officer of the United States Army. These are my tributes and my personal thanks.[39]

This message arrived at SHAEF just as Ike was preparing one of his own. He had already written to Marshall that "the strongest weapon I have always had in my hand was a confident feeling that you trusted my judgment, believed in the objectivity of my approach to any problem and were ready to sustain to the fullest limit anything we found necessary to undertake to accomplish the defeat of the enemy." He wished that in view of Marshall's "unparalleled place in the respect and affection of all the military and political leaders as well as the mass of American fighting men," Marshall could have visited the ETO to see the Army after it had attained its full growth. "Our Army and people," he wrote, "have never been so indebted to any other soldier."

Then, on receipt of Marshall's message, Ike added,

> While [I was] preparing this, your personal message of commendation was brought to me. It so overwhelms me that I now consider . . . anything I can say to be a feeble anticlimax.[40]

From that time on, Ike's preoccupations underwent a drastic change. He was now charged with caring for his former enemies—maintaining law and order, feeding and housing the population, and helping them in their first efforts to restore their lives. He also, of course, was charged with processing the mass of prisoners that had heretofore been members of the mighty Wehrmacht. In mid-June 1945, he took a representative group of some fifty war veterans back to the United States for a triumphal welcome.

As happened at other times, I made that trip as Ike's aide. We left Frankfurt by plane and flew directly to Bermuda, where a tailor awaited us and fitted us out in the tropical worsted summer uniforms that we would need in the United States. (In Europe we wore wool all the year around.) We then flew directly to Washington where a great crowd, headed by General Marshall and my mother, awaited the Supreme Commander and his entourage.

It was on that day that I saw General Marshall completely unbend. Standing behind Ike and eschewing the glare of the photographers, he beamed on Ike and Mamie with a kindly, fatherly expression. He seemed to be delighted to be present at their reunion. There was nothing of the normally aloof George Marshall in his demeanor that day. Then he faded into the background and let Ike take the stage for the rest of the day—a motorcade down the streets of Washington, and a visit to the Pentagon.

The visit home lasted about three weeks, as I recall, and soon Ike and his entourage (including me) were headed back to Frankfurt, where his headquarters were now located.

Headquarters, Allied Expeditionary Force (SHAEF), was deactivated at midnight, July 13, 1945. With that event, Ike's title as Supreme Commander became a thing of the past. He was now designated only as the Commander of United States Forces in the European Theater (USFET), again completely Marshall's subordinate.

That day, it so happened, nearly coincided with the beginning of the meeting at Potsdam between President Harry Truman, Prime Minister Winston Churchill, and Marshal Joseph Stalin. General Marshall stopped off at Bad Homburg, Ike's residence near Frankfurt, to spend the night on his way to join the meeting. I was on hand and was fortunate enough to join the intimate gathering for dinner in Ike's pleasant back yard with Marshall, Ike, and Colonel Frank McCarthy, who acted as Marshall's personal aide when he traveled.[41] There were only four of us around a small round table.

The atmosphere was quiet, and Ike excused himself for a short time to run into Frankfurt, where the members of his beloved SHAEF were having a final cocktail celebration observing the end of their association. When Ike returned, his mind was obviously wandering, and I think he can be excused for failing to listen to every word that Marshall was saying. I must say that the Chief of Staff pontificated considerably; even Ike, in our quarters upstairs, made some mention of it.

A couple of days later I delivered a message to General Marshall at Seventh Army headquarters, then at Berchtesgaden. He showed no signs of recognizing me as his former dinner companion. Perhaps he had not even noticed my presence at the table that previous evening. Perhaps he thought that first lieutenants were not to be recognized.

I might digress here about the personal aloofness commonly attributed to General Marshall in his later years. His reserve in public certainly gave him the mystery that Charles de Gaulle, in *The Edge of the Sword*, cites as necessary for personal prestige. At the same time, it seems to me that forbidding himself wide friendships outside his immediate family made Marshall's a barren life. To the outsider he seemed determined never to be friends with his subordinates. He never made any effort to develop a personal relationship with Ike off duty, no matter their mutual respect professionally. In fact, only once did he refer to Ike by that universally employed nickname, and that came as a slip of the tongue. He corrected himself by calling Ike by his last name three or four times in the next sentence. That formality bothered Ike somewhat, but after the war Frank McCarthy assured him that Marshall never referred to any officer except by his last name. The single exception to that rule was General George Patton. Marshall even bent to call him "Georgie." Perhaps, despite Patton's outstanding military qualifications, some of his personal eccentricities tickled Marshall's funny bone enough to let down the bars.

Yet Marshall was thoughtful in his own way. Whenever he would visit Ike in Europe, he would call my mother immediately on his return home to Washington to tell her that her husband was in good health. And he readily approved Ike's request that I visit him in London for a short time immediately after I graduated from West Point on June 6, 1944.

My feeling is that Marshall did the correct thing at all times, treating all persons, including himself, as parts of a gigantic team. So if he sent me to visit Ike, he did so in order to bolster the morale of the general doing the fighting. His calls to Mother conformed to the code of the gentleman. Yet, when Ike wrote and asked permission for Mother to come to join him in Frankfurt right after the German surrender, Marshall refused on the basis that such favoritism would be detrimental to the morale of the troops occupying Germany and Austria. He was able to exert no such authority over Douglas MacArthur, who had his wife and son with him during the entire war, but I am certain that Marshall would have prevented such an arrangement had he been in a position to do so.

The matter of Mother's joining Ike in Frankfurt turned out to be unimportant, because Ike returned to the United States for a visit in November 1945, and while there contracted a case of pneumonia. On his recovery, President Truman prevailed on him to remain in Washington and take over as Chief of Staff immediately. A happy Marshall went into retirement at nearby Leesburg, Virginia, on the morning of November 27. That same afternoon he received a phone call from the President sending him on a special mission to China.[42]

As Chief of Staff, Ike visited Marshall in China in late 1946. There he found Marshall suffering from both physical deprivation and acute frustration. His efforts to effect a rapprochement between Chiang Kai-shek and Mao Tse-tung were proving fruitless. Ike, expecting to bring cheer to his former chief, carried a welcome message: "The President says that you are to come home and be the Secretary of State."

Marshall sighed. He had no desire to be Secretary of State, but he was willing, if only to get home.[43] "Anything to get out of this place," he said. Actually, Ike had misquoted the President to a slight degree. Truman had said to tell Marshall that either he or Ike would be the next Secretary of State. Ike, so he told me later, left himself out of the running.

Marshall returned home to perform notable service in his new post. He was actually revered, I was later told, by the members of the State

Department, including those Foreign Service officers who customarily scorned any diplomat lacking an Ivy League background. Part of his success lay in implementing organizational improvements, one of which, brought from the War Department, was the establishment of a secretariat to bring the activities of the department's bureaus into closer coordination.

What he is most remembered for, however, was his conceiving, and

Ike and Marshall waiting to testify before Congress, July 1950. Marshall's unhappy expression may have resulted from news that he was to be called back as Secretary of Defense in the Truman administration.

Author's Collection

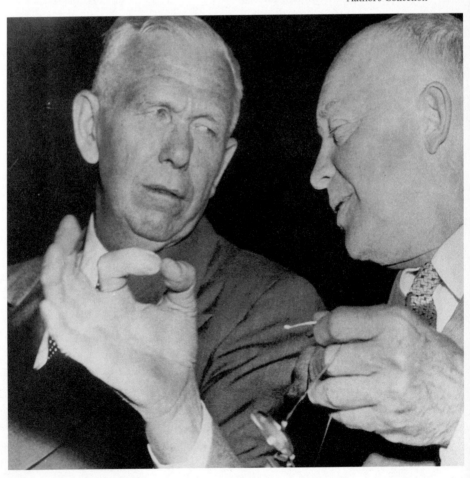

then, with President Truman's backing, selling the European Recovery Plan (which he never called by its popular name, the Marshall Plan), which did so much to promote European economic recovery after the war. For that inspired service, he was later awarded the Nobel Peace Prize. President Roosevelt's wish that Marshall be long remembered had come true, but more for his promoting that peaceful program, which took him only a short time, than for his gargantuan efforts during the Second World War.

Ike and Marshall served together once again, albeit briefly. The onset of the Korean War had demonstrated how woefully the Truman administration had allowed our military capacity to degenerate under Secretary of Defense Louis Johnson. To restore credibility to America's defense, President Truman removed Johnson and prevailed on Marshall to return to office once more. He would be named as Secretary of Defense. Marshall took the post, but only for a year.

During that time, Ike was also called back to duty, in his case from the presidency of Columbia University. Ike went into uniform once more and proceeded to Paris to begin organizing the military forces for the NATO alliance. The overlap was short; Ike arrived at NATO in February of 1951 and Marshall left the office of Secretary of Defense in September of the same year.

By June of 1952, Ike finally decided he should leave his post as Supreme Commander, Europe, and return home to run for the office of President. His astonishing victories in the New Hampshire and other Republican primaries, plus the arguments of many prominent visitors to Versailles, finally convinced him. He took the step with a great deal of ambivalence. He had previously discouraged any efforts to promote his candidacy, but he now believed that after twenty years of governmental domination by the Democratic Party, it was time for a change, a change that only he could effect.

Immediately after the Republican National Convention nominated Ike in July 1952, General Marshall penned him a note of congratulations. With it he added an explanation, as if such were necessary, why he would remain silent during the campaign. Vigorous attacks, he wrote, had been made upon him by various Republicans, and he was concerned that any public statements by him would be "picked up as the basis of some strictures detrimental" to Ike's cause.

Ike answered, expressing "very deep appreciation" for the note, and trying to pass the situation off lightly. Then, prophetically, he added, "The whole atmosphere is so different from that to which soldiers of long service become accustomed that I sometimes find it difficult indeed to adjust myself."[44]

Ironically, Ike's most serious problems stemmed from the attitude of the Republican Party itself. After twenty years of vying with Democratic presidents, the GOP congressional leaders had forgotten how to cooperate with the executive branch of government, and some of those leaders had gravitated far to the right. The most visible and vicious of them was Senator Joseph R. McCarthy, of Wisconsin, who had assumed a role as a super foe of Communism. Protected from libel suits by his privileged position on the floor of the Senate, McCarthy attacked organizations and people recklessly, often with little or no proof.

McCarthy's principal target was, of course, the Truman administration, and since General Marshall had occupied responsible positions in that administration, McCarthy attacked him also. In his first polemic, delivered a full year earlier, McCarthy had presented an astonishing list of sins: (a) Marshall's insistence on the cross-Channel attack during World War II, (b) his failure to press Ike to take Berlin and Prague at the end of the war, (c) his failure to adequately support Generalissimo Chiang Kai-shek in efforts to secure compromise with Mao Tse-tung in 1946, and above all (d) Marshall's acquiescence in Truman's relieving General Douglas MacArthur of his command in the Far East. This record, according to McCarthy, made Marshall a "dupe of the Communists."

Ike was now in a difficult position. Aside from his own campaign against the popular Adlai E. Stevenson, he faced the need to ensure Republican control of the next Congress. The contest in the Senate was so close that every seat was critical. Ike therefore found it necessary to support all Republican nominees for office, a blanket endorsement that had to include McCarthy, recently nominated for reelection by Republican voters in Wisconsin.

Ike tried in vain to separate his official endorsement of McCarthy from his personal resentment against the senator's attacks on Marshall. At a press conference in Denver on August 22, in a categorical statement of his loyalty to Marshall, he called the general "one of the patriots of this country . . . a man of real selflessness . . . the perfect example of patriotism and loyal servant of the United States." He finished up his statement by saying, "I have no patience with anyone who can find in [Marshall's] record of service for this country anything to criticize."[45]

Four days later, however, Ike made a decision that he had to live with the rest of his life. In editing the draft of a speech in Wisconsin, he gave way to the arguments of his staff,[46] on the advice of Wisconsin Governor Walter Kohler, that he delete a paragraph that repeated what he had said a few days earlier about Marshall. Ike drafted every speech many times, and paragraphs went in and out—I can attest to that personally—so the change would usually have held no consequence. However, the deleted paragraph had earlier been leaked to a reporter, and, to make matters worse, another reporter surmised falsely that McCarthy himself had bullied Ike into making the change. In the tempest that followed, a gleeful Harry Truman did not call the deletion a surrender to McCarthy, which might have been legitimate politics, but a "betrayal" of Marshall.

The incident had no effect on the outcome of the campaign. McCarthy was reelected senator in Wisconsin, but Ike ran 100,000 votes ahead of him in the state. Marshall himself, though he must have been chagrined, at least purported to understand the subtleties of the situation.[47] Forced to comment on the matter by a reporter, the general almost snorted, "Eisenhower was forced into a compromise. There is no more independence in politics than there is in jail."[48] Nevertheless, Ike never entirely forgave himself. "If I could have foreseen this distortion of the facts," he later wrote, "I would never have acceded to the staff's arguments, logical as they sounded at the time."[49]

As President, Ike never lost a chance to honor Marshall, sometimes violating protocol to do so. At White House dinners, for example, he placed the retired Marshall in precedence immediately after the Vice President and incumbent Secretary of State. At his Inaugural Parade in 1953, Ike designated the general as the Grand Marshal. At the coronation of Queen Elizabeth II of Britain the same year, Ike asked Marshall to serve as his ambassador and personal representative. Ike would have honored Marshall lavishly under any circumstances, but I suspect that the memory of the Wisconsin incident motivated him to go to the extraordinary lengths he did.

Marshall lived until 1959, and in his last sickness, Ike visited him periodically in the Presidential Suite at Walter Reed Army Hospital, where he grew increasingly comatose. Finally, Marshall was unable to recognize his visitors. He died on October 16, not quite having reached his seventy-ninth birthday. On Ike's orders, he lay in state in the Capitol Rotunda before interment at Arlington Cemetery, the latter ceremony attended, by Marshall's own direction, only by family and a few personal retainers. That modesty typified George C. Marshall.

Although my personal exposure to General Marshall was less frequent than my exposure to figures such as Patton, Monty, de Gaulle, or even Churchill, he is the one associate of Ike's who has made the strongest impression on me. That is strange, in that I respected him rather than liked him. He was an enigmatic man, and possibly more interesting simply because of his mystery.

The aspect of Marshall that I have admired, and somewhat chosen to emulate, was his conscious, clear-cut, consistent knowledge of who he was, a military man. No matter what role he was called on to play at a given moment, he always interpreted his current task as a soldierly duty. As Secretary of State, I have been told, he liked to be addressed as "General." He would serve any President willingly except in the role of partisan politician. I doubt that Marshall could have been flexible enough to serve effectively as President. He was too much the soldier to make that change.

I have also been intrigued by the personal growth that Marshall seemed to undergo between the First and Second World Wars. His published account of his services with Pershing's AEF shows him as capable, dedicated, courageous, and even sometimes gregarious—but also ambitious and vain. Given the change that twenty years brought in him, I find it quite understandable that Marshall reportedly ordered that account destroyed. Yet it is to the benefit of history that his instructions were disobeyed and that his stepdaughter, Mrs. Molly Wynn, had it published in 1976.

Dr. Forrest Pogue, Marshall's biographer, has theorized, quite reasonably I think, that Marshall cared for nobody's opinion of himself except for that of Mrs. Marshall. Such an attitude enabled him to regard himself and others as replaceable members of vast institutions. It made him a rare bird.

Ike never forgot that he owed his own extraordinary rise, which eventually led to the presidency, to General Marshall. As a competent officer, Ike would undoubtedly have attained high rank in any case, but it was Marshall who pulled him out of Third Army at San Antonio in 1941 and within six months appointed him to the top American position in Europe. With Marshall's unwavering support, Ike's stature grew to the point where he was chosen, in place of his chief, for the most important command of the war. Yet Marshall showed no resentment. He continued to treat Ike with consideration and, with Ike as President, with proper respect.

By the same token, I am sure that Marshall's gratitude to Ike was also deep. His position as Chief of Staff early in the war must have been made far less daunting when he found a loyal young officer who would take responsibility, who could send the *Queen Mary* to Australia on his own, who could make the unpopular Darlan decision, even though aware that generals in the field could be removed but officials in Washington could not. Ike went on to greater decisions—whether to give the order for the D-Day armada, how to respond to the German attack in the Ardennes, and to stop at the Elbe in the final days of the war.

Ike more than justified the confidence that Marshall placed in him back in 1942.

Ike and Monty at press conference shortly before D-Day, June 6, 1944.

National Archives

6

MONTY

Ike's Dynamic Headache

I would not class Ike as a great soldier in the true sense of the word. . . . But he was a great Supreme Commander—a military statesman. I know of no other person who could have welded the Allied forces into such a fine fighting machine in the way he did, and kept a balance among the many conflicting and disturbing elements which threatened at times to wreck the ship.

—FIELD MARSHAL SIR BERNARD LAW MONTGOMERY[1]

The United Kingdom—England, Scotland, Wales, and Northern Ireland—produced a great number of distinguished warriors in the Second World War. The list of admirable soldiers, sailors, and airmen that came from that small group of islands is long indeed. Of these, however, the name of Field Marshal Sir Bernard Law Montgomery, or Viscount Montgomery of Alamein, seems to be the best remembered. To Americans he was almost the symbol of the British war effort.

The luster that has attached to Montgomery's name—or Monty's, as he was known—was deserved, in my opinion, but not to the exclusion of others. A great many Americans disagree and contend that Monty was the most overrated general of the war.

That debate is not part of my concern. Suffice it to say that Montgomery was obviously a highly competent craftsman when it came to the handling of tactical formations. His record of victories inspired confidence, which in turn increased morale among British and Americans alike. What I will try to examine is his personality, his almost calculated arrogance, and the reason Monty was the heaviest cross that Ike had to bear in the war in Europe.

Friends sometimes say to me, "What a daunting job your dad had, being forced to contend with prima donnas like Patton and Monty." My standard answer to that is simply, "You are only half right; compared to Monty, Patton was no problem at all."

That rejoinder sometimes causes surprise; after all George Patton was at least as flamboyant as Montgomery, and just as headstrong. But Patton was an American officer, subject to the orders of his American superiors, who could promote him, decorate him, or remove him from command. Montgomery was subject to no such administrative control by the Supreme Allied Commander. He was, in fact, the British Commander-in-Chief in the Allied Expeditionary Force, and in that capacity on a par with Ike himself as the American commander. In the command arrangements agreed to by the Americans and British, he enjoyed the right to appeal to the home government if he considered an order issued by the Supreme Commander as endangering his force. Taken to the extreme, Ike might conceivably be forced to defend an order that Montgomery didn't like in the arena of the Combined Chiefs of Staff—and through them to the two heads of government.

Fortunately, no such impasse ever quite came about, though once it came close. As a rule, relations among high commanders almost always remained cordial on the surface, and Ike could usually keep Monty in harness simply by allocating and sometimes withholding resources in the form of men and supplies.*

I understand, though Ike never mentioned it to me, that he and Monty met for the first time in the spring of 1942, when Ike and Mark Clark visited the United Kingdom before Ike's assignment to Europe. The story has it that Monty, a lieutenant general, was sharp about Ike's chain-smoking in a conference. Be that as it may, they first began working together when their forces met in southern Tunisia in the spring of 1943. Ike was then Allied Commander in the Western Mediterranean and Montgomery was in command of the British Eighth Army. Monty, under Harold Alexander, had achieved a victory over German Field Marshal Erwin Rommel at El Alamein, Libya, the previous October and had joined Ike's command in southern Tunisia. Their relationships in the Mediterranean were not close, however, because Alexander, now appointed as Ike's deputy, was sandwiched between them as an army group commander. It was when Ike and Monty came to London in January of 1944 to prepare for OVERLORD that they dealt on a close basis.

It was shortly after D-Day, in June of 1944, that I first saw Montgomery. The occasion was a visit I made to Normandy with Ike during the eighteen days I spent with him immediately following my graduation from West Point. On June 15, 1944, two days after my arrival at Ike's headquarters, he took me with him on a trip to visit Monty in Normandy. It was only nine days after D-Day.

The flight to Normandy was an exciting event for a young officer

---

*For that reason, Ike once told me, the Supreme Commander in a coalition had to be the commander who administratively controlled the bulk of the resources. He had no starry-eyed illusions about cooperation. Since a Supreme Commander was short on clout by way of a stick, he had to be provided with a carrot.

who had been a cadet ten days earlier. I sat in the nose of the Boeing B-17 bomber with Air Chief Marshal Sir Arthur Tedder as we flew low over the beaches. Tedder, a wry, unpretentious man, seemed to enjoy pointing out various aspects of the activities below to a green lieutenant. At one point the Flying Fortress flew too close to the barrage balloons that protected the naval vessels, causing some edgy sailor to put a couple of 20mm rounds off one of the wings of the aircraft. The beachhead area was of course crowded, but business seemed to be going on methodically. The distance by air from London to Normandy is short, and very quickly, it seemed, we landed in an open field. Jeeps were on hand to take us to Monty's headquarters, which was located only a few miles behind the front lines just north of Caen.

Monty's headquarters, 21 Army Group, consisted of a small cluster of vans and tents in an enclosure that I remember as being some 300 yards on a side. As we drove through the entrance gate, we were amused by a sign, "All vehicle traffic keep left." It was a little touch of England; all other traffic in France, as in the United States, goes on the right.

When our jeep pulled up at Montgomery's trailer, we learned to our surprise that the general was absent. He had left shortly before to make a visit to the front. Technically, Monty was guilty of no discourtesy; Ike had previously stated to all subordinate commanders that he would take it upon himself to find whomever he was visiting.[2] And Ike was as good as his word; he did not seem to take Monty's absence amiss. To pass the time until his return, therefore, we set off on a tour around the British area by jeep. One of our stops was at the nearby headquarters of the Second British Army, where Ike had a consultation with General Sir Miles "Bimbo" Dempsey. British infantry were marching to the front. Some, seeing the stars on Ike's jeep, grinned and waved. But the atmosphere was serious.

Finally, late in the day, we arrived back at Monty's command post. In the course of the trip, I had accumulated some dust on my uniform jacket, and Ike rather sharply told me to dust myself off before being introduced. He was unusually concerned that I look my best. It made little difference. Monty did not seem to notice me or anyone else, almost including Ike.

Since Monty was a legendary figure, I observed him closely. He was an odd-looking sort of creature, and to a young American he did not live up to my concept of a general. He was wearing the informal garb that we associate him with—plain gray sweater, baggy corduroy slacks, and no jacket. His only concession to proper uniform was the black tanker's beret he had adopted.[3] In person he radiated intensity, with his sharp features, his small, wiry figure, and his restlessness. He spoke in a chirping, birdlike voice. He was known to be a loner and a confirmed ascetic who neither smoked nor drank. He was said to carry his disdain for tobacco and alcohol to the extent of denying even his most prominent guests such amenities at his table. Even Winston Churchill, known to be fond of brandy, was no exception.*

Though I was unaware of it at the time of that visit, the American commanders were already developing some doubts about Monty's aggressiveness. Such a conclusion was and is impossible to prove, especially since Monty had good reason to justify caution in facing the professional German army. The British nation was already feeling the lack of manpower reserves, and it was becoming impossible to keep British and Commonwealth units up to strength. In addition, there is no doubt that German Field Marshal Erwin Rommel, commanding in Normandy, was stacking a great amount of strength, particularly armor, on the eastern end of the Normandy bridgehead, the British and Canadian sector.

Yet Monty's personality probably contributed to his caution. He was reputed to have resolved that no matter what else happened, he was never going to risk a defeat. A stalemate, perhaps, even heavy casualties, but never a defeat. He therefore demanded a tremendous preponderance of force before launching an attack. That at El Alamein, for example, was overpowering. He was acknowledged to be a master at set-piece planning, such as preparing for the D-Day landings, but in a war of movement he was thought to be conservative to a fault. In any case, whatever one's later judgment, the American commanders by that time were beginning to perceive Monty as timid.

∞

---

*After the battle of El Alamein, in late October of 1942, the triumphant British Eighth Army captured a German General von Thoma. Monty received criticism from some elements of the press when, in old-fashioned style, he entertained Thoma at dinner. Churchill fended off the attacks with humor: "Alas, poor Thoma, I too have dined with Montgomery."

It might help here to review the command setup for the D-Day landings and the first few weeks following them. For that period, the direct ground command was to be exercised by Monty's 21 Army Group, which originally consisted of Miles Dempsey's Second British Army on the east and Omar Bradley's First United States Army on the west. Monty also claimed the title of Commander, Allied Ground Forces and, to be fair, Ike probably used the term also. But Ike always considered that title to be temporary, whereas Monty at least pretended to consider it permanent.[4]

Ike's projected organization of his command, a concept from which he never wavered, was that the forces fighting in Normandy should be under a single army group only while the Allies were consolidating their bridgehead. Then, following the expected breakout from the beachhead, General George Patton's Third United States Army was to enter the battle under 12 Army Group, and Bradley was to step up from command of the American First Army and assume command of that army group, which would now consist of the American First and Third Armies (later to be reinforced by William Simpson's Ninth Army). At about the same time as the U.S. Third Army was activated, General Henry D.G. Crerar's First Canadian Army was to became operational. Monty would then have the First Canadian and the Second British Army in 21 Army Group. Tactically, at least, Monty and Bradley would then, as army group commanders, be on a co-equal status.

Third U.S. Army entered the Normandy battle on August 1, 1944. Very soon thereafter Patton was turned loose for his spectacular drive eastward across France, and Monty was left with only one special prerogative, though an important one: until Supreme Headquarters assumed day-to-day direction—it always had full command—Monty was allowed to set the boundary between his and Bradley's commands.

I am no expert on the Normandy battle, so I may be overstating it when I say that Monty's command of 21 Army Group for those early weeks seemed far less "stitched"—to use his own term—than he later claimed. He seemed to concentrate nearly all his attention on his own army group. All the major decisions, so I can make out, were arrived at through a series of informal conferences between Ike, Monty, and

Bradley, with Ike of course carrying ultimate responsibility. In tactical matters, Bradley was largely on his own, and he later praised Monty for allowing him nearly complete latitude. For example, when the American V Corps ran into unexpected German resistance at Omaha Beach on D-Day, it was Bradley, not Monty, who seriously considered sending in reinforcements to Utah rather than Omaha Beach.

Near the end of my visit to the United Kingdom, I was able to accompany Ike on one more trip to Normandy, this time to see General Bradley in the American sector. Though I was unaware of it at the time, the meeting they held in secret was an important one. According to General Walter Bedell Smith, Ike's chief of staff, Ike had just decided on an important change in the tactics of the Normandy battle. Up to that time, the Allied high command had assumed that the breakout would be conducted by Montgomery's 21 Army Group on the east, because it was in good tank country and closer to the Seine River, where the Allies expected the Germans to make their next serious defense. But with the difficulties Montgomery was experiencing in taking Caen, originally an objective for the first day's fighting, Ike had decided that the Americans, on the right flank, should make the breakout, even though they had to fight through the nearly impassable hedgerow country to reach open terrain.[5] That was important business, and to me it is surprising that neither Monty nor a representative was present at that meeting.

Monty, as I have said, seemed to be concentrating nearly all his attention on the British and Canadian effort to take Caen. He was not, for example, present on August 8, 1944, when Ike and Bradley made the crucial decision of the campaign. At that time the bulk of Patton's Third Army was heading eastward toward Alençon, but his lifeline passed through the narrow corridor at Avranches and Mortain. Hitler, they knew, had decided to conduct a major counterattack toward the sea, with the objective of cutting Patton's supply lines to his advance elements, heading eastward. The narrow corridor through which supplies were flowing was being held open by a single division, the 30th. Other units—the 9th Infantry Division, the 2d Armored Division, and the 35th Infantry Division—were in the vicinity to reinforce if the 30th Division found the task too much.

As Bradley and Ike conferred at Bradley's headquarters, however, they saw a chance to cut off the Germans at Falaise, though that meant sending all the other divisions eastward to Patton, leaving the 30th to hold the corridor open by itself. It was a risky move, but they took it. A quick telephone call to Monty brought his ready concurrence, but the decision was Ike's sole responsibility. Even had Monty protested, there is no doubt in my mind that Ike would have gone ahead anyway. The matter is not particularly important except that it belies Montgomery's later claims that he was controlling the entire Normandy campaign in detail.

The campaign, as history has recorded, resulted in a spectacular Allied success. Patton drove eastward and then First Army, on his left, turned north and nearly closed the gap between Falaise and Argentan, south of Caen, resulting in the deadly killing ground known as the Falaise Pocket. Though the gap was not completely closed, the slaughter was tremendous, and for a while it appeared as if Hitler's entire army in the Western Theater was destroyed for good.

Once the elation of victory died down, however, a degree of rancor erupted between the British and Americans. That rancor was brought about by a misunderstanding regarding the status of Montgomery. Unfortunately, the somewhat intricate command arrangements regarding the temporary nature of Monty's overall tactical command were never announced in advance. The fact that Monty's 21 Army Group included Bradley's First Army as of D-Day was known, but the commitment of Patton's Third Army under Bradley in its dash across France was kept under wraps.[6] In the public mind, therefore, the credit for masterminding the spectacular victory in Normandy was accorded almost exclusively to Monty. The British public elevated Monty from the status of hero to one of national icon.

This exaggerated canonization of Monty was exacerbated by the fact that the British press, radio, and newsreels emphasized British accomplishments, to everyone else's expense, to a degree beyond the imagination of the Americans. Thus it is not surprising that, when Ike publicly announced his assumption of direct personal command of the ground forces on September 1, the British press and public vehemently protested. Monty, they claimed, was being "demoted" by ungrateful and jealous Americans.[7] Neither Monty nor Churchill went to any effort to explain the situation to the British public. The Prime Minister, in fact, promoted Monty to field marshal, thus elevating him once more to a grade above

Ike. And from that time on, even though he was consistently overridden, Monty never ceased to campaign for the title of overall ground commander, while at the same time insisting on retaining personal command over his own army group. An amazing demand.

In keeping his plan for future command arrangements secret at the beginning, Ike was acting according to long-accepted military procedure. The conventional military practice of keeping "order of battle" information secret from the enemy assumes that if that enemy knows who is in command at a certain time, he will know what to expect.* As it turned out, however, even Ike later admitted that the policy in the case of OVERLORD caused such a serious British-American misunderstanding that it would have been better to announce all command arrangements in advance.

In all this, the British press, and later some British historians, have looked on Ike as a tool of General Marshall, as a Supreme Allied Commander who was actually only a puppet of his American superiors in Washington. In early September, however, the pendulum swung, and many Americans found cause to criticize Ike for coming too much under Monty's sway. The episode that triggered this criticism was the disappointing Operation MARKET-GARDEN, known popularly as the offensive that went "A Bridge Too Far."[8]

As the British and Americans reached the borders of Germany in early September 1944, they felt a glimmer of hope that the war in Europe might be won within weeks, or at least before the end of the year. Montgomery, in particular, insisted that a quick victory could be won if the campaign were to be conducted according to his own "plan." This plan was simple; it simply meant placing himself in charge of all land operations of importance. If Ike were to provide Monty's

---

*Much has been made of Robert E. Lee's knowledge of the personalities of the Union commanders in the American Civil War. Lee was able to take otherwise unwarranted risks, so the theory goes, because he knew which Union commanders, such as George B. McClellan, would be overly cautious. If that is so, the principle was not followed in planning OVERLORD. That operation was intended to succeed regardless of the personality of any opposing commander.

21 Army Group with virtually all the ammunition and gasoline in the European Theater, and reinforce him with a substantial number of American troops, the new field marshal could end the war by making a long, single thrust across the North German Plain, through Holland and Germany, to seize Berlin.

This lopsided allocation of resources was out of the question from the beginning. Ike and all the American commanders dismissed it out of hand, and even the British staff members of SHAEF, such as Major General John Whiteley, scoffed at the idea. It was unreasonable, they insisted, to "keep three-quarters of the entire Allied Expeditionary Force sitting on their fannies"[9] in order to oversupply Monty, who commanded about a quarter. Such a strategy would fail to take advantage of the substantial Allied advantage in men and matériel. Furthermore, it would be politically impossible, in coalition warfare, for the troops of one nation to take all the losses and receive all the headlines. Ike refused Monty's most extravagant demands, though he conceded that Monty's army group should be given priority as the main effort. Only not to the degree that Montgomery sought.

On September 10, the day before the American First Army set foot on German soil in the vicinity of Aachen, Ike and Monty met at the newly liberated Brussels airport. In the rear of Ike's airplane,[10] which was parked on the tarmac, the two generals discussed a plan that Monty had recently proposed to seize a bridgehead over the Rhine River at the Dutch town of Arnhem, near the mouth of the river. The concept was imaginative.[11] The British Second Army, currently poised on the Escaut Canal, might drive northward, using both British and attached American troops. Three airborne divisions, one for each river obstacle along the path, were to be dropped along a single road, and the British XXX Corps, heavily armored, should push northward along the hundred-mile highway to link up with the 1st British Airborne ("Red Devils"), which was to be dropped across the Rhine. The American units, the 82d and 101st Airborne Divisions, would seize crossings over the Maas and the Waal Rivers along the way.

Ike favored the plan, but one aspect of it gave him pause: it competed for resources with Monty's other task, a drive up the northern bank of the Schelde Estuary to seize Walcheren Island, thus eliminating those German units that were capable of denying Allied use of the estuary for shipping. The importance of opening that waterway to Allied traffic was immense; Ike and his planners were counting on the port of Antwerp to supply the whole northern half of the AEF, along with the port of Marseilles to supply the south. Monty, perhaps carried away by the prospects of the more spectacular MARKET-GARDEN, assured Ike that the clearing of the Schelde would not be delayed by the simultaneous execution of MARKET-GARDEN.

MARKET-GARDEN was launched as planned on September 17, and it was clear from the beginning that it was in trouble, because German Field Marshal Walther Model had reorganized the remnants of the German army far more effectively than Allied intelligence had believed possible. Still, it might have succeeded had not foul weather, with heavy winds, driven the British Red Devils away from their objective at Arnhem. Though the American airborne divisions seized both Eindhoven and Nijmegen, the 1st British Airborne, across the Rhine, was virtually wiped out. Much of Holland had been freed, but the failure of MARKET-GARDEN to attain its final objective has stamped it with the label of failure.

It was Ike's approval of MARKET-GARDEN that brought him a great deal of criticism from American writers, because they seem to believe that Monty bulldozed him into an operation he didn't believe in. Professor Stephen E. Ambrose, Ike's biographer and a writer generally sympathetic with his views, condemns Ike's "appeasing" Monty in severe terms:

> Of all the factors that influenced Eisenhower's decisions—to reinforce success, to jump the Rhine, to bring the highly trained but underutilized paratroopers into action—the one that stands out is his desire to appease Montgomery. At no other point in the war did Eisenhower's tendency toward compromise and to keep his subordinates happy exact a higher price.[12]

Professor Ambrose thus joins others who suppose that Ike basically disapproved of the Arnhem operation. Ike always claimed otherwise. In his memoir of the war, *Crusade in Europe,* he almost heatedly denies such a notion, asserting, or at least implying, that the idea was practically his own:

I instructed [Montgomery] that what I did want in the north was Antwerp working, and I also wanted a line covering that port. Beyond this I believed it possible that we might with airborne assistance seize a bridgehead over the Rhine in the Arnhem region, flanking the defenses of the Siegfried Line. The operation to gain such a bridgehead . . . would be merely an incident and extension of our eastward rush to the line we needed for our temporary security. On our northern flank was the Rhine itself. To stop short of that obstacle would have left us in a very exposed position.[13]

Actually, it makes little or no difference where the concept of MARKET-GARDEN originated. The question is, once the idea was put forth, did Ike believe it to be a reasonable risk? The evidence is scarce. Most revealing is a message from Ike to Monty, dated September 13, 1944, which contains this paragraph:

I understand that you will launch Operation MARKET-GARDEN on the 17th. This is very encouraging, as every day gained will be to our advantage and in addition will permit the earlier reassembly of United States airborne divisions which may shortly be needed by Bradley. I also understand that you are pushing for the Scheldt [Schelde] Estuary.[14]

And in 1966, when reviewing the matter with Professor Ambrose, Ike said, "I not only *approved* MARKET-GARDEN, I insisted upon it. What we needed was a bridgehead over the Rhine. If that could be accomplished, I was quite willing to wait on all operations."[15]

Despite the doubts of many other writers, I believe that Ike, carried away by the successes of July, August, and early September, unrealistically hoped to have it both ways: the reduction of the German defenses on the Schelde Estuary and a bridgehead over the Rhine. The fact that Monty agreed does not imply "appeasement" at the expense of the mission. Ike shared a common mistake with Monty but his mistake was his own.

After the failure of MARKET-GARDEN, there followed over two months—until mid-December—of dreary disagreement between

Monty and Ike over the conduct of current operations. Undeterred by his failure to cross the Rhine in September, Monty continued his quest to attain overwhelming logistical priority for 21 Army Group plus the attachment of a ten-division American army. The division between his army group and Bradley's, he contended, should be the Ardennes; Ike insisted that it should be the Ruhr. At the same time Monty continued to seek his own appointment as overall ground commander. He conducted his campaign through two channels. First, he took advantage of Ike's invitation to express his views openly. More important, he passed his complaints against Ike's conduct of the battle to his strong ally in Whitehall, Chief of the Imperial General Staff Sir Alan Brooke. Brooke backed Monty wholeheartedly—his zeal intensified, one suspects, by his own personal disappointment. Brooke knew very well that, had it not been for his British nationality, the position of Supreme Commander would most likely have been his.

On the question of strategy, Ike and Monty continued to hold a very clear-cut difference. From the early days of planning OVER-LORD in London, it had been understood that the Allies should first clear all German forces west of the Rhine River, at least north of the Moselle, before crossing into the heart of Germany. Monty contended that such a strategy was timid, that a drive to Berlin could be conducted without first clearing the west bank of the Rhine. That optimism, of course, was part and parcel of Monty's single thrust with all the resources of the theater allocated to him.

The arguments varied but little over the two months; only the means of expressing them differed. The voluminous exchange of communications between Ike and Monty, both oral and written, was largely repetitive. It reached a climax when a letter of Monty's in late November called the current campaign a "failure" and urged that some of Patton's divisions, in 12 Army Group, be moved to positions north of the Ardennes in order to put more weight in the north. "We must concentrate such strength on the main selected thrust that success will be certain."[16]

Ike responded in anger to Montgomery's claim that the campaign was a failure simply because "all that had been hoped for had not been achieved." In what might be interpreted as a dig, he added, "We gained a great victory in Normandy. Bradley's brilliant breakthrough made possible the great exploitation by all forces, which blasted France and Belgium and almost carried us across the Rhine." He finally concluded, "I have no intention of stopping Devers' and Patton's operations so long as they are cleaning up our right flank and giving us capability of concentration."[17] Monty quickly retracted his reference to "failure," but passed his views on to Alan Brooke.

On receipt of Montgomery's message, Brooke went to Churchill with a new idea by which to promote the British, rather than the American, strategy for the campaign. He suggested that, since the Italian campaign was going to dwindle down in the near future, perhaps Ike's deputy, Air Chief Marshal Sir Arthur Tedder, could be transferred to command in Italy and Harold Alexander appointed as Ike's deputy in Tedder's place. It might be possible, he reasoned, for Alex to run the ground war, with Ike in the stratosphere, as had been the arrangement in the Mediterranean.[18] Tedder was only a pawn in this scheme. If not sent to Italy, he could be placed in the number two spot in the Air Ministry.

When Brooke presented these views to the Prime Minister, he attained little satisfaction at first. Apparently Churchill had second thoughts, however, for a few days later he wrote to President Roosevelt suggesting another summit meeting between Roosevelt, Stalin, and himself, the first since the meeting at Tehran a year earlier. If such were not possible, Churchill asked that the President send the American Joint Chiefs of Staff to London to review the conduct of the European campaign. It was an ill-timed communication. It angered Ike and it met with a rather condescending rebuff from Roosevelt, who cited his youthful biking trips in the Rhine country as evidence that the British were being overly optimistic in hoping to reach that stream so easily.[19] Nothing more came of the matter for the moment.

To resolve their differences, Ike called a meeting with himself, Bradley, and Monty at Monty's headquarters in Maastricht, Holland, on December 6, 1944. Despite the smiles they all gave the photographers, the discussions were very frank. Both sides presented their views almost exactly as they had been presenting them throughout October and November. In the end, Ike made what he considered a concession: he would, as Monty had asked, attach General William Simpson's Ninth U.S. Army to 12 Army Group on a temporary basis, thus bringing Monty's force from fifteen to twenty-five divisions. But Patton's attack into the Saar was to continue.

Monty did not believe that Ike had made much of a concession. It was the last time they exchanged views before the great German counteroffensive of mid-December, commonly referred to as the Battle of the Bulge.

On the morning of December 16, 1944, Hitler launched his operation AUTUMN FOG on the front of the VIII U.S. Corps covering the Ardennes, thus beginning the month-long Battle of the Bulge. I have described the early stages of the operation and Ike's reaction to the German penetrations in the chapter on Patton, as well as the historic meeting of December 19 at Verdun. In short, Ike ordered Patton to begin a counterattack northward from Arlon toward the Belgian road junction of Bastogne, which was at that time in the process of being surrounded.

Though Ike had ordered the first steps to squeeze the waist of the German penetration, one aspect of the situation remained to be worked out. General Omar Bradley's headquarters was still located in the city of Luxembourg, south of the penetration, and by December 19 it was already apparent that Hitler's thrust was directed to the northwest, probably to cross the Meuse River east of Namur, with a probable objective of taking Antwerp. Since Bradley insisted on keeping his headquarters in Luxembourg City, he would be virtually out of communication with the area of the main action. On Ike's return from Verdun, therefore, both he and his staff—separately, it seems—began considering the advisability of splitting the battlefield, that is, transferring command of all the First Army troops north of the Bulge from Bradley's 12 Army Group to that of Montgomery's 21 Army Group.

Besides the matter of Bradley's communication, Ike had another reason for making such a split in the battlefield. The only major reserve out of the line at the moment was the British XXX Corps, under General Sir Brian Horrocks, which was refitting after Operation MARKET-GARDEN in Holland. As Supreme Commander, Ike could doubtless have attached that British corps to Hodges and prevailed over Monty's possible protests back to London. However, it would seem more effective and more advantageous to the maintenance of Allied unity for Monty to be in charge if the employment of British forces under Horrocks became necessary.

Ike asked his chief of staff, Bedell Smith, to check with Bradley to ascertain his feelings. Bradley was of course unhappy with the prospect, but he acceded reluctantly. At the SHAEF staff meeting in Versailles on the morning of December 20, therefore, Ike announced his decision to place the northern half of the Bulge under Monty. Bradley would be left temporarily as an army group commander with only Patton's Third Army under him. Ike then called Monty and gave him his instructions.

Monty arrived at Hodges's First Army headquarters at Tongres, Belgium, later in the same day, December 20. There he sensed an aura of pessimism among the American staff. Hodges was down with a severe case of flu, essentially out of action for the moment, and his chief of staff, Major General William Kean, was running things.[20] Monty assumed personal charge—at least for the moment. As was his custom in any command, he sent his own agents, euphemistically called "liaison officers," to all major subordinate headquarters, some of which were temporarily out of contact with First Army headquarters. Soon he at least had a better idea of where those units were.[21]

It is not my purpose, in a brief chapter on relations between Ike and Monty, to make an exhaustive study of Monty's performance as operational commander of the First and Ninth U.S. Armies in the northern half of the Bulge. However, it seems to have worked out far better than the alternate arrangement, that of leaving those armies under the command of Bradley's 12 Army Group. First Army enjoyed far closer command support under Monty than it could have received from Luxembourg.[22] Monty's liaison system, while irritating to Americans, gave First Army a more detailed picture of the situation than the Americans customarily enjoyed. And Monty made another, very important move. He took the entire American VII Corps, under the aggressive commander J. Lawton Collins, out of the line and formed a mobile reserve with which to head off the westward thrust of the Germans wherever it was needed. Hodges might have done the same, but it was Monty's scheme, Monty's decision.

On the other hand, Hodges did not become mere putty in Monty's hands. When the bulk of First Army troops had fallen back northward to an acceptable defensive line, a sizable force, the 7th Armored Division, had been left stranded in a position at St. Vith which promised to be surrounded like Bastogne at any time. It had to be pulled out. Montgomery was inclined to do nothing from the north, merely to instruct General Robert Hasbrouck, commanding the division, to fend for himself. Hodges insisted on ordering General Matthew B. Ridgway's XVIII Airborne Corps to attack southwest to relieve Hasbrouck at Vielsalm and he made his position stick.

Overall, the switchover of the northern half of the Bulge from Bradley to Montgomery turned out to be successful, at least in the eyes of those on the ground in the north. When Montgomery finally surrendered control of First Army back to Bradley in mid-January 1945, his final visit to Courtney Hodges's First Army headquarters has been described as "a mutually and genuinely amiable parting."[23]

From the viewpoint of relations between the allies, however, Ike's splitting the battlefield was a move he lived to regret, for his so doing gave Monty grounds to reopen his case for his own appointment to be overall ground commander. In the outcome, Monty nearly overplayed his hand.

On December 30, 1944, Ike was chafing under Montgomery's apparent slowness in launching the planned counterattack from the north, designed to meet with Patton's attack coming up through Bastogne. At that moment he received a letter from Monty that he interpreted as an ultimatum. Ike had just reinstated Monty's authority to coordinate the boundaries between him and Bradley in cases of emergency, and he presumed that Monty would be pleased to be granted such authority, which he had enjoyed in Normandy.

Not so. Montgomery's message had waved a red flag. "If you merely use the word 'coordination,'" it said, "it will not work. The person designated by you must have the powers of operational direction and control of the operation that will follow on your directive. . . . It is then that one commander must have powers to direct and control the operations; you cannot possibly do it yourself, and so you would have to nominate someone else." He suggested a paragraph the wording of which left no doubt:

> From now onwards full operational direction, control, and coordination of these operations is vested in C-in-C, 21 Army Group, subject to such instructions as may be issued by the Supreme Commander from time to time.[24]

That drew the line.

A catastrophic situation was now threatening, and a great deal of the credit for averting it must go to a British officer who had always done so much to ease the friction between Ike and Monty, Major General Sir Francis de Guingand. A congenial, smooth bon vivant, Freddie de Guingand had been Montgomery's chief of staff from the early days in North Africa, and he was trusted by all, British and Americans alike. He often represented Montgomery at meetings with Ike when his chief decided he was "too busy." (The Americans were always relieved when that happened.)

The possibility of serious trouble between the two senior commanders first came to de Guingand's attention on New Year's Eve 1944. One of his liaison officers at Bradley's 12 Army Group headquarters reported that Bradley and his staff were infuriated by claims made in British newspapers and on the radio that Montgomery had been forced to come to the rescue of a failed American command. Worse, Monty seemed to be using the publicity to build up a campaign in public for his own advancement. When de Guingand telephoned SHAEF to confer with his friend and counterpart, Chief of Staff Bedell Smith, he received even more disturbing news.

Ike, Smith said, was contemplating a showdown with Monty: he was writing a message to the Combined Chiefs of Staff declaring that one man, either he or Monty, had to go. They could no longer work together.

De Guingand quickly took matters into his own hands. Without informing Monty, he left 21 Army Group headquarters in Brussels and took a small liaison plane through miserable weather to Orly Airfield. He sped out to Versailles to check in with Smith. Without delay he and Smith hurried to Ike's office. There they found Ike conferring seriously with Tedder.

Ike, usually effusive in greeting Freddie, was unusually curt that day. "Does Monty realize," he demanded sharply, "the effects of the line taken by the British press? And I wonder if he recognizes the effects of his continual pressing for the establishment of a land commander? I am tired of the whole business and have come to the conclusion that it is now a matter for the decision of the Combined Chiefs of Staff." He then handed de Guingand a message he was about to send to the Combined Chiefs requesting that Monty be replaced by General Sir Harold Alexander—in other words that they would now be forced to choose between Monty and him.

De Guingand, shocked, entered an earnest plea. He was certain, he insisted, that Monty had no idea that matters had become so serious, and once it was explained to him, he would cooperate completely. Finally Ike agreed to wait twenty-four hours before sending his fateful message to the CCS.

The next day, after a plane ride as harrowing as that on the previous day, de Guingand arrived at Monty's personal headquarters at Tongres. Monty was at tea when he arrived, but he detected de Guingand's distress and sensed that something was wrong. He cut his ritual short and went upstairs to confer in his office.

As de Guingand had suspected, Monty was amazed to learn of the crisis. His dismay became even worse when de Guingand assured him that, if a choice had to be made between Ike and Monty, Monty would go. It came as a double shock to realize that he, Monty, could be readily replaced by Alexander. For once the cocky field marshal seemed helpless. "What shall I do, Freddie?" De Guingand then produced the text of a message he had previously drafted. Monty approved it immediately:

Dear Ike:

Have seen Freddie and understand you are greatly worried by many considerations in these difficult days. I have given you my very frank views, because I have felt that you liked this. I am sure there are many factors which have a bearing quite beyond anything I realize. Whatever your decision may be, you can rely on me one hundred per cent to make it work, and I know Brad will do the same. Very distressed that my letter may have upset you and I would ask you to tear it up.

Your very devoted subordinate,

Monty

The next day, Freddie de Guingand was relieved to learn that, at Versailles, the original of Monty's message, along with Ike's, had been destroyed.[25]

It would be pleasant if the story ended there, with a feeling of cooperation, even if not euphoria. However, one characteristic that Monty shared with George Patton was an inability to lie low for a while once a personal crisis had passed. Once either man had survived, he acted as if nothing had happened.

Barely a week after the New Year's Eve showdown, on January 7, 1945, Monty held a press conference that dispelled any temporary truce between him and the Americans.

He started out with what he intended, no doubt, as an olive branch, expressing his devotion to Ike and citing the Supreme Commander's generosity in replacing his damaged airplane a few days earlier. He then expressed "grief" when he saw "uncomplimentary remarks" about him in the British press, claiming that "nothing of that sort has ever come from here." He finished his accolade by telling of Ike's great burdens and calling for all to "rally round the captain of the team."[26]

That bit of condescension could be tolerated, but when Monty began describing the German breakthrough of December 16, he said, "National considerations were thrown overboard; General Eisenhower placed me in command of the whole northern front."

Then Monty pictured himself as the master craftsman, telling about how he had brought to bear "the whole available power of the British Group of armies," which in fact had amounted to only one division committed late in the game. He told of pulling J. Lawton Collins's VII Corps out of the line and using it to head off the tip of the Bulge. No problem there, but perhaps the most objectionable aspect of the press conference was Montgomery's self-congratulatory attitude. His account culminated in this masterpiece:

[VII Corps] took a knock. I said, "Dear me, this can't go on. It's being swallowed up in the battle."

I set to work and managed to form the corps again.

Once more pressure was such that it began to disappear in a defensive battle.

I said, "Come, come," and formed it again and it was put in offensively by General Hodges.

The enemy was first "headed off" from vital spots, then "seen off."

He is now being "written off," and heavy toll is being taken of his divisions by ground and air action.[27]

Unfortunately the British press exaggerated Monty's statements even beyond his own words. He was pictured as having acted "on his own" to save the day. Even worse, one newspaper wrote, "Apparently the situation was so desperate that Field-Marshal Montgomery, using his own initiative, threw in all his weight and authority and asserted his leadership, which was accepted by those around him."

Monty's press conference, together with the way the British press blew it up, was too much for even the usually reticent Omar Bradley. He therefore took the rare step of calling his own press conference. By the time he did so, however, the public's attention had gone on to other things, and his remarks went nearly unnoticed.*

From a military point of view, Ike's move in giving Monty temporary command of the northern armies made good sense. The British field marshal conducted the battle with his usual caution but also his usual competence. However, from the viewpoint of Allied relations, Monty's tactlessness caused bitter feelings between Americans and British, some of which lasted for a long time. It damaged the friendship between two West Point classmates and football teammates, Ike and Bradley. For though the matter was glossed over, Bradley never

---

*Winston Churchill put the matter into perspective when he spoke before Parliament on January 17: Saying that the United States troops had done "almost all the fighting and suffered almost all the losses," he concluded, "The Americans have engaged 30 or 40 men for every one we have engaged, and they have lost 60 to 80 men for every one of ours. Care must be taken in telling our proud tale not to claim for the British Army an undue share of what undoubtedly is the greatest American battle of the war."

completely forgot the episode. Their friendship from that time on was less warm than before.

In February 1945, a circumstance arose that made Ike and Monty allies against Alan Brooke, at least for a short period of time. With the end of the Ardennes campaign, which the British press insisted on calling an inexcusable American defeat, Sir Alan Brooke revived his earlier proposal for Alexander to replace Tedder as Ike's deputy. When consulted on the matter, Ike had no objection. The position of deputy, he pointed out, was designated by the Combined Chiefs of Staff, and he had the highest regard for both Tedder and Alexander.

Perhaps Ike was being naive, for he saw nothing sinister in the proposal. Many other Americans, however, including General Marshall, saw it otherwise. In the view of the American public, they reasoned, Alexander's appointment might be construed as an admission of American failure in the Ardennes. On January 12, 1945, Ike sent Marshall a rather defensive letter about his lack of resistance to the idea, and the matter dropped again for the moment.[28]

When Roosevelt and Churchill met again on Malta in preparation for the Yalta Conference with Stalin in the second week of February, the question of Alexander came up again, and Churchill seemed to consider that the move was decided on. On his return to London, therefore, Brooke wrote Ike asking once more for his views. Ike answered again, this time expressing serious doubts. While giving no objections to the move, he wrote that taking Tedder away from him would require him to ask for Lieutenant General Carl Spaatz, currently commander of the American Strategic Air Forces in Europe, to replace him. He needed an airman who was his own man. But more important,

> It is extremely important, in my view, that Alexander should understand in advance exactly how our whole set-up is working in order that later he may not feel that he is being badly used nor his great qualities as a soldier ignored. There can be no question whatsoever of placing between me and my army group commanders any intermediate headquarters, either official or unofficial in character. . . . Day before yester-

day I saw Montgomery and he was most emphatic in insisting that the command arrangements I have made are as nearly perfect as circumstances permit. . . . [U]nless Alexander is clearly informed of all these things, he may feel that his new position is one of less influence than he should properly have.[29]

Ike's representation of Monty's views was completely accurate. Monty had no enthusiasm for having another British officer placed over him in Europe. Furthermore, Monty informed Brooke that Ike had given him all the force he needed—the Ninth U.S. Army, consisting of twelve divisions. Almost ruefully, Brooke recorded in his diary that Monty no longer desired the ground commander "that he had pleaded for so urgently before Christmas."[30]

Ike had asserted his authority once and for all.

The end of the war in Europe saw Ike and Monty working together well, even though Ike removed the U. S. Ninth Army from the 21 Army Group. Monty's major operation was to drive to the German port of Lübeck, on the Baltic. The action had a political overtone. Although the future boundary between the occupation zones of the Western Allies and Russia had been decided on the political level, the occupation zones of Denmark and Austria had not. In order to prevent a Russian occupation of Denmark, therefore, it was essential for the Allies, in Montgomery's sector, to cut Lübeck off from the east. At first Montgomery refused American help in executing that drive, but when he ran into resistance, Ike provided Ridgway's XVIII Airborne Corps to operate on his right. Montgomery drove ahead and on May 2 the British 11th Armoured Division, part of the British VIII Corps, entered the city.[31]

The relationship between Ike and Monty did not end with the Nazi surrender on May 8, 1945. From that time on, at least for a while, they were military equals, each commanding his own nation's zone in occupied Germany. (SHAEF was deactivated on July 13, 1945.) In 1946 Monty visited Ike at Fort Myer, Virginia, and when Ike and Mamie visited the United Kingdom and Germany later in the same year the two generals, both the Chiefs of Staff of their respective armies, received degrees together at Cambridge University. Monty did not seem to think that the occasion called for much effort on his part. When called on to speak, he simply reminded the audience that they still needed soldiers.

Also on that visit, Ike and Monty were guests at 10 Downing Street, the home of British Prime Minister Clement Attlee, who had replaced

Ike and Monty in June 1945, when each was commanding general in his own country's sector of Germany. Their expressions reflect the feelings they held toward each other much of the time.

National Archives

Churchill in that office in July of 1945. I was present on both occasions and cannot recall that a word passed between Ike and Monty. Of course that observation may be meaningless, as Ike was preoccupied with visiting Churchill.*

In early 1951, Ike and Monty were teamed up once again. Both had retired once from active military duty, but when the East-West crisis triggered by the Korean War caused both Britain and America to rearm and to put some real strength into the somnolent NATO alliance, both generals were called back into uniform. Ike was named Supreme Allied Commander, Europe (SACEUR). Monty, who had been serving as the head of Western European Union forces (which included those of France, Britain, Belgium, and the Netherlands), became his deputy. Monty thereupon moved up from his headquarters in Fontainebleau to become part of Ike's staff at Supreme Headquarters, just north of Versailles. This he did in good spirit, and he cheerfully underwent briefings from Ike's staff on his new role as a deputy, a position that the Victor of Alamein had never before filled.

By all accounts, the two worked harmoniously, possibly because their functions were clearly delineated. Monty's responsibilities centered on the organization and training of the combined forces of NATO,[32] and he spent a good bit of his time in the field. Ike retained direct command of all the forces, however.[33] It is not often realized that their time together between 1951 and 1952, something like eighteen months, greatly exceeded the length of time they both served in OVERLORD.

When Ike returned home in June of 1952 to run for President, the days of Ike's and Monty's professional association came to an end.

In September of 1957, the first year of Ike's second term as President, Monty visited the White House at his own invitation, and Ike welcomed him as an old comrade. As always, Monty was onstage, always

---

*Churchill and Attlee were quite cordial with each other that evening. I found it amusing, even bewildering, that on the floor of the House of Commons that day one had referred to the other as "that wicked man." I do not recall which man said it of the other, but that matter is unimportant.

seeking ways to be mildly outrageous. Soon after arrival he looked sniffingly around the walls of the stately building and harrumphed, "My regiment burned this joint down in 1814!" Ike took it in stride; Monty was just being Monty. Ike never bothered to check up as to what British regiment actually put the torch to James and Dolley Madison's White House after the disastrous battle of Bladensburg. The pair of retired generals then went off to Gettysburg to visit America's most famous battlefield.

The visit of the two most noted generals of the European war to Gettysburg was a bonanza for the American press. The sight of reporters and photographers, unfortunately, also acted as a heady stim-

Ike and Monty at Columbia University, probably 1949. When this photo was taken they had no idea they would be working together in uniform two years later.

Author's Collection

ulant to Monty. The climax came at the Virginia Monument, where the statue of General Robert E. Lee sits with deceptive serenity surveying the scene of the Confederate leader's most tragic blunder. Monty, instead of emulating the detached gaze of the Lee statue, felt impelled to put on a show for his audience. He scampered about, surveying the mile-long, mile-wide scene of Pickett's Charge, mumbling for all to hear, "Monstrous! Monstrous!"

Much to my regret, I was not present on that occasion, but I can well visualize the scene. As Monty demonstrated his agility to the onlookers, Ike's blood pressure was going up and up. Finally came the climax. "What would you do to me if I made a futile attack like this one?" asked Monty.

"I'd have fired you!" retorted an exasperated Ike.

The members of the press now had the coup they had been seeking. All other aspects of the Montgomery visit instantly disappeared. "Ike would have fired Lee!" was blazoned forth in newspapers across the South. A great admirer of Lee, Ike had always kept a portrait of the Confederate leader on the wall of the Oval Office of the White House, along with portraits of several other historical figures. It seemed to me that during the next few weeks Ike had his picture taken alongside the portrait of Lee remarkably often.

The Gettysburg visit was the last time that Ike and Monty met as friends. A year later, Monty published his *Memoirs*, which reopened old wounds from the war in Europe and made some accusations that Ike could never forgive.

From a study of Monty's *Memoirs*, I can only conclude that the field marshal never understood Ike. Monty had the ability, which Ike lacked, to separate a warm personal regard from a difference of opinion, even a serious one. On the personal side, Monty portrayed himself as genuinely fond of Ike. Besides the quote I have placed at the beginning of this chapter, he gave, on almost the last page of his book, some very lavish praise. Conceding that Ike had a "good brain" and was "very intelligent," he wrote that Ike's real strength lay in his human qualities. Ike was a "great human being." He almost overdid it:

Whenever I go to Washington I visit the Lincoln Memorial, where Abraham Lincoln sits in an imposing setting looking out over the city. I never visit that memorial without gaining inspiration; it is the same when I visit Ike. I am devoted to him, and would do anything for him. He is truly a great man, and it is a tremendous honour to have his friendship.[34]

One would think that Ike, on reading those words, would gladly forgive anything else written in Monty's book. But Monty destroyed their effect by reopening his previous arguments regarding what he considered the fleeting opportunity, in early September 1944, of ending the European war before the end of the year:

The trouble was that Eisenhower wanted the Saar, the Frankfurt area, the Ruhr, Antwerp, and the line of the Rhine. . . . To get *all* these in one forward movement was impossible. If Eisenhower had adopted my plan he could at least have got Antwerp and the Ruhr, with bridgeheads over the Rhine in the north, and would then have been very well placed. Or if he had adopted Bradley's plan he could have got the Saar and the Frankfurt area, with bridgeheads over the Rhine in the centre and south. But he was too optimistic. He compromised. He failed to get any of his objectives.

He then went on to describe his meeting with General Marshall on the 8th of October 1944 (a subject bound to irritate Ike). Monty described telling Marshall that "since Eisenhower had himself taken personal command of the land battle . . . the armies had become separated nationally and not geographically. There was a lack of grip, and operational control was lacking. Our operations had, in fact, become ragged and disjointed, and we had now got ourselves into a real mess." Marshall, Monty admitted, "said little" and appeared to disagree. Calling the events following the successful battle of Normandy "tragic," he wrote,

In Normandy our strategy for the land battle, and the plan to achieve it, was simple and clear-cut. The pieces were closely "stitched" together. It was never allowed to become unstitched, and it succeeded. After

Normandy our strategy became unstitched. There was no plan, and we moved by disconnected jerks.[35]

What Monty failed to realize is that Ike was nearly impervious to lofty expressions of admiration for his sincerity and character. He was a professional soldier and was not much interested in what Monty thought of his character. What meant most to him was approval, not of himself, but of his conduct of the European campaign. To the best of my knowledge, Ike and Monty never communicated again.

I was, of course, well aware that the rift between the generals was final; Ike was never one to keep his annoyances secret. One evening late in Ike's presidency, as the family gathered outside at the Gettysburg farm for a charcoal-broiled steak, Ike seemed preoccupied, annoyed. Apparently Monty had held a press conference that day in which he said that Ike had never had the least idea of what was going on when he was in command in Europe during the war. Ike's reaction by then, however, was confined to an unhappy shrug.

Nearly ten years later, when I was in the process of writing my account of the Battle of the Bulge, *The Bitter Woods*, I naturally sought interviews with all the surviving participants. Among them were Generals Bradley, J. Lawton Collins, and many others, including, of course, both Ike and Monty. What I learned surprised me.

Both Ike and Bradley, I discovered, were still rankled over Monty's conduct and continuing persistence in reopening old wounds, even though the war had been over for a quarter of a century. Perhaps I was brash, but I derived a certain amusement from playing the devil's advocate. "If Monty and Brooke were lieutenant generals, commanders of division and corps in 1940 when Ike and Bradley were both lieutenant colonels," I reasoned, "didn't the two Americans concede that the views of the two British generals might carry some weight?"

When I put that question to Ike, enduring his final illness in Walter Reed Army Hospital, he snorted. "You don't know Montgomery." Bradley, who gave me a few minutes in his Pentagon office, almost rose from his seat in wrath: "We wouldn't make Monty a corporal in our army!" I saw no reason to pursue the discussion with either.

In October of 1966, after I had finished the first draft of my book, I secured an interview with Monty at his home, Isington Mill, in Hampshire, England. My wife, Barbara, and I arrived in mid-afternoon. Monty, notoriously parsimonious and reclusive, showed signs of near panic for fear that I would exceed my allotted hour and expect to stay for tea. "There are others coming," he warned unconvincingly. But the interview was a treat. Once Monty gave his reasons why Allied failure to follow his plans was responsible for the fact that the Bulge had even happened, we went on for a very pleasant conversation, somewhat exceeding the hour.

What struck me most was Monty's seeming lack of rancor toward the Americans. We did not discuss Ike, but he asked with genuine interest about Bradley and others. He thought it a tremendous joke that Bradley, who had been widowed some time before, was remarrying, but he laughed kindly. He mentioned Courtney Hodges critically. "Hodges could never have done Brad's job," he said. At the end I asked him if the reason for his controversial *Memoirs* was to answer the chorus of criticism he had received from American generals, especially in Bradley's *A Soldier's Story.* "Oh no," he said lightly as we walked down the steps to the door. "They have had their say and I thought I would have mine."

The Viscount and I parted on friendly terms. Then, as was my habit, I sent him my version of our interview, with the proviso that I would not necessarily agree but wanted to get his viewpoint straight. In his answer, he addressed me by my first name and then went on with a friendly, thorough discussion, handwritten, of my account of the interview.

I do not consider it any tragedy that Ike and Monty had a final falling out. They were an unnatural pair to begin with. But in thinking over their official relationship, I am struck by two thoughts. First, the periodic conflicts of opinion caused negligible damage to the Allied war effort against Hitler. Disagreements there were, but they rarely left the discussion stage, oral or in writing. With the possible exception of Monty's neglecting the Schelde in favor of MARKET-GARDEN, Ike's decisions were carried out to the best of everyone's ability.

More important, perhaps, I wonder if Winston Churchill, had he been able to foresee the degree of animosity that Monty could evoke among Americans, would have appointed the testy Irishman rather than Alexander (another Irishman) to command 21 Army Group. The close relationship between the English-speaking peoples was a prime obsession with Churchill. Monty, whatever his capabilities—and he had many—probably did more than any other figure of World War II to damage Anglo-American friendship.

President Charles de Gaulle presents Ike with a sword once belonging to the Emperor Napoleon. In the background is Admiral Harold R. "Betty" Stark.

National Archives

7

IKE AND DE GAULLE

The Friendship That Grew

General de Gaulle, Liberator of France, will thus go down in history as the last Frenchman ever to free his country, just as General Eisenhower is now the last of the line of Supreme Commanders to lead a mighty armada to the rescue of enslaved peoples. The last statues of the last of the liberators have surely been cast.

—DAVID SCHOENBRUN[1]

*I*n mid-May 1960, when Ike had only a few months left as President of the United States, he underwent one of the most difficult ordeals of his long career. The scene was the Elysée Palace, in Paris. The four great powers—France, Britain, the Soviet Union, and the United States—were gathering for a summit conference under an ominous cloud.

The cause of the tension between the Western Allies and the Soviet Union was an unfortunate event that had occurred two weeks earlier. A United States reconnaissance plane, familiarly known as a U-2, had been shot down over Sverdlovsk, Russia, and the pilot, Francis Gary Powers, had been taken alive. That fact cast the United States, and Ike in particular, in the unaccustomed role of "threat to world peace."

That circumstance was particularly vexing for Ike because from his point of view, the accusation was totally contrary to reality. The underlying cause for the reconnaissance flights was Soviet Premier Nikita Khrushchev's spurning of Ike's offer of mutual aerial inspection offered five years earlier at Geneva, commonly known as the "Open Skies" proposal. The need to guard against a surprise Soviet nuclear attack, at least in Ike's mind, had virtually forced him, as President, to approve the CIA's ambitious reconnaissance program.* Still, the technicalities were on the Russians' side. No matter how necessary the overflights had been to United States security, Khrushchev could—and did—play the role of the injured party.

The renewed hostility between East and West was particularly disappointing, because Khrushchev had, in the months before the U-2 incident, seemed to place great store in what he viewed as warming relations with Ike.[2] He appeared to be sincere in his efforts to salvage

---

*The flights had produced invaluable intelligence, intelligence that allowed Ike to pursue a firm policy toward the U.S.S.R. secure in the knowledge of Soviet military weakness.

the newfound relationship. But his price was too high. He would forgive the transgression, he said, if the Americans would apologize, cease the flights, and punish those responsible, thus implying Ike's ignorance of the whole program. It was a futile effort. Ike had already assumed personal responsibility for the flights; he had no intention of punishing others for his own decision; and he would never apologize.

Thus rebuffed, Khrushchev flew into a rage, whether from the heart or only feigned made little difference. Even before the four-power

General Charles de Gaulle, President of France, probably in 1946.

Library of Congress

meeting formally opened, he turned to President Charles de Gaulle, presiding, and demanded the right to take the floor. That granted, he then, according to Ike, repeated all the allegations he had been making over the previous days and withdrew the invitation he had previously extended for Ike to visit the Soviet Union. Ike had to just sit and take it, resorting only to a grin when Khrushchev became ridiculously vehement.[3]

Though he tried not to show it in public, the episode had a depressing affect on Ike, because he now realized that the efforts of eight years to promote peace between the United States and the Soviet Union had been wrecked. As we sat in his bedroom at the American embassy that evening, he was sad as he told me about the meeting. Amongst all the disappointment and unpleasantness, however, one small incident had given him comfort. At the breakup of the meeting that morning, Ike had felt a touch on his elbow. Turning, he saw it was de Gaulle. "Whatever happens," de Gaulle said quietly, "we are with you."[4]

From that episode, among others, it has come to be assumed by Americans and even more so by Frenchmen that Charles de Gaulle, in later years Ike's staunchest ally, was always America's—and Ike's—first choice to be the future President of France fifteen years earlier, while France was languishing under the Nazi yoke. Such, however, was not the case. In fact, Ike and de Gaulle started out as political antagonists. How they came to be close allies, even during the war, is a long story.

Ike and de Gaulle were nearly twins, born only a month apart in late 1890.* There were similarities in their youth. Both came from large families and both were avid readers of history, especially military history. They entered their respective armies through their military academies, West Point and St. Cyr. Both worked early with tanks. And both were perfectionists, intolerant of inefficiency. In addition both were independent thinkers, often at odds with their superior military authorities.

But there the similarities ceased. Ike, well knit and coordinated, was an athlete; de Gaulle was ungainly and awkward. Ike was also gregari-

---

*Ike was born on October 14; de Gaulle on November 22.

ous, a man who liked people and mixed well. De Gaulle, oversized—his nickname was "Deux Metres," which was almost his exact height—was aloof, a loner. Unlike Ike, de Gaulle had seen much action on the Western Front in the Great War. Wounded three times as an infantry company commander, he was left for dead on the field of Verdun, only to be rescued, healed, and imprisoned by his enemies, the Germans. Ike's responsibilities in training the American 1st Heavy Tank Brigade may have far surpassed those of a company commander, but they were far less dramatic than actual battle experience.

It was in their attitudes toward established authority that the two differed most. When Ike ran into trouble from his military superiors, as with his falling out with the Chief of Infantry in 1920, he simply complied with orders. De Gaulle, on the other hand, would comply but not quietly; he was vociferous in his disagreements with the hierarchy. Ike starred at the Command and General Staff School at Fort Leavenworth, graduating number one in his class. De Gaulle, on the other hand, came out in the middle of his class at the French Ecole de Guerre. It never occurred to de Gaulle, however, that his lack of distinction was in any way his own fault. "Those bastards at the Ecole de Guerre," he was reported to have exclaimed. "I shan't stay in that filthy hole unless they make me the Commanding Officer of the college."[5]

Nationality also emphasized their differences in attitude. David Schoenbrun, de Gaulle's perceptive biographer, points out that since the days of the American Revolution the United States had never been seriously invaded; flanked on both coasts by wide oceans, the Americans have traditionally felt little fear from foreign invaders. France, on the other hand, has been invaded from time immemorial. The territory originally inhabited by the first Celtic tribes has been violated at various times by Romans, Huns, Goths, émigrés, English, Russians, Prussians (under Bismarck), and Germans (under the Kaiser). The French hero or heroine was a person who rose, like Joan of Arc, to rescue his country, not to invade foreign lands. De Gaulle, whose name derived from that of the original Celts, grew up dreaming of becoming such a hero, who would at some time rescue his beloved France from an invader. From the days of his boyhood he was, in his own mind, a man of destiny.[6]

That mysticism ran completely counter to the disposition of the practical Ike. Little wonder that Ike and de Gaulle had difficulty in understanding each other when they first met.

When Ike reached London in June of 1942, de Gaulle had been, for nearly two years, semirecognized as provisional head of the ill-defined "Free French," a rather nebulous conglomeration of overseas Frenchmen who were opposed to the Vichy regime of the aged Marshal Henri Philip Pétain. De Gaulle had little justification for his claim to be leader of the Free French, but a great many French people, unable to affect events transpiring in their homeland, looked to him as their only hope. A temporary brigadier general in the French army, he had in London miraculously laid claim to the position of the head of a republic.

De Gaulle had begun the war as a colonel. Though he had never let up in his irritating conduct toward established authority, he was given command of an armored division, with the temporary rank of brigadier general. When the German Wehrmacht unleashed its might against Holland, Belgium, France, and Britain in May of 1940, de Gaulle's 4th Armored, though ill-equipped, understrength, and lacking logistical support, comported itself well in conducting a vigorous counterattack on the flank of the Nazi blitzkrieg as it drove westward across France and Belgium to the English Channel.

De Gaulle's efforts were in vain; the narrow German corridor between the Ardennes and Boulogne, on the Atlantic Coast, survived all counterattacks. The British Expeditionary Force was evacuated by sea to Britain, and the tottering French army, under Premier Paul Reynaud, prepared to defend France along the Somme River, which runs from east to west, north of Paris. At that point, on June 5, 1940, de Gaulle was summoned to be assistant secretary for war in the Reynaud Cabinet.

As talk grew stronger in the French government for an armistice and some sort of accommodation with the German conqueror, de Gaulle found himself almost the only dissenter to this defeatist attitude, more and more separated from the rest of the government. Finally he decided to leave France, and the British were willing to help him. On June 17, 1940, a British officer visiting the French government, now at Bordeaux, walked out to his plane for his return to London. As a matter of protocol, de Gaulle accompanied him. At the plane they shook hands as if saying farewell. Then both stepped inside and slammed the door. In Churchill's description,

> The machine soared off into the air, while the French police and officials gaped. De Gaulle carried with him, in this small aeroplane, the honour of France.[7]

On June 18, the day after de Gaulle's arrival in London, two memorable speeches were beamed out to the world from London. In the morning, Winston Churchill made what was perhaps his most often quoted remarks:

> What [French] General [Maxime] Weygand called the Battle of France is over. Let us therefore brace ourselves to our duties, and so bear ourselves that, if the British Empire and its Commonwealth last for a thousand years, men will say, "This was their finest hour."[8]

That afternoon, in a less noted but also significant speech, Charles de Gaulle broadcast over the airwaves to a French audience:

> The leaders who have been, for many years, at the head of the French armies have formed a government. This government, alleging the defeat of our armies, has entered into dealings with the enemy to end the fighting. But has the last word been said? Should hope die? Is the defeat total? No. France is not alone. She is not alone. She is not alone. She can form a solid bloc with the British Empire, which commands the seas and continues the fight. This war has not ended with the Battle of France. This war is a world war.[9]

The next day de Gaulle went even further, claiming that since Frenchmen were so divided, he felt he was speaking "in the name of France."[10] De Gaulle had cast himself in the heroic role he had always dreamed of. In so doing, he was committing treason in the eyes of the French officer corps, the members of which believed themselves duty-bound to follow the dictates of the civilian government, even in surrender.

De Gaulle was never comfortable in London. A difficult man under any circumstances, he refused to cater to other large egos such as that of Winston Churchill, even though he was completely dependent on the British government for his movement's very existence. For the moment, however, he set up a London headquarters from which he could receive communications from overseas French troops not under the control of Vichy and at the same time insisted on being treated as a head of state. His effrontery in assuming such a pose caused Churchill secretly, despite his grudging admiration, to do a slow burn.

By September of 1940, after three months in London, de Gaulle decided that he would be better off if he could set up a capital in French territory. By then some of the French African colonies, starting with Chad, had joined his cause, but they were located too far from the main arenas of the war. De Gaulle decided that the best location for his capital would be Dakar, Senegal, even though that city was under the jurisdiction of the Vichy French. By this time he had accumulated some colonial troops, and Prime Minister Churchill, only too glad to get de Gaulle out of London, organized a sizable naval task force to support an occupation of that West African colony.

The effort was a disaster, due partly to de Gaulle's own miscalculations. He wrongly believed that nearly half the population of Dakar would support him, and he underestimated the formidable local commander, General Pierre Boisson, who would not give up his loyalty to Marshal Pétain. So when the joint French-British task force appeared off Dakar in the early morning of September 23, 1940, it was met with a withering fire. After a two-day effort, the expedition was withdrawn on Churchill's orders, with serious damage to several of the supporting British vessels. De Gaulle never got over that humiliating defeat. It affected his thinking from then on.

Indirectly, the Dakar fiasco of 1940 was responsible for early friction between Ike and de Gaulle when Ike began organizing his Allied headquarters for the North African invasion in late summer of 1942. Since the British blamed de Gaulle for the failure of the Dakar expedition, Ike's instructions from both the United States and British governments were emphatic that de Gaulle should be told nothing about the forthcoming invasion.[11] By this time, however, de Gaulle had developed a system of communications, particularly with the French occupation forces in Syria, so he quickly learned that some sort of military operation was afoot. He deeply resented being left out of discussions pertaining to anything French, even including Vichy French North Africa.[12]

At this stage of the war, however, friction between Ike and de Gaulle was of little importance, because de Gaulle was not considered an integral part of the North African invasion. The British and Americans, in laying their plans, were hoping that the Vichy French officers in that region, despite their enforced oaths of loyalty to Pétain, would quickly join the Allies, and that all three armies could take Tunisia and cut the Germans and Italians from their supply lines back to Italy.

To induce the Vichy officers to take such a drastic step, the Allies needed a French officer as their leader, a man who enjoyed sufficient prestige with the French army to induce the forces in North Africa to rally behind him and the Allied cause. The Allies had found their man—or thought they had found their man—in General Henri Honoré Giraud.

Giraud seemed to possess all the necessary attributes. A five-star general (a matter of some importance to the French military), he was handsome and impressive in appearance. His bravery, if not brilliance, was beyond question. He had been captured by the Germans twice, once in each war, and both times he had escaped. He was currently living in Lyon, part of unoccupied France, and the Germans had not prevailed on Vichy to turn him over.

Giraud had other facts in his favor. As an escapee from German imprisonment, he had not been paroled by the Germans and therefore had not been forced to sign the loyalty oath to Marshal Pétain required of officers on active duty. Politically he appealed to President Roosevelt, who regarded de Gaulle as a renegade at best. Since Giraud was known to be a thoroughgoing military professional, he seemed unlikely to become smitten later with political ambitions. So believed Robert Murphy, Roosevelt's representative in North Africa.

During the planning for TORCH, Giraud was still in Lyon, but a French officer friendly to the Allied cause contacted him and a British submarine picked him up in southern France in time to meet Ike and

Mark Clark at Gibraltar on November 7, the evening before the Allied landings in North Africa.

Once Giraud joined the two Americans in the tunnels of Gibraltar, it was immediately obvious that he was going to be a problem. For starters, he expected to be placed in personal command of the entire TORCH expedition, commanding American and British (though no French) troops at the outset. Ike and Clark had an anguished six-hour confrontation with Giraud before he finally agreed to play the role the Allies asked.

The whole exercise turned out to be futile. When the American landing parties set foot in Algiers, Oran, and Casablanca, the local French command declined to pay any attention at all to Giraud's order to cease fire.

The problem, as mentioned in the chapter on Marshall, was solved by the deal that Ike and Clark made with Admiral Jean François Darlan, the commander-in-chief of the Vichy French armed forces, who happened to be in Algiers when the Allies landed and was immediately taken into Allied custody. The admiral would be recognized by the Allies as the French authority in North Africa if he would give the order to the French commanders to cease all military resistance and join the Allied cause. Darlan's orders were effective. Resistance soon ceased, though not by order of Henri Honoré Giraud.

De Gaulle, still in London, was angered when he learned what had happened. So when the press in Britain and America raised a furor over the Darlan deal, the Gaullists joined in the chorus, adding as much fuel to the flame as possible. The political crisis was solved only by the dramatic assassination of Darlan by a fanatic young Frenchman on Christmas Eve in Algiers. Ike, with political authority, of course, thereupon appointed Giraud as both military and civil governor of French North Africa.

Meanwhile de Gaulle, still in London, continued to seethe. Not only did he dislike Giraud's appointment to succeed Darlan, but the assassination affected his own plans. President Roosevelt canceled de Gaulle's long-planned trip to Washington. At this point, de Gaulle and his followers were condemning everything the Allies were doing.

For the rest of the Tunisian campaign, Ike had little or no contact with de Gaulle. In January of 1943, when Roosevelt and Churchill met at the famous Casablanca Conference to discuss immediate future strategy, Ike was there for only one day. De Gaulle was pressured to attend despite his protesting a meeting of the "Anglo-Saxons" on "French" soil. While there, de Gaulle managed to infuriate Churchill and Roosevelt by his insistence on French sovereignty in North Africa, which area the Allies regarded for the moment as "occupied territory." Nothing came out of the Casablanca Conference from de Gaulle's viewpoint, except for a famous and misleading photograph of him and Giraud shaking hands in the garden of Roosevelt's villa while a beaming President and Prime Minister looked on.* de Gaulle then returned to London.

On May 20, 1943, the Allies staged a victory parade in Algiers to observe the end of the Tunisian campaign on May 13. Troops from several nations marched past in review. It was a gala occasion, made more optimistic by the fact that the French had now joined the British and Americans as full-fledged partners in the victory, having contributed the French XIX Corps in the Tunisian battle. Giraud, standing next to Ike, was at the zenith of his power. Unbeknownst to him, however, the seeds of his downfall had been planted. For the procession included a contingent of Free French (Gaullist) troops, who refused to march in the same part of the line as Giraud's XIX French Corps. The significance of their finding a separate place in the order of march seems not to have been noticed.

The end of the Tunisian campaign brought with it a new relationship between the French and the Allies in North Africa. First, that territory was no longer a battleground, so it no longer need be considered as part of an Allied combat zone. Second, the French had participated in the Tunisian battle and deserved a place in formerly "Anglo-Saxon" circles. Third, the undercover activities of the Gaullists had successfully begun the process of undermining Giraud in the minds of the French.

---

*The meeting is better remembered for Roosevelt's announcement of a policy of Unconditional Surrender, uttered at the same time as the photograph of the two Frenchmen was taken.

Perhaps the most important reason for the change in French attitudes came out of the Tunisian victory itself. In earlier days, before the Allies had scored any victories against Nazi Germany, the peoples of Europe had every reason to assume that Hitler would never be defeated. Resistance to German rule seemed pointless, and the name of de Gaulle was not taken very seriously. Now that El Alamein and the fall of Tunisia held out the probability of Allied victory, pockets of French resistance in the colonies and in Metropolitan France began to cast about to find a leader. The figure that appealed most was the charismatic Charles de Gaulle, and it was now time for him to enter the active arena, which meant coming to North Africa to join Giraud.

Giraud, despite his temperament, was generous and trusting, and he had been in communication with de Gaulle for some time. It had not been Giraud who had prevented de Gaulle's coming to North Africa before this; it had been Ike. The Allied commander had been concerned over the trouble that de Gaulle's presence might stir up among the French, and he had enough on his hands fighting a war against the Germans and Italians in the Tunisian campaign. He had therefore simply denied de Gaulle the use of a British or American airplane to make the trip. But now that Tunisia was in Allied hands, Ike had no logical reason to object, so he informed de Gaulle that he would be glad to meet with him. De Gaulle accepted immediately.

De Gaulle arrived in Algiers on May 30, only ten days after the Tunisian victory parade, to be welcomed by Giraud with great cordiality and hospitality. He set his guest up in a comfortable villa, assuming, of course, that the two would work together for the future of France.

Giraud had put his trust in the wrong man. The same afternoon that Giraud welcomed him, de Gaulle set off down the hill to the Monument des Morts to preside over a special political ceremony arranged by his supporters. Preparations had been thorough; leaflets bearing de Gaulle's likeness were distributed among the roaring crowd. He then returned to his villa with a motorcycle escort, standing erect in the back of his open car. At a press conference later that day he made caustic references to all French leaders, leaving out a direct attack on Giraud, though Giraud was obviously his principal target.[13]

The next morning, Giraud and de Gaulle met with their followers to set up the body that would govern a unified French war effort, the

French Committee of National Liberation (FCNL). Supposedly it was balanced; Giraud and de Gaulle were co-chairmen, alternating in presiding. Yet Giraud, whose interests were primarily military, was obviously doomed as France's leader.

De Gaulle moved with amazing speed in taking over. With the aid of the French banker Jean Monnet, who ironically had been sent by President Roosevelt, Giraud signed away his powers to de Gaulle on June 4, less than a week after de Gaulle's arrival in Algiers. When Robert Murphy, the American political representative, saw what the general had done, he was aghast when Giraud admitted that he had not read the document whereby he had ceded power.[14]

Now solidly in charge, de Gaulle lost no time in replacing French officers he disapproved of, even though they had functioned satisfactorily in supporting the Allies during the fighting. First of these, not surprisingly, was Pierre Boisson, Governor of Dakar, who had humiliated de Gaulle nearly three years earlier. Since de Gaulle's actions were taken in the name of the Committee of National Liberation, Ike had no cause to object, so long as the officers being installed would continue to support the Allies as they prepared to invade Sicily.

Still, Roosevelt was determined to avoid having any single Frenchman recognized as the provisional head of France until the war should be over. Accordingly, he attempted to control French political matters from Washington, thousands of miles away, through Ike. This placed Ike in an awkward position. His main concern was only harmony with the French, not control over them.

On June 19, 1943, Ike and de Gaulle met face-to-face to discuss their problems. De Gaulle arrived at the meeting late, a ploy he had used when dealing with Roosevelt and Churchill at Casablanca. He then spoke first, declaring himself the President of the French government:

> I am here in my capacity as President of the French Government. For it is customary that during operations the chiefs of state should come in person to the headquarters of the officer in command of the armies they have entrusted to him. If you wish to address a request to me concerning your province, be sure I am disposed beforehand to give you satisfaction, on condition, of course, that it is compatible with the interest of my charge.[15]

Ike shrugged off this piece of histrionics, and in his report to the Combined Chiefs later in the day he made no mention of it. The meeting set forth Ike's and de Gaulle's positions, which were far from compatible.

Absorbed with the impending invasion of Sicily, Ike was quite willing to allow de Gaulle to assume political control in North Africa, so long as he gave the Allies his full support. Ike did, however, ask that de Gaulle retain General Giraud as the French military chief. He could not enforce that request, of course, because the Allied troops that gave him control of the country were almost ready to leave for Sicily. He was left with only a single though substantial bargaining chip in dealing with de Gaulle. The FCNL had no sources of supply and equipment except those supplied by the Allies. Without such logistical support, neither de Gaulle nor Giraud could maintain an army.

De Gaulle saw things differently, and one must admit that he had much logic on his side. Ike, as an American, never claimed the right to designate who should command British troops, so why should he assume such authority with French troops? As to the status of French North Africa, it was no longer a war zone. It was territory ruled by the FCNL, and the Allies were there only at French sufferance. That view he carried so far as to express regret that the Tunisian battlefront had not been commanded by a Frenchman rather than an American or British officer.

Ike's use of the French supply situation to influence the actions of the FCNL also rankled de Gaulle. As an argument he harked back to the First World War, only twenty-five years earlier, in which the French had supplied the Americans with airplanes, artillery, and even tanks without demanding the right to tell the Americans who their commander should be. As a result of these differing viewpoints, from which neither man was willing to retreat, the meeting ended at an impasse. Ike reported the meeting back to Washington and went on planning for Sicily.

But despite the firmness with which he expressed his views, de Gaulle had a realistic side in his pursuit of sometimes unreal objectives, so for the moment he recognized that French command of Allied troops was out of the question. Further, if his French Committee of National Liberation was considered to be the French authority in the region, a hollow title for Giraud could do little harm. He left the general in his position, at least for the moment.

Despite the seeming intransigence of both men when they were arguing their positions, a mutual appreciation was developing. De Gaulle noted that Ike tried to be pleasant and was sure that the American was acting under orders from Washington. And Ike received the support he needed. Giraud remained in nominal control of the French army in North Africa until finally replaced for good in February 1944. By then Ike was long gone from the Mediterranean.[16]

Another meeting, far more promising than that of June, occurred on December 30, 1943, when Ike was leaving North Africa to command OVERLORD. Now convinced that de Gaulle was the one man who could rally all Frenchmen fighting Hitler, Ike paid a call on de Gaulle to solicit his support. Ike made no mention of the meeting in his book *Crusade in Europe*, but de Gaulle later recorded his own version of Ike's words:

> "You were originally described to me in an unfavorable sense. Today, I realize that the judgment was in error. For the coming battle, I shall need not only the cooperation of your forces, but still more the assistance of your officials and the moral support of the French people. I have come to ask for your assistance."
>
> "Splendid!" I replied. "You are a man! For you know how to say, 'I was wrong.'"[17]

Assuming that the above exchange was accurately described by a reporter who was also a participant in the exchange, all signs were that Ike and de Gaulle had become allies. That does not mean, however, that the road ahead would always be smooth between them.

Ike was sincere in looking to de Gaulle as the true leader of French resistance, but his authority with regard to such matters was limited. Shortly after his visit with de Gaulle in Algiers, Ike went back to the United States for his short visit of rest and conferences, and during that time he vigorously sought support for his policy of dealing with de Gaulle as the head of the French. His efforts, however, met with strong resistance from the Combined Chiefs and the President. Roosevelt, who still detested de Gaulle, seemed to fear that the authoritative Frenchman would try to make himself dictator once France had been liberated. In the meantime, Roosevelt feared, treating with him as the interim authority would only facilitate his doing so. Secretary of State Cordell Hull was no help to Ike. He simply expressed the hope that the French would "subordinate political activity to the necessity for unity in ejecting and destroying the enemy."[18] Since it seemed that nobody in Washington could decide on anything, Ike dropped the matter until he arrived back in London on January 12, 1944. Then, before doing anything else, he sent a message back to General Marshall for the Combined Chiefs:

> It is essential that immediate crystallization of plans relating to civil affairs in metropolitan France be accomplished. This requires conferences with properly accredited French authorities. I assume, of course, that such authorities will be the representatives of the Committee of Liberation.[19]

Roosevelt got around to answering Ike's plea two months later. He somewhat relaxed his restraints on Ike's dealings, giving him permission to "consult" with anyone he liked on French civil affairs. He directed, however, that Ike secure guarantees to ensure that the Committee would do nothing to entrench itself pending a free choice of the French people.[20] Late in arriving as it was, that permission gave Ike the elbow room he needed.

During the early months of 1944, when the Allies were preparing for OVERLORD, de Gaulle and the FCNL remained in Algiers, making no move to come to London. Ike was happy with that arrangement, considering the record of indiscretion on the part of some of de Gaulle's people. A crisis broke out as D-Day drew near, however, when the British government, at Ike's urgent request, put a clamp of censorship on all diplomatic traffic going in and out of Britain. Foreign diplomats, even those of neutral countries, were forbidden to enter or leave the United Kingdom. The British government bore the brunt of foreign outrage against that arbitrary restriction, but the Prime Minster was willing to undergo that opprobrium in the interests of security. The major complication arose from the fact that the edict included the FCNL under de Gaulle. De Gaulle would not submit to what he considered censorship by the Anglo-Saxons, and as a recourse he simply ceased communicating with General Pierre Koenig, his emissary in London. Rather than cut off all communications with de Gaulle, therefore, Ike and Churchill

De Gaulle and Churchill visit Ike at his Portsmouth trailer on June 4, the day on which Ike deferred D-Day for twenty-four hours.

National Archives

decided to invite him to come to London. Churchill sent de Gaulle a conciliatory message of invitation, capping it off by offering to send his own private plane to Algiers. De Gaulle accepted and arrived in London in the early morning hours of June 4, 1944, as Ike was making his difficult decision to postpone D-Day for a day, from June 5 to June 6.

As always, de Gaulle's meetings with the Americans and British were mixed affairs of mutual admiration and mutual recrimination. Churchill had established a temporary headquarters in the vicinity of Portsmouth, near Ike's camp close to the British Naval War College. There de Gaulle's lunch with the Prime Minister started out on a warm note. Churchill began by describing the nature of the invasion force, emphasizing its immense size and justifiably boasting that the initial, naval phases of the operation would be conducted primarily by the British—the Royal Navy. De Gaulle graciously attributed this triumph to the "courageous policy which [Churchill] himself had personified since the war's darkest days." Whatever would happen, France was "proud to be in the line of attack at the side of the Allies for the liberation of Europe."*

The rosy glow soon came to an end, however, when the two men began addressing the procedures by which de Gaulle could best contribute to the Allied effort. Churchill felt that de Gaulle's first objective should be to establish himself with the Americans, President Roosevelt in particular. To that end, de Gaulle should fly to Washington as soon as possible so that the President would "grow less adamant and will recognize your administration in one form or another."

De Gaulle bristled. "Why do you seem to think that I need to submit my candidacy for the authority in France to Roosevelt? The French government exists. I have nothing to ask, in this sphere, of the United States of America nor of Great Britain."[21] Soon both men were raising their voices. Churchill admitted to being guided largely by Roosevelt, but he exclaimed that if forced to choose between de Gaulle and Roosevelt, he would always choose Roosevelt. De Gaulle, looking around the room, sensed that Churchill was speaking for himself rather than

---

*The American contribution, while substantial, was only a small part of the vast armada, which was British. De Gaulle, *Memoirs*, p. 556.

for the whole British Cabinet.[22] However, there the matter stood; it was time to leave for Ike's headquarters.

Churchill and de Gaulle found Ike nervously pacing up and down at his small camp. Ike was glad to see them both and was probably relieved to have someone to share his burdens, because he was undergoing the agony of having suspended the invasion for twenty-four hours. He took de Gaulle into his headquarters tent and gave him a complete briefing on the OVERLORD operation. Then he politely asked what he, de Gaulle, thought of the situation. De Gaulle, though flattered to be asked, insisted that the decision was Ike's alone. Having said that, however, de Gaulle added that he thought the invasion should go without delay, because the "atmospheric dangers seem less than the disadvantage of a delay of several weeks." Morale and secrecy would be at risk.[23]

Again the cordial atmosphere disappeared, however, when Ike showed de Gaulle the proclamation he would read when the invasion was launched:

Citizens of France! I am proud to have again under my command the gallant forces of France. Fighting beside their Allies, they will play a worthy part in the liberation of their homeland. Follow the instructions of your leaders. A premature uprising of all Frenchmen may prevent you from being of maximum help to your country in the critical hour. Be patient. Prepare.

As Supreme Commander of the Allied Expeditionary Forces, there is imposed on me the duty and responsibility of taking all measures necessary to the prosecution of the war. Prompt and willing obedience to the orders that I shall issue is essential. Effective civil administration of France must be provided by Frenchmen. All persons must continue in their present duties unless otherwise instructed. Those who have common cause with the enemy and so betrayed their country will be removed. As France is liberated from her oppressors, you yourselves will choose your representatives and the government under which you wish to live.[24]

Nothing about the proclamation pleased de Gaulle. He resented the fact that Ike's first message was to be beamed to the people of Norway,

Holland, Belgium, and Luxembourg in his capacity as a soldier and having nothing to do with their future political destiny. In his message to the French, by contrast, Ike had urged the French to carry out his orders. All of this seemed to imply, de Gaulle wrote later, that Ike "appeared to be taking control of our country even though he was merely an Allied general entitled to command troops but not in the least qualified to intervene in the country's government." Further, the draft proclamation made no mention of de Gaulle or the FCNL, a sore point indeed. Accordingly de Gaulle made revisions, which he sent to Ike, only to be informed that the text of the talk had been approved by both Roosevelt and Churchill. It had, in fact, been previously recorded. It would have to be transmitted as written.

De Gaulle therefore refused to follow Ike's message with one of his own. Such a procedure, he reasoned, would place him in a position subordinate to Ike.[25] Soon, however, de Gaulle came to realize that this was no time to appear unnecessarily intransigent. His presence in London was known and he could never be seen as refusing to throw his weight in with the Allies. If he failed to do so, he would bear the taint of failure to help when needed. Accordingly, he composed his own message and delivered it late in the morning of June 6, allowing enough time to elapse after Ike's proclamation to give it a status of his own:

> The supreme battle has been joined. It is, of course, the Battle of France, and the battle for France! For the sons of France, wherever they are, whatever they are, the simple and sacred duty is to fight the enemy by every means in their power. The orders given by the French government and by the leaders which it has recognized must be followed precisely. From behind the cloud so heavy with our blood and our tears, the sun of our greatness is now reappearing.[26]

De Gaulle's statement was a masterpiece of deft wording. It implied strongly that he was broadcasting as the Provisional President of France, though he did not say so, and any member of the Resistance would have to assume that the "leader which the French government has recognized" was Ike. It maintained de Gaulle's pose as the head of France but did nothing to interfere with or contradict the proclamation that Ike had issued. Throughout this confrontation, de Gaulle, as usual, held nothing against Ike personally. He knew by now that Ike, given a free hand, was the best friend he had in Allied circles. He also knew that Ike's hands were tied by the attitudes of his two political superiors.

Once de Gaulle was in Britain, it would be unrealistic for the Allies to expect him to sit quietly in London. However, Ike considered it reasonable that de Gaulle should inform the Allies as to what he was up to. He did not do so.

On June 15, nine days after D-Day, when I accompanied my father to Normandy to visit General Montgomery, Monty was, it will be recalled, absent from his headquarters when Ike arrived, and Ike killed time by driving around to visit various British headquarters. I was riding in the back of the jeep, and Ike was in the front. Monty's Royal Air Force aide was driving. Almost casually, the aide told Ike for the first time that de Gaulle had come ashore the day before and had visited Monty. From there de Gaulle had gone to attend a pre-arranged rally in Bayeux, in which he had harangued the crowd with the claim that the French were returning to liberate themselves "with the aid of the British and Americans." I could see the back of Ike's neck grow red. He was furious.[27]

The incident, while unimportant in the long run, points up once more the differences in viewpoint between Ike and de Gaulle at that time. Ike felt a proprietary interest in the invasion and in the European Theater of Operations (ETO) in general. Nobody was supposed to go ashore in the combat zone without his permission.[28] Ike felt that de Gaulle was violating the rules of his theater of operations. On the other hand, de Gaulle did not regard France merely as a part of Ike's European Theater of Operations. Instead he felt that he was coming home to his beloved France and needed nobody's permission to do so.

In any event, de Gaulle later made the trip to Washington that Churchill had requested. By the time he did so, however, he had established himself as provisional leader of France.

During the summer of 1944, de Gaulle's position vis-à-vis the Anglo-American Allies grew stronger day by day, and he lost no chance to consolidate it. He issued a fiat incorporating the French Forces of the Interior, as the French Resistance was called, into the regular French army. He laid down the law with respect to those Resistance fighters with Communist leanings. The Allies cooperated by bringing General Jacques Leclerc's 2d French Armored Division to Normandy from Morocco. De Gaulle could now wield power, not simply bluff.

By mid-August 1944, the Americans had headed south from the Normandy beachhead and cut off the Brittany Peninsula. Ike and Bradley had sent the bulk of General George Patton's Third Army eastward. Patton planned to cross the Seine River south of Paris, leaving the French capital in the zone of the American First Army, specifically V Corps, under General Leonard Gerow. At first Gerow planned to bypass the city as his V Corps drove eastward. Doing so would force the retreating Germans to feed the population for a few more days and avoid the need to clear out the city, street by street, a costly prospect.

Those plans were soon discarded, however, because of a new turn of events. French Resistance elements in the city could no longer wait, and the development that Ike had tried to warn against, a premature uprising, was beginning. De Gaulle became concerned, not only for fear of German reprisals against the Resistance elements, but also for the political setback to himself if the Communists could manage to associate themselves in the minds of the public as the liberators of Paris. He therefore sent Ike an urgent message asking him to change plans and take Paris without delay.

Ike immediately complied. He moved Leclerc's 2d French Armored Division to the vicinity of Paris and on August 25, 1944, Leclerc and his men entered the city. There they were greeted, showered with flowers, and kissed. It was a memorable experience for many, no doubt, but the celebration slowed down the progress of the fighting. So far behind schedule was Leclerc that Gerow committed the 4th U.S. Infantry Division to fight alongside the French, and together the two divisions did the job of mopping up remaining elements of resistance.* De Gaulle, showing remarkable physical courage, entered Paris later in that same day, August 25, and took charge of the French government even though snipers were still raking the streets along which he paraded.

---

*With no fanfare for the American 4th Division, of course.

By this time, even the authorities in Washington had come to recognize de Gaulle's power, and they authorized Ike to deal with his government on an interim basis. Ike, conscious of de Gaulle's immense symbolic value, went a step further; he paid a formal call on de Gaulle as the provisional President of France on August 27, 1944, thus further consolidating de Gaulle's position of power in the eyes of the world. De Gaulle never forgot that gesture, even with the passage of years.

By early September 1944, Allied forces were knocking on the doors of Germany. De Gaulle was formally installed as Provisional President of France. Ike's French troops were considered to be provided by de Gaulle and he, on his part, was careful to ensure that the long supply lines that ran across France functioned well. On August 15, 1944, the American VI Corps, under General Lucian Truscott, landed near Marseilles, and as part of the U.S. Seventh Army drove northward up the Rhone Valley, and on September 11, 1944, they joined with Patton at Dijon. Coming up from Italy were the seven French divisions that had been fighting with distinction as part of Clark's Fifth Army. These French divisions were soon formed into the First French Army, under the overall command of Lieutenant General Jacob Devers's Sixth Army Group.

De Gaulle would have liked a different command arrangement. He wished that the Supreme Commander of all the forces fighting Germany could have been a French officer. At the very least he wished that the French First Army, under the command of Jean de Lattre de Tassigny, could be fighting further north in the critical zones, rather than in the Vosges Mountains to the south. But de Gaulle knew how far he could push his point of view. He supported the Allied war effort against Germany as a full ally, though his main attentions were focused on consolidating his position in France.

The war, despite some hopes, did not end in the fall of 1944, and fighting bogged down. On December 16, 1944, Hitler launched his last great effort to drive the Allies into the sea, hoping thereby to ensure his own survival. He amassed three armies, heavy in tanks, to attack through the Ardennes region[29] to split the Americans armies from those of the British and to take the all-important seaport of Antwerp. For a week, the situation looked serious to the Americans, whose front was hit, but by December 26, ten days after the assault, Hitler's forces reached their high-water mark a few miles short of the Meuse River, where they were stopped. (See Map 6.)

Hitler, however, had one more shot in his bag, which he called Operation NORDWIND. Instead of driving westward, this attack was directed southward from Lorraine toward Switzerland, on the west bank of the Rhine. If successful, Hitler hoped to destroy General Jacob Devers's Sixth Army Group, which consisted of the French First Army and the American Seventh.

When Patton's Third Army had turned left toward Bastogne on December 19, 1944 (see Patton chapter), Devers's front in the north had been extended northward to cover the Saar. It therefore held a very sharp corner in the north, along a line that approximated the boundary between Lorraine and the German Palatinate. It was a vulnerable salient, and Hitler decided to hit it at 11:00 P.M., New Year's Eve 1944.

Ike was not very much concerned about Hitler's latest attack, because it led to no important strategic object such as Antwerp. His plan to cope with it, therefore, consisted of a withdrawal from the banks of the Rhine into the easily defended ground of the Vosges Mountains. By so doing he would gain several divisions for use in the Ardennes. The territory that he voluntarily gave up could be retaken after Hitler's Ardennes drive was defeated.

From a military viewpoint, Ike's plan was good, but politically it had a serious flaw. Within the territory to be given up was the Alsacian city of Strasbourg. If the Germans retook that city, as many as 100,000 people might have to be evacuated ahead of time to escape severe reprisals.[30] In addition, Strasbourg held a symbolic significance to the French as the most important city in Alsace-Lorraine.

De Gaulle was determined to prevent Ike from going through with his plan to withdraw to the mountains. He tried working through the staffs to no avail. He then sent messages to Roosevelt and Churchill asking them to intervene with Ike. Roosevelt refused to interfere in a military matter, as did Churchill officially. The Prime Minister, however, decided to pay Ike a visit at Versailles, timed to coincide with a meeting with de Gaulle. If Ike knew the purpose of Churchill's visit on January 3, he made no sign of it. They had a pleasant luncheon and then prepared for the inevitable confrontation with de Gaulle.

De Gaulle, though determined, presented his viewpoint calmly. Admitting the military merits of Ike's plan, he asked that it not be carried out because of the political considerations. If Strasbourg were to fall to the Germans, the reprisals against civilians would be brutal, and de Gaulle would be blamed for doing nothing to avert such a disaster. At first Ike refused to consider any change in his plan. He was fighting a military, not a political war; further, I suspect, he was frazzled from the strains of the Battle of the Bulge.

The discussion rose in intensity, with both men standing firm. At one point, de Gaulle threatened to withdraw the seven divisions of the First French Army from Ike's command. At that point Ike reportedly lost his temper. Reminiscent of their confrontation in North Africa eighteen months earlier, he threatened to withhold any more supplies—food, ammunition, clothing, whatever—from the French army. He then pointed out that the failure to reduce the Colmar Pocket, one of the causes of the present emergency, lay at the feet of the First French Army itself. Throughout Ike's tirade, Churchill sat silently and de Gaulle apparently held his temper admirably.

Fortunately, Ike took time to reconsider. Certainly he held the card of French supply in his hands, but de Gaulle held impressive cards also. Ike's supply lines, one from Cherbourg and the other from Marseilles, ran through French territory, and to guard them against French sabotage would require many divisions. Both men thus had telling weapons to use against the other. But if either were to use such weapons, the result could only be a bonus for Hitler.

So Ike decided to compromise. The VI U.S. Corps on the north, he reasoned, could be pulled back from its most extended salient, but at the same time Ike could provide additional troops to protect Strasbourg. He canceled his plan for withdrawing voluntarily to the mountains.

De Gaulle was satisfied. The French leader's main political fear had not been so much the prospect of losing Strasbourg as of giving it up without a fight. Now that Ike had promised to fight for it, he left Versailles happily, according to Ike, "in good humor, alleging unlimited faith in my military judgment."[31]

Churchill had stayed completely out of the discussion, but once a solution had been resolved, he said quietly, "I think your final conclusion was absolutely correct. A break with General de Gaulle would have been bad. Could we have a whiskey soda before we go to bed?"[32]

Nearly four months later, during the last days of the war, Ike and de Gaulle had one last disagreement, this time minor, and far less important than the New Year's crisis in Alsace. As the Allies drove eastward across Germany, the city of Stuttgart fell into the area of General Devers's Sixth Army Group, a region of Germany that was under consideration as part of the future French occupation zone.

For some reason, General Devers had originally included Stuttgart in the zone of the First French Army, but at the last minute switched the boundary to give it to the American Seventh. The French, however, crossed the new boundary and occupied Stuttgart before the Americans could reach it. On learning of this development, de Gaulle in Paris ordered the French commander to hold the city in spite of Devers's orders to withdraw. He needed assurance, de Gaulle reasoned, that the French would later be given that area for occupation. Devers appealed to Ike, who took the matter up with de Gaulle. De Gaulle refused to budge. When the issue was referred back to Washington, de Gaulle also defied the angry reaction of President Harry Truman, who had succeeded Roosevelt after the latter's death at Warm Springs, Georgia.

Fortunately, Ike and de Gaulle solved the dilemma amicably. Their exchanges of messages exuded expressions of mutual respect and admiration. De Gaulle explained that the American Seventh Army was free to use the city as part of its supply line. He insisted, however, that he would keep a force there. Ike again gave way. He had no intention of causing hard feelings between the Americans and French when the war had obviously been won. He made accommodations and the matter came to naught.[33]

With the end of the war came a temporary end of the Ike–de Gaulle relationship, and nobody could foresee that it would ever resume. Ike returned to the United States in late 1945, and de Gaulle stayed on as Provisional President of France. He resigned his presidency in 1946, angry over the failure of the Constituent Assembly to give him the power he demanded in the new constitution for the Fourth Republic. Though politically active for a while, he was essentially out of power for the next dozen years. When in 1951 Ike returned to France as Supreme Allied Commander in Europe, under NATO, de Gaulle was far from the French political scene.

In de Gaulle's absence, France's position in the world suffered, especially as the shaky French Empire melted away. In 1954 the treasured possession of Indochina was lost to the newly independent South Vietnamese Republic and to the independent republics of Laos and Cambodia. Even worse was the uprising in Algeria, a country that the French officially but unrealistically called part of Metropolitan France. During the course of that upheaval, one government after another ruled France, most of them with very short tenures in office. Finally, on June 1, 1958, with the Algerian crisis at its most intense, de Gaulle was called out of retirement and made Premier of France. He drew up a new constitution vesting the French President with strong executive powers. Submitted to a popular referendum, de Gaulle's constitution was adopted, and he was elected President of the Fifth Republic by an overwhelming majority on December 1, 1958.

I had not kept up with events pertaining to de Gaulle through those years; and like other young officers in the Army, I had not been a de Gaulle fan. Accordingly, when de Gaulle returned to power, I regarded it as an unfavorable development. One evening, as a new member of the White House Staff, I approached my father as he sat reading his newspaper in the West Hall of the second floor of the White House. I expressed my misgivings, expecting that the Boss, as we called him, would agree. Ike looked up from his paper and said quietly, "It's okay. I think the French need to be told what to do for a while."

That was a period of intense crisis between the Americans and the Soviets. Only a few days before, on Thanksgiving Day, Soviet Premier Nikita Khrushchev had issued an ultimatum: the United States, Britain, and France must leave West Berlin in exactly six months. If they failed to do so, he would turn over control of all access routes to the East Germans, who would in turn put an end to Western occupational rights, with a virtual certainty of war. Considering the nature of the war that would follow, it is easy to imagine why de Gaulle was of secondary interest to Ike at that moment.

The next six months after this episode saw a masterful diplomatic performance on the part of Ike and his dying Secretary of State, John Foster Dulles, who during the latter part of that period was replaced by Christian Herter. Once Ike had convinced Khrushchev of his determination to defend Western rights in Berlin with force, he was able to steer discussions into diplomatic channels. The spring and summer of 1959 saw a series of East-West conferences in which reasoned exchanges of views made the world forget about Khrushchev's ultimatum. In fact, on the day of Secretary Dulles's funeral, the foreign ministers of the three Western allies and the Soviets, in Washington to attend rites for their fellow diplomat, seized the opportunity to recommence conferring. The ultimatum was forgotten.

The East-West issue had now broadened to include all of European security, and the tensions between the two sides had subsided considerably. Ike and Khrushchev initiated exchanges of cultural activities, including a Soviet art exhibit in New York and an American art exhibit in Moscow. Two high-ranking members of the Politburo, Anastas Mikoyan and later Frol R. Koslov, visited the United States, Mikoyan to see Ike in the Oval Office. In the flush of this somewhat artificial good will, the State Department, misunderstanding Ike's instructions, invited Khrushchev to visit the United States in the early fall.[34] On learning of the error, Ike felt he had to make the invitation official. Khrushchev accepted with alacrity.

Ike was now in an embarrassing position. He had to avoid appearing to speak for all the Western powers, going over the heads of the French, British, and West Germans. To rectify that impression, Ike decided to visit Bonn, London, and Paris to assure Chancellor Konrad Adenauer, Prime Minister Harold Macmillan, and de Gaulle that he was not proposing to speak for all of them.

I was put in charge of arranging this trip as the President's representative, probably because he was spending the summer at Gettysburg, where my family was located. We set up a summer White House in the

Gettysburg Hotel on the town square, and from there planned the trip. At first Ike suggested arriving in Paris on August 27, the anniversary of Ike's calling on de Gaulle just after the liberation of Paris fifteen years earlier. To Ike's mild surprise, however, de Gaulle demurred on the basis that he would be in Algeria on that day. As finally settled, the schedule called for a trip directly from Washington to Bonn, thence to London, and an arrival in Paris on September I.

The trip was exciting, and Ike was surprised at the enthusiasm of the crowds in Germany, the country he had been instrumental in conquering fifteen years earlier. He was also surprised at the enthusiasm of his reception in London, where he was concerned that his stern action against the British and French governments in connection with the Suez Crisis in 1956 might have diminished his popularity. The itinerary included a visit to Balmoral Castle with the British royal family, as well as a couple of pleasant days with Prime Minister Harold Macmillan at the historic Chequers, so fraught with memories of the Second World War for Ike.* Still, the high point, if only for its novelty and suspense, was the visit with de Gaulle, the last official stop of the trip.

All of us on the new Boeing 707, the first Air Force One, harbored silent apprehension as the plane taxied up to the ramp at Orly Airport. We were wondering what kind of reception de Gaulle would render. He could play the visit down or welcome Ike warmly; we had no idea which way he would go.

Our doubts were soon dispelled, however. *Le Grand Charlie* pulled out all the stops in his zeal to make the welcome warm. The Republican Guard was on hand with all its splendor, and the French President's words were warm. The ceremonies were brief, and soon Ike and de Gaulle were riding side by side into Paris.† After a pleasant luncheon at the Elysée Palace, the two Presidents, with their advisers, met

---

*Chequers was the country home of the Prime Minister, used by Churchill during the Second World War.

†De Gaulle and Ike felt cramped in the back seat of their car, so they instructed the driver to take the canvas top down. He agreed to do so but stalled until he was ready. The route went through a Communist district and the French Sureté had told the driver when the car should be opened. The word of the Sureté took precedence over the orders of the Presidents.

at the French Foreign Office on the Quai d'Orsai. It was now 4:00 in the afternoon.

De Gaulle had been out of the American public eye for years before being recalled to power, and I, for one, had no idea of how he would look or act. To my surprise, he seemed very different in appearance from the gaunt giant of the Second World War. He had gained a good deal of weight, and much of that weight had settled in a large paunch. His corpulence was not overly noticeable until he donned a uniform, which he did on occasion. His figure then approached the grotesque. For some reason, probably a gesture of defiance against the conventional French military, he continued to wear the uniform of a brigadier general, nothing higher. It was as a brigadier that he had left France in 1940, and from then on he claimed to have been a statesman, not a general.[35] He had also aged, of course, and his black eyes seemed even blacker than ever, with great circles under them. But his aura of dignity remained, even enhanced.

In the afternoon's meeting, I was seated behind my father and, since the two principals sat across from each other at the elongated table, I was able to observe de Gaulle head-on. His main impression was that of calm bordering on detachment. He spoke quietly but with no apologies for his views, taking the attitude more of a teacher than of one pleading a case.

De Gaulle's preoccupations bore some resemblance to those he held during the Second World War: they were all concentered around France and her position in Europe rather than around any mutual enemy the Americans and French were facing. His first concern was the degenerating position of the French in Algeria, which he still insisted on calling a part of Metropolitan France, and his second was the position of France in NATO. Just as during the war he had assumed that the Allies would defeat Hitler, he now seemed to show little interest in Ike's problems with the Soviet premier, Nikita Khrushchev. These questions were not his focus of interest.

When de Gaulle discussed Algeria, Ike had little to say. The United States, with its anti-colonial tradition, could never side with the French, the colonial power, but Ike listened patiently to de Gaulle's discourse.

The matter of NATO was something else, because of Ike's dedication to the NATO concept.[36] De Gaulle disliked the principle of French participation in the military side of NATO, emphasizing that the French soldier fights best under his own flag. Ike of course disagreed. He had not objected when de Gaulle had previously withdrawn the French fleet from the command of Supreme Allied Headquarters,* but he objected to the idea that French ground forces, operating independently, could cooperate with NATO armies as effectively as they could if they were part of the peacetime military structure.

Neither Ike nor de Gaulle had ever held any hope of changing the other's mind, so the parties simply agreed to disagree. The issues that interested the two of them were different anyway. But de Gaulle, despite his views, did nothing to remove French troops from the military command of NATO so long as Ike was President.

The rest of the visit was largely ceremonial. After a night spent in the sumptuous Quai d'Orsay guest house, Ike transferred to the American embassy, where he could relax. At the Hôtel de Ville the next day, de Gaulle went all out to express friendship for the Americans in general and Ike in particular:

> Long live General Eisenhower! Long live the President of the United States! Long live America, forever the friend and ally of France![37]

Ike's final evening in France was spent at the historic Rambouillet, some miles out of Paris. Business finished, all was relaxation and comradeship. As Ike and de Gaulle sat on the back veranda that pleasant September evening, Ike called me over and directed me to recite a passage from Shakespeare's *Henry V*. How he knew I had memorized it while studying Shakespeare at Columbia University ten years earlier, I do not know. Even less do I understand why he desired a rendition of King Henry exhorting his troops to do battle with the French at Agincourt. Nevertheless, so he did, and I, feeling like a schoolboy going through a recitation, complied. De Gaulle, as I studied his face, seemed unmoved.

The next morning Ike and his party left Rambouillet, departing by

---

*The American Sixth Fleet remained under national control during peacetime, earmarked for NATO only in case of war.

helicopter. De Gaulle had planned to accompany him to Orly Airport, but Ike was afraid that his so doing would set a precedent for him back in Washington. When de Gaulle came to the United States, Ike, out of courtesy, would be forced to reciprocate, and other heads of state would henceforth expect the same courtesy. De Gaulle reluctantly agreed to say goodbye at the helicopter pad, though I am not certain whether he understood.

The two men met twice again before the abortive Paris summit of May 1960. One visit, part of Ike's Eleven-Nation Trip of December 1959, was short.[38] After a relaxing trip from Athens to Marseilles aboard a cruiser of the Sixth Fleet, Ike's party took a high-speed train to Paris for a short visit. All I remember, egotistical though it may be, was my chagrin at de Gaulle's cold reception on the steps of the Elysée Palace, in contrast to his usual friendly greeting. On going inside, however, de Gaulle donned his eyeglasses, the result of a recent cataract operation. Vanity had made him greet his visitors outside without seeing who they were.[39]

In the spring of 1960 de Gaulle visited the United States, principally to prepare for the coming summit meeting with Khrushchev. By this time Ike had developed a routine of taking his visitors to Camp David, in the Catoctin Mountains, for their conferences. Camp David was only a few minutes by helicopter from Ike's Gettysburg farm, so Ike customarily brought his distinguished visitors to the farm as part of the package. In this instance, he brought de Gaulle to the modest house where my family lived, about a mile away from Ike's house and on the edge of his farm. There de Gaulle unbent, sitting comfortably on our glassed-in breezeway. He spoke good English, though in public he made a point of speaking only French. When our youngest daughter, Mary, age five, toddled up to his chair and reached for his thick glasses, de Gaulle was very gentle. Wistfully, he said, "I must wear these to see: poor me!" De Gaulle had a persona around families completely different from that he wore in public.

Time passed; the U-2 went down, the Paris summit of May 1960 collapsed. De Gaulle was staunch. Eight months later Ike was out of office. His last official relationships with Charles de Gaulle were at an end.

❧

My last view of de Gaulle is the one I treasure most. When Ike died at Walter Reed Hospital, Washington, D.C., on March 28, 1969, dignitaries from around the globe attended the funeral. But among that glittering array, Charles de Gaulle stood out. Though still President of France, he appeared officially in his brigadier general's uniform. I stood by while he came up and leaned over to speak to my mother.

He was a strange figure, bent over with his long nose and ungainly figure. But what he said, always quietly, made my eyes glisten. *"Vous savez,"* he said, *"que le general était près de mon coeur."*

Churchill and Ike confer at Ike's forward headquarters, Reims, on March 5, 1945.

National Archives

8

IKE AND WINSTON CHURCHILL

Soldier and Statesman, but Comrades-in-Arms

In war [Churchill] was aggressive, combative, and inspirational in his leadership. In most questions arising out of the conduct of the war, he and I found ourselves almost always in full agreement. On those few occasions when we did not see eye-to-eye, the quality of our friendship was never diluted in any way.

When finally he laid down the mantle of his high office, I could not help feeling that, for me, a treasured partnership had been broken.

—DWIGHT D. EISENHOWER[1]

In the early days of June 1944, tension reigned in London. Everyone in the United Kingdom, even the man in the street, knew that a cataclysmic event was approaching, the outcome of which would shape the course of history. The great Allied invasion force, building up for months in Britain, was about to be hurled against the coast of France. Nobody knew the exact day that would happen, not even Ike, the Supreme Commander. But it would have to come soon. The south of England had already been sealed off; diplomatic communications from London to the world's capitals had been curtailed; Admiral Sir Bertram Ramsay, commanding the naval forces of OVERLORD, had assumed command of the English Channel. The moment was near.

Ike, as the man on whose shoulders the success or failure of the campaign rested, bore the heaviest burden of anyone, for it was he who would make the final decision as to the exact day to go. His options were narrow. Certain predictable meteorological conditions were required, such as the phase of the moon and the time of low tide. Those limitations dictated that D-Day would have to fall on one of three days: Monday, June 5, Tuesday, June 6, or Wednesday, June 7. The first day would be preferable, but any one of the three would be satisfactory. The final choice would depend almost entirely on the weather, a factor that could not be predicted with certainty. Everything hung on that one decision, Ike's alone. Outwardly, Ike showed the strain less than did many others, but his burden was heavy enough to break a lesser man.

Each high-ranking Allied official coped with the tension in his own way. Ike, for one, resorted to taking strenuous walks up and down the small dirt road that led from his trailer in his forward encampment to the main hall of the British Naval War College, where he would make the final decision. Prime Minister Winston Churchill, on his part, took refuge in submerging himself in boundless details, wrestling with matters very few of which would normally have called for his personal attention. As part of that therapy, Churchill sought relief in laying plans to participate personally, and he began making arrangements to witness the landings from the bridge of a British warship.

Word of the Prime Minister's plans soon reached Ike, and he was shocked. Churchill, in his view, had no right to expose himself to death or wounding by such an act of bravado. His knowledge and wisdom, not to mention his status as a symbol of Allied determination, made Churchill indispensable to the Allied cause. Ike protested vigorously, but to no avail. Unable to deter the Prime Minister by sheer reasoning, he appealed on the basis that he himself was already carrying enough of a load without having to worry about Churchill's safety. Ike hoped that a touch of generosity would induce the Prime Minister to cancel his plans without appearing to back down.

It did not work. Instead of evoking Churchill's sympathy it caused him to bristle at what he considered Ike's presumption. Half the troops under Ike's command, he pointed out, were British, and Ike himself was at least partially Churchill's subordinate—through the Combined Chiefs of Staff, of course. Even conceding that Ike was in sole charge of this operation, Churchill rightly claimed that the Supreme Commander's authority did not include a right to interfere with the personnel composition of one of His Majesty's ships; Churchill could merely sign on as a seaman aboard a British naval vessel, and Ike would have no legal basis on which to protest.

Ike, temporarily defeated, still did not give up. In desperation, he appealed to King George VI, with the hope that Churchill would defer to the wishes of his monarch. Even then, it required a great deal of persuasion on the part of the King. Even a threat by the King to participate himself fell on deaf ears. It finally required a personal pleading as a friend to induce Churchill to relent.

This small incident, a mere footnote to history, serves to illustrate what an indefinite set of roles Ike and Churchill played at times during the conduct of the European war. Ike was, admittedly, Supreme Commander only at Churchill's and Roosevelt's sufferance, but times arose, as in this instance, in which he was in charge. This was one of the few occasions when his will and that of the Prime Minister clashed. But whatever the outcome of any such differences, their friendship survived and even flourished.

❧

In viewing the relationship between Ike and Churchill, I cannot, of course, speak for Churchill. Nor, for that matter, can I write confidently about Ike's opinions. He was a very complex man and beneath his disarming grin, highly judgmental. The expression "does not suffer fools lightly" applied to him in spades, and his opinion of an individual could vary according to the situation. But Churchill was a great exception. Of all the prominent men Ike ever dealt with, I am confident that Churchill was his favorite. Never once did I ever hear Ike say a derogatory word about him. Naturally, he loved to tell stories of Churchill's foibles, but he did so affectionately.

Ike certainly gave every indication of his feelings in his declining years. After he retired to his Gettysburg farm following his presidency, I was part of a gathering one evening at which a guest asked him to name the five greatest men he had dealt with in his public career. Such a request ran counter to Ike's inclinations, because he held little brief for the concept of "great men." But to accommodate the friend, he reluctantly sat down with a pad and pencil. In a remarkably short time he produced a list: General George C. Marshall, Secretary of State John Foster Dulles, British Air Chief Marshal Sir Peter Portal, General Charles de Gaulle, and not surprisingly Winston S. Churchill. A year later, in the company of other friends, I asked Ike to repeat the procedure, expecting to find at least one discrepancy. To my surprise, the list was unchanged. He never set a priority among the names, and my guess is that he would have utterly refused to do so. But it is noteworthy that the list includes two Englishmen and one Frenchman. It omits some very prominent Americans.[2]

At this point, let me flash back to a moment sixteen years earlier, to June 1944, when I was visiting my father in London. One day, June 20, we found ourselves thwarted in our effort to make a visit to Normandy, because a virulent storm had broken out over southern England and the English Channel.* While the two of us were cooling our heels unhappily

---

*The storm is one of the most neglected episodes in history. It demolished the "Mulberry" (artificial harbor) on Omaha Beach and tied up shipping in Portsmouth, England, for several days. It delayed, if not endangered, the whole venture.

at Telegraph Cottage, his home south of London, Ike brightened up with an idea: we should pay a visit on the Prime Minister up in London.

We arrived at Whitehall, in which Churchill had an office in his role as British Defence Minister, in a driving rain, and we were immediately admitted into Mr. Churchill's office. As I recollect the scene over the span of many years, the office was remarkably spare. We sat, just the three of us, almost silently around a large conference table. Churchill barely looked up. He squirmed in his chair, mumbling to himself: "THEY have no RIGHT to give us weather like this!" Not far from our minds was the fact that, if Ike had been forced to postpone the Normandy landing from June 7, the last day meteorological conditions permitted, the next possible day would have been June 19, the day before our visit to Whitehall. Around us was raging the worst storm that had hit the English Channel in fifty years.

After a short visit, Ike and I slipped out of the Prime Minister's office, hardly noticed. If Ike had hoped to bolster either his own morale or Churchill's, the effort appeared to be a colossal waste of time. But I have always suspected that Ike, with a sense of history, had an ulterior motive; he wanted me to see the Prime Minister in informal circumstances. During the war and thereafter Ike often took me with him when we met with most of the world's prominent figures, including Soviet dictator Joseph Stalin, but this was the only instance when I sensed his going out of his way to ensure that I met any one of them.

Ike was always conscious that the Prime Minister was a piece of history. Born in 1874, Churchill was sixteen years older than Ike, a prominent figure on the world scene when Ike was still a cadet at West Point. In 1915, the year of Ike's graduation, Churchill had already been the British First Lord of the Admiralty for some years. In that capacity, he had been instrumental in the conception and planning of the ill-fated British campaign at Gallipoli. A member of Parliament for nearly his entire life, Churchill was in and out of high political office. Though relegated to the political wilderness during the 1930s, he had been notable as the one voice crying out for arming Britain for the Second World War that he saw coming.

Churchill had reached the zenith of his career in June 1940, when he held Britain together in defiance of Adolf Hitler, whose panzers had just swept across France, demolishing the French army, driving the British Expeditionary Force into the sea, and threatening to invade Britain. Churchill's stirring oratory in those dark days inspired the free world and remains his "finest hour." This was happening during a time that Ike was a lieutenant colonel, executive officer of the 15th Infantry at Fort Lewis, and the United States had not even begun mobilizing for possible war. That momentous climax to Churchill's career had occurred only four years before Ike took me to visit him in Whitehall.

After the Japanese attack on Pearl Harbor and Hickam Field on December 7, 1941, the United States was thrust into the war on the side of the British, and an elated Churchill saw America's entry as assuring ultimate victory.

Somewhat to President Roosevelt's discomfort, Churchill had insisted on visiting the United States immediately after the attack in order to coordinate the war efforts of the two new allies. With him he brought an entourage of high British officials. His first act, as befitted a world figure of Churchill's stature, was to address a joint session of Congress. There, on the day after Christmas 1941, Churchill's eloquence captivated the American public. He inspired the Yanks with his expressions of grim determination and outrage against the Axis powers. But to Americans the most memorable aspect of that monumental speech was his reference to his American mother, Jennie Jerome. He declared,

> I cannot help reflecting that if my father had been born American and my mother British, instead of the other way around, I might have got here [into the United States Congress] on my own.[3]

The effect was deep and lasting. Americans immediately embraced Churchill as one of their own.

They were, however, at least partly misled. Churchill has been aptly described as "half American and all British," and I can think of no better way to put it. He did, of course, hold a strong affection for the land of his mother's birth, and he prided himself in his knowledge of American history. His long-term aims as a statesman, however, were all British aims, sometimes contrary to the aims of the Americans.

The American public, and I presume the British public as well, were treated by their propaganda machines to a soothing picture of seamless Anglo-American harmony in conducting the crusade against Hitler. In the broadest sense that was true, but the general spirit of cooperation did not preclude the fact that in many instances the British and American war aims diverged. The Americans were intent on taking direct action against the common foe, which meant defeating the Axis—Hitler's Germany, Fascist Italy, and Imperial Japan—as quickly as possible. The British, while agreeing with that objective, combined it with another one, equally important to them, which was to maintain the British Empire as it had existed before the war. Churchill made that point clear in an important speech in November 1942. Unrest had recently broken out in India, the British possession regarded as the "Jewel in the Crown" of the empire, and the American press had been making remarks favorable to India's aspirations for independence and critical of British imperialism. At a dinner for the Lord Mayor of London, Churchill stated meaningfully,

> Let me make this clear, in case there should be any mistake about it in any quarter: we mean to hold our own. I have not become the King's First Minister in order to preside over the liquidation of the British Empire. For that task, if ever it were prescribed, someone else would have to be found.[4]

Churchill pursued his dual objective with astonishing persistence and flexibility. Though personally a prima donna, he subordinated himself totally to the interests of his cause. To do so must have been difficult at times, because pursuing his objective in dealing with the Americans subjected him at times to rebuff, disappointment, and even personal humiliation. Perhaps the first such instance occurred in the private conferences conducted on Churchill's early visit to Washington when he addressed the Congress. The fact of overpowering American potential strength forced the Prime Minister to accept American dominance in the structure for the conduct of the war. The Anglo-American Combined Chiefs of Staff, the body that would direct the military conduct of the war, would be located in Washington, not London. From time to time during the war, Churchill would appeal to President

Roosevelt to override American (often Ike's) actions, only to receive a condescending lecture.

Yet Churchill achieved his broad objective. The end of World War II in Europe found Britain still regarded as America's co-equal partner, even though the United States by that time was supplying the bulk of the manpower and matériel for the war. To me, Churchill's ability and

Prime Minister Winston S. Churchill announcing the end of World War II in Europe, May 8, 1945.

National Archives

willingness to play the "lieutenant" in pursuit of his cause was the
most impressive evidence of his greatness.[5]

CHURCHILL AND IKE DURING THE WAR

The relationship between Ike and Churchill, which eventually
grew to intimacy, began in late June 1942 when Ike arrived in London. Perhaps following the practice of Prime Minister David Lloyd
George in the First World War in courting General John J. Pershing,*
Churchill lost no time in establishing a relationship with the somewhat brash, relatively young American. But Churchill carried the
courtship far beyond the practice of his predecessor. He began a routine of lunching with Ike every Tuesday and asking him to dinner at
the Prime Minister's country home, Chequers, every Friday evening.
Somehow their personalities were compatible, and Ike developed a
genuine fondness for the Prime Minister. In contrast to Alan Brooke,
who loathed the late evenings at Chequers, Ike enjoyed them.[6] At the
beginning of their association, Ike was still only an American, not an
Allied, commander.

A dramatic change in Allied strategy occurred in July 1942, after
Ike had been in London for a little over a month. Churchill had put a
final end to any chance of executing SLEDGEHAMMER, the cross-
Channel invasion, in 1942 (see Marshall chapter), but since Roosevelt
insisted that American troops had to fight somewhere before the end
of 1942, the two heads of government decided on a compromise:
British and American forces would enter and occupy French North
Africa.

The decision to go forward with the North African operation
thrust Ike into the position of Allied commander. The reason for his
selection was political, based on his nationality, because of the bitter
resentment against Britain that prevailed among the French military.
Even Churchill agreed that the North African expedition should carry
an American complexion.[7] Ike, already in London, was chosen.

---

*Lloyd George, a mentor and ally of Churchill's, got along very poorly with his British gen-
erals. He went out of his way, however, to stay on cordial terms with the American commander, General Pershing.

Then followed a period in London that Churchill later called the "most anxious months" of the war,[8] those leading up to the landings in North Africa, scheduled for early November 1942. Everything pertaining to TORCH, as the operation was called, hung in the balance. This first Allied action could not afford to fail, and yet the British and Americans were acting without precedent and without established procedures, planning to invade a continent hundreds of miles from either the U.K. or the United States. They were without knowledge of how either the people of the region or the Vichy government would react. At that time Ike and Churchill worked together very closely. Churchill made full use of Ike's warmth of feeling toward himself to manipulate the American, but though a master of such techniques, he was not a howling success. Ike had his own convictions, and at times he was subject to strict instructions from his own government. But Ike's affection for Churchill made him rueful when he could not meet the Prime Minister's wishes or hurt when he sensed that Churchill was being unsupportive.

Planning for the invasion was hampered by the fact that the amount of shipping available to the Allies was sufficient to allow only three landings on the North African coast, even though there were four possible landing areas. The choice of the three to be selected differed among the planners, largely along nationalistic lines. The British, whose lifeline to India ran through the Mediterranean to Suez, felt at home in that region; the Americans, on the other hand, viewed a passage through the Strait of Gibraltar as tantamount to entering some great black hole from which an expedition might never return. The British, therefore, tended to be bold, advocating landings at Bône, Algiers, and Oran, all in the Mediterranean and close to Tunisia, the Axis lifeline between North Africa and Italy. The Americans, on the other hand, insisted on including a set of landings on the Atlantic coast of French Morocco.

The key factor in American caution, as we have seen, was lack of intelligence regarding the possible response of General Francisco Franco, the dictator of Spain. Franco was known to be an Axis sympathizer, and the Americans were concerned that if he chose, he could close the Strait of Gibraltar between Spain and Spanish Morocco, thereby cutting the Allies off from the Atlantic. Possession of French Morocco, the terminus of a railroad bypassing Spanish Morocco to the south, might provide the Allies a means of withdrawal if Franco chose to act. General Marshall therefore insisted that Patton's task force, coming from the United States, should make landings on the Moroccan coast of the Atlantic. (See Map I.)

This was early in the war, and Ike had not yet been able to establish his authority. The decision as to the choice of landing areas was therefore not left up to him, as it would be later in the war; in fact he was treated as only one of the participants in the discussions. But Churchill quickly recognized that Ike was thinking along the same lines as Churchill himself, advocating landings as far to the east as possible, close to Tunisia, the ultimate goal. Always quick to make use of an ally, Churchill made a point of emphasizing Ike's authority by all means possible whenever dealing with the officials in Washington. At one point he recommended to Roosevelt that the choice of landing spots be left exclusively to Ike (an idea that was quickly turned down) and at another time he offered to come to Washington himself, with Ike accompanying him.

A compromise was finally reached in the "cross-Atlantic slanging match," as Ike called it. Of the three landings, George Patton's task force, sailing directly from the United States, was to make three landings on the Atlantic coast of Morocco. Charles Ryder's task force was to pass through Gibraltar and land at Algiers; Lloyd Fredendall's force was to land at the Algerian port of Oran. The initial assault troops were all to be American, under American command. The follow-up troops would be largely British, and eventually the Allied ground forces would be organized into the First British Army.

The attitude of the Vichy French officers in North Africa was a serious unknown factor. Would they join with the Americans and British in a campaign to destroy Hitler's army in North Africa? Would the French officers, all of whom had signed oaths of loyalty to the Vichy President, Marshal Pétain, resist the Allies according to their orders from France? Washington was eager to know, and their way of getting information led to one of the dramatic exploits of the war. On Sunday morning, October 18, a message arrived at Norfolk House, Allied Force headquarters in London, requesting that a high-ranking American officer be sent clandestinely to North Africa. There he would meet secretly with Robert Murphy, the American representative in the region, and certain French officers known to be friendly to the Allied cause. This was a touchy matter indeed.

Ike discussed the matter with his deputy, Major General Mark Clark, and they quickly decided that Clark was the man to go. As the implications for the British were great, Ike placed a phone call to Churchill, who was, as usual, spending the weekend at Chequers.

Ike could not, in these circumstances, observe protocol. He had no time to run up to Chequers; the telephones were not sufficiently secure; nevertheless, the Prime Minister needed to be informed, so Ike urged Churchill to cut his weekend short and come to London. When Churchill pleaded that the telephone lines were sufficiently safe, Ike stood his ground: they were not. Finally Churchill gave in, a Prime Minister giving way to a general. "All right, I'll meet you at No. 10 [Downing Street] this afternoon."[9]

A few hours later, when Ike and Clark arrived at 10 Downing Street, Churchill was already there, accompanied by some key advisers.[10] Despite Churchill's initial irritation at being called on to interrupt his weekend, he was soon glad he had come. Delighted, he plunged into every detail of the trip. Clark and four others were to be taken by a British submarine to a lone house on the shore of the Mediterranean some miles west of Algiers. It would be a dangerous mission. "The entire resources of the British Commonwealth are at your disposal," he said to Clark. "I want to assure you once more how important it will be to get this information and to cut down French resistance. Keep in mind that we will back you up in whatever you do."[11]

The Clark mission was soon under way, and after some hair-raising squeaks with suspicious French police, it was successful in somewhat clarifying the situation in Morocco and Algeria and in making plans with French officers sympathetic to the Allied cause. Only two weeks after Clark's return, TORCH was launched.

Ike left London early in the morning of November 5, 1942. Churchill's relations with the Americans would never be closer than they were during the three "most anxious months."

TORCH began auspiciously. The American assault forces, followed up by the British, quickly consolidated their landings at Casablanca, Oran, and Algiers. Nevertheless, French resistance was more determined than expected, and the result was the Darlan deal, which I have described in earlier chapters. As a result, both Roosevelt and Churchill, who could understand Ike's reasoning, were put very much on the defensive.

The furor over Darlan was particularly strong in Britain.* The press and later Parliament took Churchill's acceptance of Ike's action as a further sign of Churchill's subservience to Roosevelt. Further, the British had a more personal cause for disliking Darlan. When the Royal Navy attempted to make a peaceful occupation of Madagascar the previous May in order to protect the sea-lanes of the Indian Ocean, Darlan had notified the local French commander,

> Do not forget that the British betrayed us in Flanders, that they treacherously attacked us at Mers-el-Kebir, at Dakar, and in Syria, that they are assassinating civilians in the home territory [by bombing] and they have sought to starve women and children in Djibouti.[12]

In the light of this background, it was difficult for Churchill to stand behind Ike both in public and in Parliament. But he did so stoutly. As Harold Macmillan described it,

> Churchill, who shared to the full the British disappointment at what had happened, with his usual magnanimity stoutly defended General Eisenhower's decision, and was not prepared to sacrifice the fruits of his long wooing of the President and the American Chiefs of Staff.[13]

The furor subsided with Darlan's assassination on Christmas Eve, but the episode had made Churchill uncomfortable. As a result, Churchill, with Roosevelt's blessing, sent a British minister, Harold Macmillan, to act as Ike's political adviser in Algiers. Fortunately, Ike and Macmillan soon began a friendship that lasted throughout their lifetimes. Though Ike made good use of Macmillan's services, it is

---

*A few weeks later, according to Robert Sherwood, Stalin wrote Churchill, "It seems to me that the Americans used Darlan not badly in order to facilitate the occupation of Northern and Western Africa. The military diplomacy must be able to use for military purposes not only Darlan but, 'Even the Devil himself and his grandma.'" Sherwood, *Roosevelt and Hopkins*, p. 651.

obvious that even Macmillan, in the first days of TORCH, could not have affected Ike's decision to use Darlan.

In January and early February of 1943, Churchill and Roosevelt met at Anfa, just outside Casablanca, Morocco, for their famed Casablanca Conference. High-level planning always entails future operations at least one step ahead of current events, and this one was directed toward deciding what the Allies should do once Tunisia fell. With the victory of Alexander's and Montgomery's British forces at El Alamein, in the eastern desert, the chances of trapping and destroying all Nazi forces between Alexander and Eisenhower in North Africa were virtually certain.[14]

At Casablanca, the British strongly advocated invading Sicily after the predicted fall of Tunisia. Their viewpoint eventually won out over the resistance of the Americans, who feared further operations in the Mediterranean. It was not so much conviction that won the day as the fact that the British chiefs were better prepared in their arguments.[15] Then, when Tunisia fell to the Allies in May and the invasion of Sicily was decided, the old argument arose again between Washington and London as to the next objective after Sicily. Marshall, as always, opposed further operations in the Mediterranean, and Roosevelt tended to back him. A meeting in Washington between the two governmental leaders and their staffs resulted in an impasse.

At that point, Churchill came up with a proposal for reaching some sort of agreement. He prevailed on President Roosevelt to send a reluctant General Marshall with him to Algiers to discuss strategy with Ike.* It was a shrewd move. Ike, he knew, would be loyal to Marshall's wishes in principle, but as the commander on the spot, he would be emotionally inclined to utilize what forces he had available to continue pursuit of a retreating enemy.

They met at the St. George Hotel, Ike's headquarters in Algiers. Other than Ike and Marshall, nearly all the participants were British— Tedder, Alexander, Montgomery, Brooke, and Andrew Cunningham.

---

*This meeting has been described in the Marshall chapter, but it is a necessary part of this story.

In that atmosphere, Churchill was able to prevail over the strong objections of Marshall and the more tentative objections of Ike. Since it was already well along in the year, Churchill argued, the cross-Channel assault against northern France, ROUNDUP, was definitely out of the question for the remainder of 1943. To ease Marshall's doubts, Churchill promised that a follow-up campaign in Italy would not endanger the timetable for the cross-Channel operation in 1944. An invasion of Italy would come after Sicily was taken.

Historic meeting between Ike and Churchill at Marrakech, Morocco, on New Year's Eve, 1943. With them in the front row is General Sir Henry Maitland "Jumbo" Wilson, Ike's successor as Allied commander-in-chief, Mediterranean. Between Ike and Churchill, in the second row, is General Sir Harold Alexander. Walter Bedell Smith, Ike's chief of staff, is on the extreme right, behind Wilson.
National Archives

The landings in Italy took place in early September. General Montgomery's Eighth Army crossed the Strait of Messina against almost no resistance, but Mark Clark's landing at Salerno encountered heavy German resistance and counterattacks. Eventually, British and American forces linked up, and the Naples area was occupied. In view of the success of Sicilian operations, the resultant removal of the dictator Benito Mussolini, the landings in Italy, and the Italian surrender, Churchill regarded his role in pushing the Mediterranean over American objec-

tions with a great deal of exuberance and personal pride. The Americans regarded it in a more jaundiced manner.

Churchill, however, had further ambitions in the Mediterranean. At the eastern end, in the Aegean Sea, nestled up against Turkey, are the islands of Rhodes, Cos, Leros, and Samos, collectively called the Dodecanese Islands (see Map I). Despite their geographical position along the Turkish coast, they were politically owned by Greece. Ordinarily, the Dodecanese would hold little strategic value, but Rhodes boasted several airfields, one of them significant, and Cos also had a field. Those airfields had inspired Churchill, from as far back as early 1943, to dream of seizing the islands. If the Dodecanese were brought into Allied hands, he argued, Turkey might enter the war on the side of the Allies, thus opening the Dardanelles to shipping convoys to resupply the Soviets through the Black Sea. The need for the cold and dangerous convoys up north around Norway to Murmansk and Archangel would therefore be eliminated.[16] Churchill doubtless had an additional reason for wanting to emphasize the Eastern Mediterranean: its importance to the future of the British position regarding Suez. However, he did not employ that argument in discussions with the Americans.

The Americans, not surprisingly, had always been cold to any action in the Eastern Mediterranean. Operations in that region, they believed, would constitute just one more diversion from the main effort toward Germany. Accordingly they had always been content to allow the Mediterranean Theater to be split under two commands, the Middle Eastern, under British General Sir Henry Maitland Wilson, and the Western, under Ike. The Americans saw to it that nearly all the resources for fighting Hitler were assigned to Ike's western half.

When Roosevelt and Churchill had met at the Quebec Conference in August of 1943, the Prime Minister had proposed an operation against the Dodecanese. Finally, after much discussion, he secured General Marshall's grudging agreement to execute such a move provided that it was conducted solely by forces currently assigned to General Wilson, as commander in the Middle East.[17] That agreement, while seemingly a concession, effectively killed any prospects for action in the region, because Wilson lacked sufficient force. His activities were therefore limited to training the 8th Indian Division for an eventual attack on Rhodes.

When the Italian government under King Victor Emmanuel and Marshal Pietro Badoglio surrendered to the Allies on September 8, 1943, Churchill believed that the time had arrived for him to push for his Dodecanese project. At first he held a glowing hope that the numerically superior Italian garrison of Rhodes might overcome the Germans stationed there and take them prisoner. That hope turned out to be unrealistic, however. The Germans quickly subdued the Italians and then began reinforcing Rhodes with German troops from elsewhere. A vastly disappointed Churchill directed General Wilson to seize the other islands. During the next two weeks, Wilson occupied Cos, Leros, and Samos with an infantry battalion on each island. Rhodes would have to come later.

Churchill then turned to Ike for help. Despite the fact that Wilson's Middle East Command was separate from the Western, the Prime Minister sent Ike a message on the 25th of September in which he listed what, in his mind, should be the priorities in the Mediterranean as a whole:

> Four fifths of our effort should be the buildup of Italy. One tenth should be our making sure of Corsica (which will soon finish) and in the Adriatic. The remaining tenth should be concentrated on Rhodes.[18]

Ike did not leap at the opportunity to give up a division or two in the middle of a hard battle in Italy, so he answered merely that he was "closely examining resources" and felt sure that he could "meet minimum requirements of Mideast."[19]

In the meantime, Adolf Hitler and his generals met on that same September 25 to determine their Mediterranean strategy. They decided to hold Crete and certain islands in the Aegean and to send air reinforcements to the region. Churchill later conceded ruefully that Hitler's decision was justified. The Nazis, he said, had "gained large profits" at a small cost.[20]

On October 3, 1943, the first blow fell on the British troops occupying the three Dodecanese islands that had fallen into British hands. A small German force of paratroopers and seaborne troops attacked and quickly occupied the island of Cos. This loss only strengthened Churchill's resolve to take Rhodes, whose airfields dominated all the others. He began planning such an operation, which he called ACCO-LADE.

Ike wanted to help, if only by providing Wilson with air support. He therefore consulted Sir Arthur Tedder, his air commander, to see what could be done. But prospects were not encouraging. When the Italian government had surrendered, the Germans under Albert Kesselring and Erwin Rommel had subdued the Italian armed forces and set up a series of strong delaying positions designed to hold the Americans and British as far south on the Italian peninsula as possible. The line at that time ran across the boot north of Naples and south of Cassino. The German ground forces were strong, with German divisions actually outnumbering the Allied. Further, Ike had received no instructions from the Combined Chiefs to assist Wilson. Putting all that together, Ike and Tedder agreed that their options for assisting Wilson were narrowed down to bombing German air bases in Greece. Ike so advised the Combined Chiefs of Staff.* He also notified General Marshall that he would be meeting with his three commanders-in-chief—Alexander, Tedder, and Admiral Sir Andrew Cunningham—on October 9.

Churchill considered Ike's offer of help inadequate, and as was his wont he appealed to Roosevelt. By now the President was rapidly losing patience with Churchill's persistence,[21] and he answered that he was "opposed to any diversion which will in General Eisenhower's opinion jeopardize the security of the current situation in Italy."[22] Roosevelt also spurned Churchill's offer to go personally to join in Ike's forthcoming meeting with his commanders in Algiers. Probably recalling his earlier success at Algiers, Churchill had hoped that General Marshall could fly the Atlantic and accompany him.[23]

The next day, October 9, Ike held his scheduled meeting with Tedder, Cunningham, and Alexander. Together they agreed that no further action should be taken in support of ACCOLADE, that

our resources in the Mediterranean are *not* large enough to allow us to undertake the capture of Rhodes and at the same time secure our

---

*If, against his judgment, they directed him to assist Wilson, he could provide some B-17 bombers, B-25 bombers, and P-38s. He added, however, that the effect of these diversions on the operations in Italy would be most serious. Hopkins, III, pp. 1488–89.

immediate objectives in Italy. To us it is clear that we must concentrate on the Italian campaign.[24]

On November 14, Leros, like Cos, fell to the Germans and the entire Dodecanese island group was in enemy hands. In the course of the debacle, the British lost a brigade of troops, six destroyers, and two submarines. Eight other ships were also damaged.[25]

Though he stood alone in his views, separated from both the Americans and his British colleagues, Churchill seemed to blame Ike:

> The painful episodes of Rhodes and Leros . . . constitute, happily on a small scale, the most acute difference I ever had with General Eisenhower.[26]

Yet Churchill was too big a man to allow a single such episode to destroy his relationship with Ike. In fact, on the very day that Leros fell, Ike met the Prime Minister at Malta and no acrimony was recorded by either man. Churchill even informed Ike confidentially that the selection of Marshall to command OVERLORD was not yet settled and that Ike, in fact, was being considered as an alternative.

Churchill was adamant on one point, however: that the command of the Mediterranean Theater must pass to the British when an American was named commander for OVERLORD. That meant that Ike would leave his present position, no matter where he went, whether to London or Washington.* "I am sure you will realize, my dear general, that we are quite happy with you," Churchill told him, "but it would obviously be unfair to us to be foreclosed from both major commands in Europe." Ike said that he understood.[27]

From Malta, Churchill went on to conferences with President Roosevelt at Cairo and Tehran, at which he felt obligated to agree to the invasion of northwest Europe on May 1, 1944, and a simultaneous landing in southern France, code-named ANVIL. At the second Cairo conference, following that at Tehran, Roosevelt made his fateful decision: Ike, not Marshall, would command OVERLORD, the new code name for ROUNDUP. General Sir Henry Maitland Wilson would

---

*It was generally assumed that if Marshall assumed command of OVERLORD then Ike would go to Washington to serve as Acting Chief of Staff in Marshall's place.

take command of the newly consolidated Mediterranean Theater.

Ike left the Mediterranean Theater with some regrets, but he was eager to get started on his new challenge.[28] When he arrived in London on January 13, 1944, it was with an optimistic spirit. "Now began the task of preparing for an invasion," he later wrote, "but by comparison with the similar job of a year and a half earlier, order had replaced disorder, and certainty and confidence had replaced fear and doubt."[29] Ike and Churchill would be once more working together. Churchill resumed his invitations to lunch every Tuesday and the two again worked hand in hand.

In some ways, however, the relationship between them was more difficult in 1944 than it had been in 1942. TORCH had been a mere expedition, and the forces earmarked for it were separate and distinct from the rest of the British armed forces. OVERLORD, on the other hand, was an all-encompassing effort, demanding everything available in Britain to support it. Ike, having gained much in confidence over the past eighteen months, was demanding control of practically all forces on hand in the U.K. In those demands he met resistance from Churchill.

The most serious issue revolved around control of the Strategic Air Forces, the long-range bombers that operated directly under the control of the Combined Chiefs of Staff. Ike considered airpower as vital, and with the near disaster of Salerno fresh in his mind,[30] he was determined never again to have to negotiate for the forces he needed. So he set out to secure and control all the air forces available in Britain and the Mediterranean until it was certain that his landings in Normandy were secure.

He did not expect to encounter the difficulties he met, because Churchill, when Ike visited him at Marrakech the previous December, had promised him that he would get what he wanted in that regard. Ike now realized, however, that Churchill had developed second thoughts, possibly under the prodding of Air Marshal Sir Arthur "Bomber" Harris, whose heavy bombers were hitting Germany at night. For whatever reason, Churchill backed away from Ike's understanding of his earlier assurances, once he and Ike found themselves together in London.

The controversy was long and drawn out, and it carried strong overtones of the schism between tactical and strategic airmen. But Ike eventually won out when the CCS gave him control of the Strategic Air Forces from April to September 1944, by which time it was presumed that OVERLORD would be well established on the continent of Europe. One of the circumstances that prompted this decision was the good sense of Ike's deputy, Sir Arthur Tedder, and British Chief of the Air Staff Sir Peter Portal (hence Portal as one of Ike's "greats"). A more critical element was Ike's own determination. If not given control of strategic air, he later wrote, he threatened to resign his position: the Western Allies would have to get a new commander. Such a development would, of course, have been unacceptable to both governments and publics alike.[31]

All through the planning days, up to early April 1944, Churchill was uncomfortable with the idea of OVERLORD. Still haunted by memories of the terrible slaughters of the First World War and their impact on British society, he felt an apprehension that Americans could never be expected to understand. Since I cannot express his attitude better than Ike, I cite *Crusade in Europe:*

> In all our conferences, Mr. Churchill . . . gradually became more optimistic than he had earlier been, but he still refused to let his expectations completely conquer his doubts. . . . More than once, he said, "General, if by the coming winter you have established yourself with your thirty-six Allied divisions firmly on the Continent, and have Cherbourg and Brittany peninsulas in your grasp, I will proclaim this operation to the world as one of the most successful of the war." And then he would add, "And if, in addition to this, you have secured the port of Le Havre and freed beautiful Paris from the hands of the enemy, I will assert the victory to be the greatest of modern times."
>
> ". . . Liberate Paris by Christmas and none of us can ask for more."

Ike would always reassure him that by the coming Christmas the Allies would be on the border of Germany.[32]

Unfortunately, another clash was now forced on Ike similar to that of the Dodecanese the previous summer. This time the issue between Churchill and the Americans was ANVIL, the plan, agreed to at Tehran, for landing ten divisions in southern France. These divisions, of which three were American and the rest French, were to come from Italy.

ANVIL was an operation that Churchill dearly wanted canceled. His reasoning was consistent with his ongoing desire to emphasize the status of "Jumbo" Wilson's Mediterranean Theater. Sending so many divisions from Italy to France, where they would immediately be absorbed into OVERLORD, would drastically weaken the campaign that British General Alexander was conducting in Italy under Wilson.

Though Churchill had earlier agreed to ANVIL—or at least had grudgingly acceded to it—there is no evidence that he was ever reconciled, and the wily Prime Minister felt free to keep the question open regardless of any "formal" agreements made at a summit conference. (As it turned out, he considered the question of ANVIL settled only when the first troops actually hit the beaches in southern France in mid-August.)

In the spring of 1944, fate presented Churchill with a new argument that might reasonably relieve him of his agreement at Tehran: the shortage of landing craft. Ike, upon assuming command in London, had upgraded the original OVERLORD landing plan to a five-division assault rather than the three divisions originally visualized. The increased size of the landing force meant a shortage of landing craft. This was measured in general terms by LSTs (Landing Ships, Tank), seaworthy vessels each capable of carrying the personnel of an infantry battalion. Even with OVERLORD delayed from early May to early June, the only way to execute OVERLORD concurrently with DRAGOON (as ANVIL had been renamed) would be to stagger their timing. The LSTs that transported the troops of OVERLORD into northwest France would have to return to the Mediterranean to deliver troops for DRAGOON some time later. Churchill could now argue that DRAGOON had become unnecessary, since it would not be executed together with the main assault. He carried this argument to the Combined Chiefs in Washington, to Marshall, and to Roosevelt.

If Churchill was determined, however, so were the American Joint Chiefs. They turned down his arguments as well as his invitation for them to fly to Britain to discuss the matter. Instead, on February 9, 1944, they deputized Ike to represent them in any further discussions on the subject. At the same time, they refused to send Ike any additional landing craft. This assignment was hardly a welcome chore for Ike.

Ike did his best. Proposals and counterproposals went on, somewhat eased by an unexpected but welcome supplement of some additional LSTs from the United States. Finally, on April 3, Churchill invited Ike to lunch, both men resolved to work out a compromise. Their answer was to set priorities for the Mediterranean versus DRAGOON. First priority, they agreed, would be the capture of Rome. DRAGOON would be planned for, but the target date for its execution would be delayed until July 10, not June 6. By then Roosevelt and Marshall, tired of the controversy, agreed. When Rome fell on June 4, 1944, the matter seemed resolved for good.[33] The way was clear for DRAGOON, once the LSTs should become available.

Yet the question of DRAGOON arose again in early August, two months after D-Day. Paradoxically, it came up as the result of success. The Americans had broken through the German front at St. Lô and Patton was about to set out eastward across France, so Churchill saw a plausible argument for canceling a landing at Marseilles. The seizure of the Brittany ports—Brest, St. Nazaire, St. Malo, Lorient, Quiberon Bay, and others—would make Marseilles unnecessary as a port through which to move American men and supplies, he declared. He made a trip to Normandy, where he and Ike debated the issue of DRAGOON off and on over a period of days.

Churchill was at his most persuasive. He dwelt on the success of General Alexander's drive up the Italian boot, exploiting his capture of Rome the previous June. Possibly such success, he added, would encourage a major uprising against the German occupation of the Balkans.

In his choice of information sources, Churchill was cleverly selective. Ignoring an optimistic intelligence study made by Supreme Headquarters (SHAEF), he harked back to a British study that predicted three months as the time it would take for a force landed at Marseilles to drive up the Rhone to Lyon. Further, he pictured a hotly fought landing, with the beaches running red with the blood of Allied soldiers. "And if that series of events should come about, my dear general," he said, "I would have no choice but to go to His Majesty the King and lay down the mantle of my high office."[34] He conveniently overlooked the fact that virtually none of the blood shed would be

British; it would all be American and French. The Americans, making the actual assault, would suffer the most.

As the debate dragged on, Ike came to realize that the Prime Minister's motives for wanting to cancel DRAGOON were political, an effort to keep the Mediterranean Theater force as strong as possible. Churchill, however, would never admit it; as a political leader he refused as a matter of principle to make such an admission to a general. So the debate was confined to military considerations, in which Churchill's arguments were weak.

Ike was completely sure of his own position. The only major French port taken thus far was Cherbourg, and its capacity was proving disappointing. The ports of Brittany, on which Churchill placed such stress, were not yet in American hands and when they did fall, they might be severely damaged. Not only was Marseilles closer to Germany than were Normandy and Brittany, but it would probably suffer minimum destruction at the hands of the hastily retreating Germans.

On the tactical side, Ike was convinced that, even though German strength in southern and southwestern France was weak, the right flank of Patton's army as it drove eastward would be exposed until the front could be solidified by meeting a drive coming up the Rhone from the south. The Loire River, which Patton depended on for flank protection at the moment, was a formidable but not impenetrable obstacle. Finally, the seven French divisions earmarked to land at Marseilles would obviously fight better on French soil than on the Italian front.

Churchill gave up. A week later he was on a British warship witnessing the landings near Marseilles. Ike, always sorry when he had to deny anything to Churchill, was struck by the Prime Minister's magnanimity. Though he lost the argument, he believed in fighting the German anywhere and wanted to be part of it.[35] Despite that magnanimity, however, Churchill always insisted that the invasion of southern France was a mistake.

By September 11, 1944, less than a month after the landing in southern France, British and American forces were at the borders of Germany. On that date, the American Seventh Army, driving northward from Marseilles, joined up with Patton's right flank. German forces in southwest France surrendered by the tens of thousands. One infantry lieutenant, Sam Magill, a platoon leader in the 83d Infantry Division guarding the Loire, found himself accepting the surrender of some 20,000 German prisoners. The fugitives were seeking any American officer, even a lieutenant, to whom they could give themselves up.[36]

By then, however, the force of the Allied drive eastward was spent, not so much from German resistance, though that stiffened when Hitler's Wehrmacht began defending German soil, as from lack of supply. Ninety days after landing in Normandy, the Anglo-Americans had expected to occupy only a "lodgment area" between the Loire and the Seine Rivers, reaching about to the Paris-Orléans gap. With all the ports of Normandy and Brittany beginning to operate, that territory could be amply supplied. But in fact the advance of the front-line troops had vastly outstripped that area in the planned amount of time. The capacity of the ports and the French road and railroad nets could not keep the combat units supplied, especially with gasoline. The Allies were now forced to fight on a shoestring, and a dreary autumn set in, with heavy casualties in drives toward Walcheren Island (after the failure of the Arnhem operation), toward Aachen, and in the south toward Metz. Churchill's attitude at that time was disappointing to Ike, especially when the Prime Minister sent a proposal to Roosevelt calling for another "summit" meeting where "the whole stormy scene can be calmly and patiently studied with a view to action as closely concerted as that which signalized our campaigns of 1944."[37] Ike reacted, concerned that the Prime Minister was seeking to give him new directives, to bind his hands:

When [Ike] learned of this communication, for one of the few times in their long, close association General Eisenhower was irked at his friend Churchill. He recalled the early spring of 1944, during the preparations for OVERLORD, when he personally had constantly assured the Prime Minister that the Allied forces would be on the border of Germany by early winter. His optimism at the time was gently but invariably derided by Churchill. He recalled Churchill's often expressed doubts about executing OVERLORD at all, and Field Marshal Brooke's arguments at the conference in Algiers in June, 1943, when Brooke had gone so far as to urge Eisenhower to abandon any thought of land operations in Europe during the next year.

Now, with things going almost exactly as he had predicted, Eisenhower found himself harassed by outside pressure to change his plan radically. He flatly refused.*

The Battle of the Bulge, which began on December 16, 1944, settled the issue.

One final difference of opinion between Ike and Churchill manifested itself in March and April 1945, when the Allied armies were overrunning Germany. This entailed Ike's decision to stop at the Elbe River and meet the Soviets along that line rather than attempt an attack on Berlin. The divergence of views was complicated once more by the thin line between military and political considerations—and the fact that Ike, whether he liked it or not, had one foot in both doors.

At Yalta the previous January, Churchill, Roosevelt, and Stalin had agreed on the zones that each country would occupy in Germany once the enemy had surrendered. The lines between national occupation zones had been drawn up on the assumption that the Soviets, not the Western Allies, would overrun most of Germany. Success in the west, however, had now made it certain that the Western Allies would wind up farther east than had been anticipated at Yalta. So even if Ike stopped at the Elbe, which he intended to do, the Americans and British would still be required to drop back some distance when the respective forces settled into their previously agreed zones of occupation. Churchill and Roosevelt disagreed in one important respect on this matter. Roosevelt considered the Yalta agreement on occupation zones binding, a promise he had made to Stalin. Churchill considered the agreement negotiable.

Ike's intention to stop at the Elbe was based solely on military considerations. His armies, with their centers of gravity west of the Rhine River, would be stretched if he attempted to send a few divisions into Berlin. In addition, he feared the prospect of a clash between friendly

---

*Bitter Woods, pp. 93–94. This passage is included at length because these words were carefully studied by General Eisenhower himself during the writing of that book.

Field Marshall Sir Alan Brooke, Chief of the Imperial General Staff, accompanies Ike and Churchill on a tour of the front in the dreary days of autumn 1944.

National Archives

forces. There was always a chance that, even if some American divisions could drive those last fifty miles into the German capital, they might accidentally be ground up by the vastly superior Russian juggernaut. The Russians had been building up their force only thirty miles away from Berlin for months. And, considering the 20 million estimated dead they had suffered in fighting the Germans, they were far more passionate about taking the German capital than were the Western nations. Ike considered the Elbe, which is a wide, unmistakable river, to be an ideal demarcation line.[38]

Ike was also well aware of the accord that had been signed at Yalta. As he had been directed to do (or at least as he interpreted his directions), he sent a message to the American Military Mission in Moscow on March 28 asking them to inform Stalin of his plans. He would make his main drive, not to Berlin but to Leipzig, where he would meet the Russians on the Elbe. Stalin answered enthusiastically.

Churchill objected to Ike's actions on two bases. He was still strongly in favor of a drive toward Berlin, presumably with Montgomery commanding, and as a matter of procedure he objected to Ike's communicating directly with Stalin. In sending a message to the Russian head of government Ike was, Churchill claimed, exceeding his purview as a military commander. He also protested that Ike had not informed the British Chiefs of Staff (BCOS), Tedder, or Montgomery before sending the message.

Ike was unrepentant. Stalin, he claimed, was the de facto general in charge of the Russian armies, in that respect his own counterpart. Churchill then protested to Roosevelt and the American Joint Chiefs, receiving rebuffs from both quarters.

After considerable flurry of messages back and forth, Churchill gave in graciously. On April 5 he sent a message to Roosevelt:

> I still think it was a pity that Eisenhower's telegram was sent to Stalin without anything being said to our Chiefs of Staff or to our deputy, Air Chief Marshal Tedder, or to our Commander-in-Chief, Field-Marshal Montgomery. The changes in the main plan have now turned out to be very much less than we had first supposed. My personal relations with General Eisenhower are of the most friendly character. I regard the matter as closed.[39]

That was the last of the controversies. In my judgment, Ike's decision to meet the Russians at the Elbe was correct, particularly—and this is overlooked—in that Roosevelt and the Americans were counting on Russian help against Japan in the Far East. His communicating directly with Stalin is more questionable and I must admit that Ike stretched the limits of his powers at times, because, I think, he found the channels for formal approval in Washington and London far too slow.

The matter of Ike's failure to inform the BCOS—or Tedder— before sending the controversial message is interesting, and to me it indicates that Ike was thinking so "Allied" that his actions had nothing to do with nationality, at least in his mind. Here he differed with Churchill, who never failed to look at things from a British viewpoint, and who considered Ike's British staff officers as his own agents.

As a personal aside, I might add that I was able to drop into SHAEF in early April 1945, shortly after the matter had been settled, and I noticed no appreciable sign of strain on Ike's part. But I had no idea of the difficulties he had been undergoing in the weeks before my short visit. In mid-March, I understand, Ike's chief of staff, Bedell Smith, seemed to be worried that Ike was completely exhausted and persuaded him to visit his villa at Cannes for a couple of days. By the time the Allies crossed the Rhine at Wesel on March 24,* Ike did not look tired. Photographs taken at the time show Ike and Churchill standing together looking pensive but relaxed. Not only Ike's disposition, but his relationship with the Prime Minister, showed remarkable resiliency.

IKE AND CHURCHILL IN PEACETIME

With the war in Europe finished, not only Ike but Churchill also seemed to let down. The fighting in the Pacific was not over, to be sure, but Ike's combat role was finished, and Churchill's main preoccupation had always been with Hitler, not Hirohito. On June 12, 1945, a little over a month after V-E Day (May 8), Ike flew from his headquarters in Reims to London, where he was honored by an enthusiastic British public and government. He was awarded a specially designed "London Sword," modeled after the sword on the SHAEF shoulder patch. He was also presented with the Honorary Citizenship of London at the famous Guildhall, or City Hall, of London, where he made perhaps his greatest speech (see Appendix B).

---

*This was the first planned crossing of the Rhine, but as things turned out, it was, actually, the third that occurred. On March 7, Combat Command B of the 9th Armored Division seized an intact bridge in the vicinity of Remagen. On March 23, General Patton sent the U.S. 5th Infantry Division across near Oppenheim, a day before the Wesel crossing.

Churchill was glowing, at his best. At lunch in the Guildhall, he toasted Ike by predicting that his influence in the world would always be "one of bringing our countries together in the much more difficult task of peace in the same way he has brought them together in the awful cataclysm of war." Referring to Ike's decision of June 5, 1944, in which he ordered the invasion to begin, Churchill called it "the mightiest of the war," to which nothing could be compared. He concluded by saying that Ike had not only taken the risk and arrived at the fence, "but he cleared it in magnificent style."[40]

Shortly after the Guildhall speech, Ike went home to the United States for a triumphal welcome, accompanied by a representative group of soldiers and airmen. He then returned to his headquarters, now located at Frankfurt, Germany. His immediate contact with Churchill was at an end, especially since, at Churchill's insistence, SHAEF was dissolved at midnight on July 13, 1945.

It was shortly after that, in late July, that Ike was able to make a gesture to express his friendship for the Prime Minister. In the middle of the Potsdam Conference between Stalin, Churchill, and President Truman, word came in that Churchill, after leading his nation though five years of war, had been voted out of office. The British public, ready for a change and looking now toward domestic considerations, had replaced Churchill with the Labour Party leader, Clement Attlee.

Churchill was devastated. True, he had often referred to the possibility of his being replaced in office during the war, and he was well aware that his government was not a Tory, but a coalition government, with Attlee as his deputy. Still, he felt that the British public, out of gratitude to him personally, would certainly vote him back into office. They did not.

Churchill had no place to go to rest, to be away from it all. He turned to Ike and to Alexander, in Italy, asking if they could provide him a refuge. Both agreed with alacrity. Ike arranged for Churchill to occupy the villa that the Army had rented for his use near Cannes. There Churchill could stay as long as he liked. Despite the sadness, Ike felt some warmth at being able to do something tangible for his wartime friend and ally.

In early November of 1945 Churchill sent Ike a telegram which illustrates the sensitivity of top leaders to criticisms of the actions they had taken during the war. It was written from Strasbourg, France, where Churchill was making a visit at the invitation of the city. Churchill's telegram said that "certain statements" had been published regarding his supposed role in dissuading Ike from leaving the city exposed during the German offensive in January 1945 (see de Gaulle chapter). The allegation gave unjustified accolades to the Prime Minister for allegedly forcing Ike to change his plans and defend the city.* Churchill was asking if Ike wanted him to make a refutation in public.

Ike responded immediately that such a gesture would be unnecessary. He reiterated his thanks for the full support the Prime Minister had demonstrated a year earlier in leaving the decision up to him, but noted that "many interesting incidents of the war have been more distorted in the telling than has that one." He added, however, that he had no objection if Churchill thought that some statement of the facts might be proper.

Churchill took advantage of Ike's generosity and decided to say nothing; it would have been awkward for him to refute what was probably the major reason for his invitation to visit Strasbourg. In 1949, however, four years later, Churchill finally set the record straight. The French were presenting him with an honorary citizenship of Strasbourg, this time openly based on the Versailles incident, and he brought them up short. In the ceremony he paid tribute to Ike, calling him "that great American soldier who was willing to assume additional risks rather than expose the people of Strasbourg to German vengeance."[41]

In late November, only a couple of weeks after the exchange of messages on Strasbourg, Ike left his headquarters in Frankfurt for a trip to the United States, presumably for a little rest and consultation. Sickness and other circumstances prevented his return to Germany, however, and he remained in the United States. Ike was quick, once he had recovered, to assure Churchill that he had not intended to slight him by his abrupt departure:

---

*Churchill, as both men recalled clearly, had merely sat and listened at that Versailles meeting, never uttering a word.

Dear Mr. Churchill, I am sure you understand that I would never have deliberately separated my official connection with the European Theater without paying a final call on you. My plans had called for me to return to Europe in late November for a brief visit involving several engagements in Scotland and England. I hope that circumstances will yet permit me to come back to your wonderful country sometime during the next few months and, if that should eventuate, that I may have the honor of calling on you personally.[42]

That visit never came to pass, but a few months later, in the early spring of 1946, the two men, with their wives, had an even better

Ike and Churchill at Williamsburg, Virginia, in March of 1946.

Library of Congress

reunion. The four of them left Washington on March 8, 1946, for a tour of the restored colonial village of Williamsburg, Virginia. Both men addressed the Virginia House of Burgesses. Two days earlier, at Fulton, Missouri, Churchill had rocked the world with his speech warning of the danger of an aggressive Soviet Union, perhaps unexpectedly introducing a new term into the English language, the "Iron Curtain."

From then on, up to 1951, the correspondence between Ike and Churchill became less frequent. Both were busy men: Ike was Chief of Staff of the Army and later was immersed in organizing the Office of the Joint Chiefs of Staff—and trying to function as president of Columbia University at the same time. Churchill, for his part, was busy writing his six-volume account of the years of World War II.

Nevertheless, a couple of letters are worth noting. One was written by Ike in 1948, a year after the publication of his block-busting bestseller, *Crusade in Europe.* Some people had called his attention to the amount of controversy between Americans and Britons in that book, and thought that more emphasis should be given to the times in which the two nations cooperated. Ike could not rewrite his book, but he wrote Churchill:

> All this brings to my mind that I may not have sufficiently pointed up, in my own simple account of the war, the fact that I was aware of and always counted upon your own essentially aggressive and positive attitude toward the conflict as a whole. While I did attempt, seriously, to hold up the truth of the broad British-American agreement as the true miracle of the war and I discussed differences of opinion and conviction only as a means of proving that this great accord, under the leadership of yourself and the President, persisted in spite of these natural differences, yet I regret that I did not somewhere find occasion to emphasize from the very beginning you were a tireless advocate of the offensive. If ever again there comes any occasion for me to write anything about the war, I am most certainly going to take the opportunity to do just that.[43]

In late 1950, Ike wrote Churchill another interesting letter involving the writing of books. *The New York Times,* on Churchill's behalf, had sought Ike's permission to use his words verbatim in Churchill's account of the meeting at Algiers in June of 1943. In that letter, Ike expressed the philosophy that he followed in all his writings. He had

> no objection whatsoever to your using the minutes because—while I do not recall the exact details of the presentation—the minutes certainly expressed what everyone else understood that I meant. Consequently, they are part of history.[44]

It was in that letter, incidentally, that Ike confessed to having taken up Churchill's lifelong hobby of painting. He was almost boyish about it:

> I have had a lot of fun since I took up, in my somewhat miserable way, your hobby of painting. I have had no instruction, have no talent, and certainly no justification for covering nice white canvas with the kind of daubs that seem constantly to spring from my brushes. Nevertheless, I like it tremendously and, in fact, have produced two or three little things that I like well enough to keep.[45]

Three months following that letter, Ike would be recalled to active duty as Supreme Allied Commander, Europe, the military arm of NATO.

I saw the two statesmen together several times after that, the first instance occurring in the summer of 1951. On the 3d of July 1951, Ike and Mamie, accompanied by my wife, Barbara, and myself, made the trip from Ike's Supreme Headquarters at Versailles over to London. Ike had a full schedule: a memorial service in St. Paul's Cathedral to dedicate a corner honoring the 28,000 American airmen who died in bombing raids over Germany while based in Britain during the Second World War; a dinner of the English-Speaking Union, to be held at the Grosvenor House; and a dinner exclusively for Ike's wartime British comrades, given by Sir Hastings Ismay, Churchill's military assistant during the war. Barbara and I were included in the St. Paul's ceremony and the dinner at the Grand Ballroom of Grosvenor House for the English-Speaking Union.[46]

The ceremony at St. Paul's was impressive. Queen Elizabeth[47] was there in the absence of her ailing husband, King George VI, along with the two young princesses, Elizabeth and Margaret. For me the most memorable part of the visit was the large, spectacular dinner at Grosvenor House that included nearly a thousand guests in the brightly lighted ballroom. Prime Minister Clement Attlee was present, along with his Foreign Secretary, Herbert Stanley Morrison.

Despite the glitter and the rank, the focus of attention was Winston Churchill, still out of office. He had aged visibly since I had last seen him nearly five years earlier. He was heavier, slower, and harder of hearing. When introduced to Barbara, he beamed for a moment, as any old man might when a pretty young woman is introduced, but then he seemed to settle back with his own thoughts.

Ike was the main speaker, and his talk that evening was remarkable for the fact that it was one of the earliest public proposals for the establishment of what would later become the European Common Market. The critical paragraphs of his speech covered matters he had been thinking about a long time.

He began with remarks about Anglo-American friendship, referring to the circumstances that had prompted the American Declaration of Independence, but hastily adding that those conflicts had long been transcended by the values shared by the two countries. He warned of the threat to the freedom of the people of Western Europe by an "ideological front that marshals every weapon in the arsenal of dictatorship." That was a standard reference to Communism, in keeping with the circumstances of the time.

Ike then went on to a further thought, the need for European unity. Strength was demanded, of course, but "without unity, the effort becomes less powerful in application, less decisive in result." He then applied this to Europe. "It would be difficult indeed," he said, "to overstate the benefits, in these years of stress and tension, that would accrue to NATO if the free nations of Europe were truly a unit."

He admitted the difficulties brought about by European "history, custom, language and prejudice." He tossed the task of achieving unity out as one "to challenge the efforts of the wisest statesmen, the best economists, the most brilliant diplomats."

Finally, he paid a heartfelt tribute to Churchill:

European leaders, seeking a sound and wise solution, are spurred by the vision of a man at this table—a man of inspiring courage in dark hours, of wise counsel in grave decisions. Winston Churchill's plea for a united Europe can yet bear such greatness of fruit that it may well be remembered as the most notable achievement of a career marked by achievement.[48]

Churchill listened carefully as Ike talked. Then, a few days later, he penned a letter. "As I am getting rather deaf," he began, "I could not hear or follow your speech when you delivered it." Having obtained a copy, however, he called it "one of the greatest speeches delivered by any American in my lifetime—which is a long one—and that it carries with it on strong wings the hope of salvation of the world from its present perils and confusion."[49]

Ike was abashed by such praise. On July 11 he responded,

It would be quite impossible for me to tell you how flattered I was by the nice things you had to say about my talk. While I have no great hope that the timorous leadership of Europe will, under the spell of Eisenhower eloquence, suddenly begin with head up and chest out to march sturdily forward along the rocky road to unification, yet the making of the talk did me the personal good of putting into public words something that I believe in very deeply.[50]

This was more than "old boy" flattery. From my viewpoint, that moment illustrated a dramatic change in the relations between Ike and Churchill, that Churchill had now recognized Ike as a statesman, not a mere soldier. It was well that Churchill did so, because later that year he himself was back in his old place as Prime Minister of Britain, and a year later Ike would be elected President of the United States.

Ike and Churchill served together as the heads of government of the United States and Britain for a little over two years, until Churchill gave in to advanced years at age eighty-one and resigned all his offices except that of Member of Parliament. From the viewpoint of drama, those years were an anticlimax of a long relationship, but compared to the war years, the problems were just as knotty. For Ike, at least, it was a comfort to have Churchill at the helm of this nation's strongest ally.

They did not work together as closely as had the two nations during the war. Certainly they did not associate themselves as closely as Churchill would like. Again, it was Ike who had to say no, though the no was done far more subtly than in the days of arguments over ANVIL-DRAGOON.

On Ike's return from his noted trip to Korea in December of 1952, before inauguration,* he learned that Churchill was coming to New York to pay a visit. When they met at the home of Bernard Baruch, Churchill's friend from the days of the First World War, Churchill lost no time in proposing a sort of unofficial alliance of the "English-speaking peoples," namely the United States and Britain. It would be a continuation of the old wartime alliance. Ike demurred without hesitation. He was willing, even eager, to consult with Churchill and attempt to reach common positions, but such consultations should not be trumpeted to the whole world. Any appearance that the two strongest powers in the West were operating as a "gang" had to be avoided. Churchill, always greedy to have a say in the employment of America's vast resources, had to accept Ike's viewpoint once more.

Churchill, contrary to his advocacy of a union of English-speaking peoples, was not overly supportive of Ike when, in April of 1954, the French military situation in Indochina was degenerating into a crisis. The French were fighting a losing battle against the native Indochinese who, under the leadership of Ho Chi Minh, were impressively throwing off French domination.

Ike was not adamant in his refusal to aid the French, but he planned to do so through an alliance of the French, British, Americans, Australians, New Zealanders, Thais, and Filipinos. He also proposed including the "Associated States," as the Indochinese were then called. He was certain that the United States Congress would never consent to unilateral action on the part of the United States. He did not envision the use of either British or American ground forces.[51] Churchill demurred, thus throwing some doubt on his constant advocacy of Americans and British acting together in the postwar world.[52]

◌

---

*During the 1952 presidential campaign, Ike had promised to visit Korea, where war was dragging on, if elected. After his election, he fulfilled the promise with a visit of several days.

Churchill left the office of Prime Minister in April of 1955, only a month before the historic summit meeting of four powers at Geneva. Though Ike expressed sincere regret that Churchill could not attend, all were tacitly agreed that the old man's absence was for the best. Churchill lived for another nine years, but his failing faculties had made it impossible for him to participate in fast-moving situations such as faced the West and the Soviets in the mid-1950s.

In the spring of 1959 Churchill visited Ike and Mamie in the White House. As always, the honored guest was accommodated in the Queen's Room, at the far end of the second-floor hall, some distance from the west end, where the family gathered. One evening the family met for an informal dinner in the Family Dining Room, on the ground floor.* Barbara and I, along with our children, were included. As the time to go down to dinner approached, Ike, Barbara, and I stood in the West Hall, waiting for Mr. Churchill to come and join us. When the aged statesman stepped gingerly into the hall, his walk was so laborious as to cause us pain to watch him. He had suffered some minor strokes, not to mention several small heart attacks during his life, and his eighty-five years told on him. So deaf was he that Ike, turning to Barbara, said as he approached, "I wish you could have seen him in his prime." There was no danger of Churchill's hearing.

At dinner that evening, I was seated next to Churchill, and I was flattered that he made a sincere effort to understand what I was saying, casual though it was. The next day Churchill departed from the White House, and I will never forget the scene. He sat alone in the back seat of a limousine, heading out the northwest gate of the White House grounds and therefore passing in front of the West Wing. The entire White House Staff stood out on the curb, clapping but at the same time feeling awed. We all sensed we were witnessing a historic moment. Churchill responded by simply holding his felt hat out in front of him, smiling slightly, gazing passively at the reverent crowd.

---

*In 1959 there was no family dining room on the second floor of the White House. The so-called Family Dining Room on the ground floor was hardly an intimate affair, and its designation served principally to differentiate it from the State Dining Room. The two are adjacent at the west end.

That was the last time Churchill came to Washington. I saw him only once again, in September of the same year, 1959. But then it was in a crowd. Prime Minister Harold Macmillan hosted a dinner at No. 10 Downing Street in conjunction with a joint television program depicting a debate between him and Ike regarding the latest Berlin crisis and Khrushchev's pending visit to the United States. Also present that evening, besides Churchill, were two other ex–Prime Ministers, Clement Attlee and Anthony Eden. It was a large, impersonal affair, so in my memory, the last time I saw Churchill was in the Family Room of the White House the previous spring.

During the years following Ike's presidency, the two corresponded sporadically, primarily over such matters as "permissions" to use quotations from their mutual correspondence. As I was helping Ike in writing his memoirs, *The White House Years*, we were disappointed (and also amused) by Churchill's caution in granting such permissions. He pleaded security. We were sure that he was writing his own book, somewhat in competition with Ike's.

Ike saw Churchill one more time. In 1962 he visited the sinking man in a London hospital. Churchill was barely able to communicate, but on recognizing his visitor he was able to squeeze his hand. It was a poignant farewell between two old comrades.

Winston Spencer Churchill died on January 24, 1965, at age ninety. His death, while not unexpected, was sad. It did, however, give Ike an unusual opportunity to express his affection and admiration in public.

The unusual opportunity came about through a diplomatic gaffe on the part of President Lyndon Johnson. Not noted as the most sensitive of men, Johnson apparently listened too closely to the advice of the State Department, whose protocol section advised that, since Churchill had been a mere head of government rather than a head of state, attendance by the President at the funeral would be improper for a President of the United States. (This is conjecture on my part.) No matter on whose advice, Johnson declined to attend. To represent him he sent the Chief Justice of the Supreme Court, a considerable figure, of course, but not the President.

The British public was insulted. Johnson had failed to realize that in the hearts of Englishmen, Sir Winston Churchill stood a great deal higher than most, if not all their monarchs. Whether in response to the uproar or whether out of courtesy I do not know, but Queen Elizabeth II graciously invited Ike to come to London as her personal guest to attend the ceremonies. When Ike arrived, British television asked him to deliver a eulogy, to be aired concurrently with the live coverage of the funeral cortege as Churchill's casket left Westminster Abbey and proceeded to the wharf where it was loaded on a barge and taken up to Churchill's ancestral churchyard near Blenheim Palace.

Ike outdid himself. Not given to poetry, he delivered a eulogy that came from the heart:

At this moment, as our hearts stand at attention, we say our affectionate, though sad, goodbye to the leader to whom the entire body of free men owes so much.

In the coming years, many in countless words will strive to interpret the motives, describe the accomplishments, and extol the virtues of Winston Churchill—soldier, statesman, and citizen that two great countries were proud to claim as their own. Among all the things so written and spoken, there will ring out through all the centuries one incontestable refrain: Here was a champion of freedom.

May God grant that we—and the generations who will remember him—heed the lessons he taught us: in his deeds, in his words, in his life.

May we carry on his work until no nation lies in captivity; no man is denied opportunity for fulfillment.

And now, to you Sir Winston—my old friend—farewell![53]

EPILOGUE

The Ike I knew before and during the Second World War faded away, so the old Army song goes, when he returned to Washington from Frankfurt in November 1945. From that time on, his military duties were largely administrative. Furthermore, political pressures weighed heavily on him. As a result, he became a different man from the one I have been attempting to throw light on in this book.

When the European war ended in the spring of 1945, Ike still had nearly a quarter century of public service ahead of him. Those years included, besides the eight in the presidency, a term as Army Chief of Staff, military adviser to President Truman in setting up the new Department of Defense in 1949–50,* and the organizer, as first Supreme Allied Commander, Europe (SACEUR), of the military side of that alliance. Those years, however, have been covered extensively in other books.[1] They are the story of the man I think of as the "second Ike."

I am sometimes asked whether or not I consider Ike a "great general." I regard that question as inane. For one thing, I cannot as Ike's son be expected to give any answer other than a resounding yes. In addition, I have yet to see a definition of a "great general" that comes close to satisfying me. General Montgomery's criterion, for example, that a "great soldier" must have experienced battle at all levels of command

---

*As president of Columbia University, Ike came to Washington for two days a week to serve as the first, though ex officio, Chairman of the Joint Chiefs of Staff. He organized that office and set up the Joint Staff.

seems ludicrous, and I have cited it as an illustration of Monty's mind-set, not as an evaluation of Ike. Such a limitation would rule out Robert E. Lee, Julius Caesar, and Napoleon, just for beginners.

Parenthetically, I think I can speak for most of the families of prominent generals, people who are left at home poring over the newspapers for any hint of how military operations are going. That worried group cares little whether or not the relative is termed a "great soldier" by some colleague in memoirs written years after the fact. The prospect that the cruel vagaries of war could turn a wrathful hand on any military leader is all too vivid. The fates of Admiral Husband E. Kimmel and General Walter C. Short at Pearl Harbor are difficult to put out of mind.

That said, it is quite obvious that Ike was one of the most successful military commanders of all time. On February 14, 1944, he received a directive from the Combined Chiefs of Staff:

You will enter the continent of Europe and, in conjunction with other Allied Nations, undertake operations aimed at the heart of Germany and the destruction of her Armed Forces.[2]

Less than a year and a half later, in the early morning hours of May 7, 1945, Ike was able to report, from Reims, France,

The mission of this Allied force was fulfilled at 0241, local time, May 7th, 1945.[3]

Even with the passage of fifty-eight years that exchange still gives me pride.

The term "brilliant" is sometimes applied to successful military commanders, but the term should mean effectiveness in execution rather than mere originality of concept. Ike was highly intelligent and his standing number one in his class at Leavenworth in 1926 would attest at least to his grasp of the theories of strategy and tactics, but his greatest claim to "brilliance" rests on his utter relentlessness in the pursuit of his goal, the destruction of Hitler. He understood the army he was commanding and the nature of its troops and its tactics, but above all, he was strong and stable.

Ike often quoted Napoleon, who, he claimed, defined the military genius as "the man who can do the average thing when all those around him are going crazy." That was Ike to a T. My favorite example of such an ability was his lonely decision, made during the early morning hours of June 4, 1944, to defer the launching of the OVERLORD armada, scheduled for June 5. He had polled his top commanders. Admiral Ramsay of the Royal Navy and Air Marshal Leigh-Mallory of the Royal Air Force recommended delay; General Montgomery, in direct command of the ground forces for the landing, recommended going ahead at once. Ike delayed. The next day, with the weather somewhat more favorable, Ike ordered the landing to proceed.

A student in a military staff college might very well, when presented with the facts available to Ike that early June morning, come up with the same answers that he did: to postpone the assault on the morning of June 4, and on June 5, order the assault to go ahead on June 6. However, that student would reach his conclusions with no more pressure on him than the outcome of an examination; Ike had the fate of untold thousands on his hands, even the outcome of the war. Quite a difference.

In my experience as an observer, it seems that the first thing a people forgets is the fear it felt when their sons and daughters were committed to a military action in which heavy casualties were expected. With the passage of the years, it is impossible to reconstruct the tensions that gripped the American people at times such as D-Day in June of 1944 or in the winter of that year when news came in of another full-scale German attack through the Ardennes, the Battle of the Bulge. Ike was responsible in both cases, and he bore up with grit and determination. His sheer personal strength and the confidence he inspired in his commanders and in the people of the Western nations were critical.

There was another side of Ike that bespeaks his greatness, his ability to make concessions to strong-willed associates when doing so furthered the end he was pursuing. His relations with General Bernard Law Montgomery serve as a case in point. Time and again, Ike put up with the foibles, discourtesies, and downright arrogance of his official subordinate, while at the same time insisting that his major decisions be carried out.* More significant, however, were the instances in which Ike gave way to the will of French President Charles de Gaulle. In recognizing de Gaulle as the provisional wartime leader of France in early 1944, in the confrontation over Ike's plans to abandon Strasbourg in early January 1945, and in the lesser matter of French occupation of Stuttgart at the end of the war, Ike swallowed his pride. He was well aware that de Gaulle, as an ally, promised indispensable support; as an antagonist, he could severely damage the objectives Ike sought. Ike never forgot that his enemy was Adolf Hitler, not de Gaulle. He made concessions in these matters and de Gaulle rewarded him.

British Prime Minister Winston Churchill possessed the same quality. Despite Churchill's personal prestige, which in 1940 and 1941 far overshadowed that of President Franklin Roosevelt, Churchill conceded important tactical points perhaps more often than not. He suffered many personal humiliations. But in the end, he performed the miracle of keeping Britain on a co-equal status with those of the United States and Russia as one of the three major victors over Hitler's Germany.

For that reason, I view Churchill, de Gaulle, and Ike, despite the invaluable accomplishments of many others, as the giants of the European war.

Ike made mistakes—most of them, in my opinion, in failing to predict the effects of his actions on public opinion in the United States and even more in Britain. From my comfortable office in eastern Maryland, I can say that I think he erred in keeping the temporary nature of the command arrangements for the Normandy battle secret from the public. It seems from where I sit that Ike later gave Monty too much latitude, especially in setting the boundaries between the British and American army groups at Falaise and Argentan in August of 1944. And rather than turn over the northern half of the Ardennes battlefield to Monty in December of that same year, I think it would have been better to order (not request) General Omar Bradley to move

---

*Here I cannot help thinking of President Abraham Lincoln's tolerance of his treatment by General George B. McClellan so long as "Little Mac" promised to give him victories.

his tactical headquarters from Luxembourg to Namur, where he could control the main battle to blunt the German spearheads.

These are, however, judgments open to question. I prefer to end my evaluation of Ike by repeating the generous words of George C. Marshall:

> You have commanded with outstanding success the most powerful military force that has ever been assembled.
>
> You have made history, great history for the good of all mankind and you have stood for all we hope for and admire in an officer of the United States Army.[4]

APPENDIX A
THE GUILDHALL ADDRESS
(London, June 12, 1945)

The Guildhall Address is one of Ike's most noted. It was delivered on June 12, 1945, only a little more than a month after the end of the European phase of World War II. It is notable for the tone of modesty, which was very genuine. The words "humility must be the portion . . ." are among Ike's immortal expressions of the role of the commander.

The occasion was a grand one. The Guildhall is London's City Hall, and all the dignitaries, including Churchill and the Lord Mayor, were present. Ike was made an Honorary Citizen of London and presented with the magnificent "London Sword," specially cast to resemble the sword on the Supreme Headquarters shoulder patch. Ike spoke without notes, having memorized every word.

The high sense of distinction I feel in receiving this great honor from the City of London is inescapably mingled with feelings of profound sadness. All of us must always regret that your great country and mine were ever faced with the tragic situation that compelled the appointment of an Allied Commander-in-Chief, the capacity in which I have just been so extravagantly commended.

Humility must always be the portion of any man who receives acclaim earned in blood of his followers and sacrifices of his friends.

Conceivably a commander may have been professionally superior. He may have given everything of his heart and mind to meet the spiritual and physical needs of his comrades. He may have written a chapter that will glow forever in the pages of military history.

Still, even such a man—if he existed—would sadly face the facts that his honors cannot hide in his memories the crosses marking the resting places of the dead. They cannot soothe the anguish of the widow or the orphan whose husband or father will not return.

The only attitude in which a commander may with satisfaction receive the tributes of his friends is in the humble acknowledgment that no matter how unworthy he may be, his position is the symbol of great human forces that have labored arduously and successfully for a righteous cause. Unless he feels this symbolism and this rightness in what he has tried to do, then he is disregardful of courage, fortitude, and devotion of the vast multitudes he has been honored to command. If all Allied men and women that have served with me in this war can only know that it is they whom this august body is really honoring today, then indeed I will be content.

This feeling of humility cannot erase of course my great pride in being tendered the freedom of London. I am not a native of this land. I come from the very heart of America. In the superficial aspects by which we ordinarily recognize family relationships, the town where I was born and the one where I was reared are far separated from this great city. Abilene, Kansas, and Denison, Texas, would together equal in size, possibly one five-hundredth of a part of great London.

By your standards those towns are young, without your aged traditions that carry the roots of London back into the uncertainties of unrecorded history. To those people I am proud to belong.

But I find myself today five thousand miles from that countryside, the honored guest of a city whose name stands for grandeur and size throughout the world. Hardly would it seem possible for the London Council to have gone farther afield to find a man to honor with its priceless gift of token citizenship.

Yet kinship among nations is not determined in such measurements as proximity, size, and age. Rather we should turn to those inner things—call them what you will—I mean those intangibles that are the real treasures free men possess.

To preserve his freedom of worship, his equality before law, his liberty to speak and act as he sees fit, subject only to provisions that he trespass not upon similar rights of others—a Londoner will fight. So will a citizen of Abilene.

When we consider these things, then the valley of the Thames draws closer to the farms of Kansas and the plains of Texas.

To my mind it is clear that when two peoples will face the tragedies of war to defend the same spiritual values, the same treasured rights, then in the deepest sense those two are truly related. So even as I proclaim my undying Americanism, I am bold enough and exceedingly proud to claim the basis of kinship to you of London.

And what man who has followed the history of this war could fail to experience an inspiration from the example of this city?

When the British Empire stood—alone but unconquered, almost naked but unafraid—to defy the Hitler hordes, it was on this devoted city that the first terroristic blows were launched.

Five years and eight months of war, much of it on the actual battle-line, blitzes big and little, flying V-bombs—all of them you took in your stride. You worked, and from your needed efforts you would not be deterred. You carried on, and from your midst arose no cry for mercy, no wail of defeat. The Battle of Britain will take its place as another of your deathless traditions. And your faith and endurance have finally been rewarded.

You had been more than two years in war when Americans in numbers began swarming into your country. Most were mentally unprepared for the realities of war—especially as waged by the Nazis. Others believed that the tales of British sacrifice had been exaggerated. Still others failed to recognize the difficulties of the task ahead.

All such doubts, questions, and complacencies could not endure a single casual tour through your scarred streets and avenues. With awe our men gazed upon the empty spaces where once had stood buildings erected by the toil and sweat of peaceful folk. Our eyes rounded as we saw your women, serving quietly and efficiently in almost every kind of war effort, even with flak batteries. We became accustomed to the warning sirens which seemed to compel from the native Londoner not even a single hurried step. Gradually we drew closer together until we became true partners in war.

In London my associates and I planned two great expeditions—that to invade the Mediterranean and later that to cross the Channel.

London's hospitality to the Americans, her good-humored acceptance of the added inconvenience we brought, her example of fortitude and quiet confidence in the final outcome—all these helped to make the Supreme Headquarters of the two Allied expeditions the smooth-working organizations they became.

They were composed of chosen representatives of two proud and independent peoples, each noted for its initiative and for its satisfaction with its own customs, manners, and methods. Many feared that those representatives could never combine together in an efficient fashion to solve the complex problems presented by modern war.

I hope you believe we proved the doubters wrong. And, moreover, I hold that we proved this point not only for war—we proved it can always be done by our two peoples, provided only that both show the same good-will, the same forbearance, the same objective attitude that the British and Americans so amply demonstrated in the nearly three years of bitter campaigning.

No man alone could have brought about this result. Had I possessed the military skill of a Marlborough, the wisdom of Solomon, the understanding of Lincoln, I still would have been helpless without the loyalty, vision, and generosity of thousands upon thousands of British and Americans.

Some of them were my companions in the High Command. Many were enlisted men and junior officers carrying the fierce brunt of battle, and many others were back in the United States and here in Great Britain in London.

Moreover, back of us always were our great national war leaders and their civil and military staffs that supported and encouraged us through every trial, every test. The whole was one great team. I know that on this special occasion three million American men and women serving in the Allied Expeditionary Force would want me to pay a tribute of admiration, respect, and affection to their British comrades of this war.

My most cherished hope is that after Japan joins the Nazis in utter defeat, neither my country nor yours need ever again summon its sons and daughters from their peaceful pursuits to face the tragedies of battle. But—a fact important for both of us to remember—neither London nor Abilene, sisters under the skin, will sell her birthright for physical safety, her liberty for mere existence.

No petty differences in the world of trade, traditions, or national pride should ever blind us to our identities in priceless values.

If we keep our eyes on this guidepost, then no difficulties along our path of mutual co-operation can ever be insurmountable. Moreover, when this truth has permeated to the remotest hamlet and heart of all peoples, then indeed may we beat our swords into plowshares and all nations can enjoy the fruitfulness of the earth.

My Lord Mayor, I thank you once again for an honor to me and to the American forces that will remain one of the proudest in my memories.

Appendix B
The English-Speaking Union Address

Ike's speech before the English-Speaking Union at Grosvenor House, London, was delivered on July 3, 1951, when he was Supreme Allied Commander, Europe, the military wing of the North Atlantic Treaty Organization (NATO). It is notable principally for its early advocacy of European unity. Ike, in fact, delivered this talk some time before the "Father of the Common Market," Jean Monnet, began his campaign for such unity. The setting is also remarkable because it illustrates the prestige then enjoyed by SACEUR, a soldier speaking before an attentive audience that included not only Churchill but Prime Minister Clement Attlee and his Cabinet.

One hundred seventy-five years ago, the founding fathers of the American republic declared their independence of the British Crown. Little could they have known—in the heat and bitterness of the hour—that the severance, accomplished in passion, would through the years flower into an alliance of such fitness and worth that it was never recorded on legal parchment, but in the hearts of our two peoples. The bond that joins us—stronger than blood lines, than common tongue and common law—is the fundamental conviction that man was created to be free, that he can be trusted with freedom, that governments have as a primary function the protection of his freedom.

In the scale of values of the English-speaking people, freedom is the first and most precious right. Without it, no other right can be exercised, and human existence loses all significance. This unity of ours in fundamentals is an international fact. Yet on more than one occasion, it has been obscured in Britain and in my own country by concern with trifles and small disputes, fanned into the flames of senseless antagonisms.

Serious differences in conviction must be beaten out on the anvil of logic and justice. But scarcely need they be dragged into the public forum, in the petty hope of capturing a fleeting local acclaim, at the expense of an absent partner! There are men in this room with whom, in World War II, I had arguments, hotly sustained and of long duration. Had all these been headlined in the press of our two countries, they could have created public bitterness, confusing our peoples in the midst of our joint effort. Decisions were reached without such calamitous results, because those at odds did not find it necessary to seek justification for their personal views in a public hue and cry. Incidentally, a more personal reason for this expression of satisfaction is a later conclusion that my own position in the arguments was not always right. In any case, may we never forget that our common devotion to deep human values and our mutual trust are the bedrock of our joint strength.

In that spirit our countries are joined with the peoples of Western Europe and the North Atlantic to defend the freedoms of western civilization. Opposed to us—cold and forbidding—is an ideological front that marshals every weapon in the arsenal of dictatorship. Subversion, propaganda, deceit and the threat of naked force are daily hurled against us and our friends in a globe-encircling, relentless campaign.

We earnestly hope that the call for a truce in Korea marks a change in attitude. If such a welcome development does occur, the brave men of the United Nations forces did much to bring it about. We entered the conflict one year ago, resolved that aggression against free and friendly South Korea would not be tolerated. Certain of the nations furnishing forces had heavy demands elsewhere, including postwar reconstruction at home. Nevertheless, every contingent added evidence of the solidarity and firmness of the free nations in giving an object lesson to aggression. Our success in this difficult and distant operation reflects the fortitude of the allied troops and the leadership that guided them.

The stand in Korea should serve notice in this area, as well as in the Far East, that we will resist aggression with all the force at our command. Our effort to provide security against the possibility of another and even greater emergency—an emergency which will never be of our making—must go forward with the same resolution and courage that has characterized our Korean forces. The member nations in the North Atlantic Treaty Organization need not fear the future or any communistic threat if we are alert, realistic and resolute. Our community possesses a potential might that far surpasses the sinister forces of slave camp and chained millions. But to achieve the serenity and the confidence that our potential can provide, we must press forward with the mobilization of our spiritual and intellectual strength; we must develop promptly the material force that will assure the safety of our friends upon the continent and the security of the free world.

This is the challenge of our times that, until satisfactorily met, establishes priorities in all our thoughts, our work, our sacrifices. The hand of the aggressor is stayed by strength—and strength alone!

Although the security of each of us is bound up in the safety of all of us, the immediate threat is most keenly felt by our partners in Europe. Half the continent is already within the monolithic mass of totalitarianism. The drawn and haunted faces in the docks of the purge courts are grim evidence of what communistic domination means. It is clearly necessary that we quickly develop maximum strength within free Europe itself. Our own interests demand it.

It is a truism that where, among partners, strength is demanded in its fullness, unity is the first requisite. Without unity, the effort becomes less powerful in application, less decisive in result. This fact has special application in Europe. It would be difficult indeed to overstate the benefits, in these years of stress and tension, that would accrue to NATO if the free nations of Europe were truly a unit.

But in that vital region, history, custom, language and prejudice have combined to hamper integration. Progress has been and is hobbled by a web of customs barriers interlaced with bilateral agreements, multilateral cartels, local shortages and economic monstrosities. How tragic! Free men, facing the spectre of political bondage, are crippled by artificial bonds that they themselves have forged, and they alone can loosen! Here is a task to challenge the efforts of the wisest statesmen, the best economists, the most brilliant diplomats.

European leaders, seeking a sound and wise solution, are spurred by the vision of a man at this table—a man of inspiring courage in dark hours, of wise counsel in grave decisions. Winston Churchill's plea for a united Europe can yet bear such greatness of fruit that it may well be remembered as the most notable achievement of a career marked by achievement.

The difficulties of integrating Western Europe of course appear staggering to those who live by ritual. But great majorities in Europe earnestly want liberty, peace and the opportunity to pass on to their children the fair lands and the culture of Western Europe. They deserve, at the very least, a fair chance to work together for the common purpose, freed of the costly encumbrances they are now compelled to carry.

Europe cannot attain the towering material stature possible to its peoples' skills and spirit so long as it is divided by patchwork territorial fences. They foster localized instead of common interest. They pyramid every cost with middlemen, tariffs, taxes, and overheads. Barred, absolutely, are the efficient division of labor and resources and the easy flow of trade. In the political field, these barriers promote distrust and suspicion. They serve vested interests at the expense of peoples and prevent truly concerted action for Europe's own and obvious good.

This is not to say that, as a Commander, I have found anything but ready cooperation among the Governments of Western Europe. Time and again, I have saluted from my heart the spirit of their armed services—of officers and men alike—from the mountains of Italy to the fjords of Norway, from Normandy to the Curtain. Within political circles, I have found statesmen eager to assure the success of their current defense programs. I have no doubts as to the capacity of NATO to surmount even the formidable obstacles imposed upon us by the political facts of present day Europe. Yet with the handicaps of enforced division, it is clear that even the minimum essential security effort will seriously strain the resources of Europe. We ignore this danger at our peril since the effects of economic failure would be disastrous upon spiritual and material strength alike. True security never rests upon the shoulders of men denied a decent present and the hope of a better future.

But with unity achieved, Europe could build adequate security and, at the same time, continue the march of human betterment that has characterized western civilization. Once united, the farms and factories of France and Belgium, the foundries of Germany, the rich farmlands of Holland and Denmark, the skilled labor of Italy, will produce miracles for the common good. In such unity is a secure future for these peoples. It would mean early independence of aid from America and other Atlantic countries. The coffers, mines and factories of that continent are not inexhaustible. Dependence upon them must be minimized by the maximum in cooperative effort. The establishment of a workable European federation would go far to create confidence among people everywhere that Europe was doing its full and vital share in giving this cooperation.

Any soldier contemplating this problem would be moved to express an opinion that it cannot be attacked successfully by slow infiltration, but only by direct and decisive assault, with all available means.

The project faces the deadly danger of procrastination, timid measures, slow steps and cautious stages. Granted that the bars of tradition and habit are numerous and stout, the greatest bars to this, as to any human enterprise, lie in the minds of men themselves. The negative is always the easy side, since it holds that nothing should be done. The negative is happy in lethargy, contemplating, almost with complacent satisfaction, the difficulties of any other course. But difficulties are often of such slight substance that they fade into nothing at the first sign of success. If obstacles are of greater consequence, they can always be overcome when they *must* be overcome. And which of these obstacles could be so important as peace, security and prosperity for Europe's populations? Could we not help? We, the peoples of the British Commonwealth and of the United States, have profited by unity at home. If, with our moral and material assistance, the free European nations could attain a similar integration, our friends would be strengthened, our own economies improved, and the laborious NATO machinery of mutual defense vastly simplified.

A solid, healthy, confident Europe would be the greatest possible boon to the functioning and objectives of the Atlantic Pact.

But granting that we cannot reach maximum security without a united Europe, let us by no means neglect what is within our immediate grasp or deprecate the achievements already attained.

Look back, I ask you, over a space of two years only. Consider the dangerous level to which morale and defensive strength had descended: the despairing counsel of neutralism, appeasement and defeatism that then existed. Against such a backdrop, the accomplishments of the North Atlantic Treaty Organization are magnificently manifest. We are joined together in purpose and growing determination; we know the danger, we have defined our goals. Each day we make headway. The basic economies of European nations are on the upswing: the chaos and floundering of the postwar years are definitely behind. The international forces of Atlantic defense are no longer merely figures on paper; the international organization is no longer a headquarters without troops. The forces—ground, naval and air—are assembling. They are training together and the spirit of mutual respect and cooperation that marks their joint maneuvers is heartening and encouraging. Still far too few in numbers and short of equipment, their ranks are filling; machines and weapons reach them in a steady stream. The military and political leaders of the participating nations no longer slowly feel their way forward in an endeavor without guiding precedent. Caution that is inescapable in a new and unique enterprise has been replaced by confidence born out of obstacles overcome. The Allied Powers in Europe are constituting a team for defense, one capable of assuring a lasting and secure peace.

The winning of freedom is not to be compared to the winning of a game—with the victory recorded forever in history. Freedom has its life in the heart, the actions, the spirit of men and so it must be daily earned and refreshed—else like a flower cut from its life-giving roots, it will wither and die.

All of us have pledged our word, one to the other, that this shall not be. We have cut the pattern for our effort—we are devoting to it available resources for its realization. We fight not only our own battle—we are defending for all mankind those things that allow personal dignity to the least of us—those things that permit each to believe himself important in the eyes of God. We are preserving opportunity for men to lift up their hearts and minds to the highest places—there must be no stragglers in such a conflict.

The road ahead may be long—it is certain to be marked by critical and difficult passages. But if we march together, endure together, share together, we shall succeed—we shall *gloriously* succeed together!

Appendix C
Joint Session of Congress
March 27, 1990

John S.D. Eisenhower

The year 1990 saw many observances of Ike's 100th birthday anniversary. Celebrations were held in Washington, Abilene, and Paris (the latter in conjunction with the birthday celebrations for Charles de Gaulle). One of the significant occasions was the convening of a Joint Session of Congress, on March 27. I was one of the speakers. Others included newscaster Walter Cronkite, golfing champion Arnold Palmer, Truman presidential adviser Clark Clifford, and Winston S. Churchill II, the Prime Minister's grandson. It was an occasion of great goodwill. All members of Congress, regardless of party, sported "I Like Ike" campaign buttons.

Mr. Speaker, Mr. President pro tempore, Senator Dole, Mr. Churchill, distinguished members of Congress, friends:

It is a great pleasure for me to be here today to participate in this tribute to my father, Dwight D. Eisenhower. Our previous speakers have given us vivid and inspiring and heartwarming glimpses of Dwight Eisenhower from several different viewpoints: from those of politics, the television media, business, and sports. I would like to speak a little more personally, however, and venture an opinion as to how General Eisenhower himself would like to be remembered. I believe he would like to be thought of simply as the Good Soldier.

Ike Eisenhower was a complex man, full of contradictions. Beneath the well-known grin, he was a serious, purposeful leader. He made no pretense at intellectual brilliance, but he was contemplative and literate. He walked with kings but he never forgot his home in Abilene, Kansas.

He was the vaunted warrior who hated war. He was the five-star general who warned of the dangers of an *unbridled* military-industrial complex.

But despite those complexities, my father was consistent in following the code of the Good Soldier. But with Ike the term "Soldier" meant more than an infantryman, more than a general, more even than a supreme commander. Ike thought of himself primarily as a dedicated public servant, one who placed his country above himself. And serving his country in an ever-shrinking world meant serving the whole of mankind as well.

Both as a general and as a president, Ike viewed the high positions he held as fiduciary trusts. He did not crave fame, for his personal self-esteem was too strong for that. But responsibility was something else. Throughout his career he prepared himself for the day when he might be called on to carry heavy responsibilities, and when that call came, he was ready. His preparations made him confident, and he did his job with zest. But he was never reckless; he was ever conscious that the lives and well-being of others depended on his good judgment.

On occasion I was a witness to my father's ability to concentrate on the problem at hand. In Normandy, during mid-June, 1944, I was struck by the way in which he shrugged off the historic role he was playing on the world stage. Only the week before, he had launched the vast D-Day armada under harrowing weather conditions, but the memory of that anguished moment had already faded. Ike's eyes were always on the task at hand, not on himself.

Ike's record as President is a matter of history. He accomplished much. And in guiding the Western World through the most unstable and frightening period of the Cold War, he was, I believe, nearly indispensable. The people of the United States and the world were lucky during the 1950's to have Good Soldier Ike in control of our nuclear arsenal.

When his time was up in January, 1961, President Eisenhower turned over the reins of office with good will. As a new private citizen, Ike now supported presidents Kennedy and Johnson as he had earlier served other presidents, from Wilson through Truman. As a Republican, he could never approve all that his Democratic successors did, but Good Soldier Ike was ever conscious that they, not he, were now carrying the responsibility for governing. When once advised to speak up he said, "I'm *not* going to make it tougher for the fellow who's trying to run the country."

Ike is now part of history, gone from us for twenty-one years tomorrow, and one sentimental line of the West Point Alma Mater comes to mind. The words read, "And when our work is done, Our course on earth is run, May it be said, 'Well done; be thou at peace.'"

That is the way that Dwight Eisenhower would like to be remembered by those he has left behind.

Thank you.

Notes

Chapter I: Early Influences

1. Dwight D. Eisenhower, personal diary entry, 15 June 1932, *Eisenhower: The Prewar Diaries and Selected Papers, 1905–1941*, Daniel D. Holt and James W. Leyerzapf, eds. (Baltimore: Johns Hopkins University Press, 1998), p. 224.

2. I do not know in what area Ike lectured, but I suspect it was the internal combustion engine, at which he was an expert for the time. Patton, basically a horse cavalryman, might well have learned about motors from his compatriot.

3. Eisenhower, "A Tank Discussion," *Infantry Journal*, November 1920, in Carlo D'Este, *Patton: A Genius for War* (New York: Harper Collins, 1995), p. 297.

4. For a detailed account of their service together at Fort Meade, see Dwight D. Eisenhower, *At Ease: Stories I Tell to My Friends* (Garden City: Doubleday, 1967), pp. 169–79.

5. Ibid., p. 184.

6. Virginia Conner, *What Father Forbade* (Garden City: Doubleday, 1951), pp. 120–121.

7. *At Ease*, p. 185.

8. Ibid., p. 187.

9. Ike to Fox Conner, 4 July 1942, *The Papers of Dwight David Eisenhower* [hereinafter *PDDE*] (Baltimore: Johns Hopkins University Press, 1970–2001), I, p. 369.

10. The mails were extremely slow at that time. Ike was upset by my own supposed failure to write. On August 28, however, he received a letter dated June 28, sixty days earlier. Several others were en route. Dwight D.

Eisenhower, *Letters to Mamie,* ed. John S.D. Eisenhower (Garden City: Doubleday, 1978), p. 39.

11. Conner, *What Father Forbade,* pp. 121–23.

12. *PDDE,* I, p. 370.

13. Xen Price gave Ike his only bad efficiency rating of his career. Part of the reason was that Price was an Engineer officer, a branch notorious for rating each other poorly. It does not seem to have been a matter of personal animosity, because Price kept up a cheerful and friendly correspondence after Ike left Paris in 1929.

14. "In his later years, I visited General Pershing in his rooms at Walter Reed Hospital. He became weaker and weaker and it became almost impossible to talk with him. But whenever he spoke from his hospital bed, it was always as a senior commander. He managed to convey how much he appreciated visits by younger officers." *At Ease,* p. 209.

15. Ibid., p. 207.

16. Ibid., pp. 208–9.

17. In the last days of the Meuse-Argonne campaign, Pershing ordered the American First Army to cross its assigned boundary and take Sedan, a city of great psychological and patriotic importance to the French. When the French protested, the Americans, embarrassed, withdrew into their own sector.

18. Pershing was said to be angry when Ike, on being sent to command the European Theater in the Second World War, did not come to pay a call on him. "I don't even know the man," he is reported to have declared. Richard O'Connor, *Black Jack Pershing* (New York: Doubleday, 1961), p. 382.

19. DDE to JJP, through Marshall, 8 May 1945, *PDDE,* VI, p. 20. Fort Sill is the home of the Artillery School; Fort Riley that of the Cavalry.

20. *At Ease,* p. 210.

CHAPTER 2: IKE AND MACARTHUR

1. When those departments expanded and moved into separate offices, the State-War-Navy Building became the Executive Office Building of the White House. Today it is named the Eisenhower Executive Office Building.

2. At the height of the Depression, some 18,000 to 20,000 veterans of the First World War marched on Washington to try to induce Congress to

pay them their wartime bonuses, to which they were entitled, at once. Those bonuses were meant to be distributed later in life, but they needed the money then. President Hoover refused, and went so far as to call out a contingent of Army troops to keep the marchers across the Anacostia River, away from the streets of downtown Washington. It was a fairly mild affair, but public sympathy was on the side of the protesters, and MacArthur, against Ike's advice, chose to command the troops personally. It represented a black mark on MacArthur's record in the public mind. See *At Ease*, pp. 215–18.

3. Ike was less impressed than most people with MacArthur's spectacular record for valor in the Great War, because he viewed most of the general's feats of daring as unnecessary to the proper performance of his duties.

4. I still, remembering those dreadful occasions, get a hollow feeling in my stomach when the Army-Navy game is in progress, much as the event has been downgraded in the public mind.

5. The term "insurrection" was coined by the Americans. Possession of the islands was supposedly ceded to the United States by Spain in 1898, but the Filipinos saw themselves as fighting a new master for their independence. The war went on for three years, costing dearly in lives and property.

6. Both Ike and Ord were majors, but Ord was going to assist Ike. Ord's assignment was a concession that MacArthur made to induce Ike to go to Manila. Once there, Ike and Ord worked as a team.

7. *At Ease*, p. 223.

8. Just before we left for the United States in December of 1939, Ike received his private pilot's license, a source of much pride to him. He was later the first licensed pilot to occupy the White House.

9. *At Ease*, p. 221.

10. Stephen E. Ambrose, *Eisenhower*, Vol. I: *Soldier, General of the Army, President-Elect, 1890–1952* (New York: Simon & Schuster, 1983), p. 106.

11. Eisenhower, *Prewar Diaries*, pp. 306–7.

12. Dwight Eisenhower to author, date of conversation unknown.

13. *Prewar Diaries*, p. 326.

14. *At Ease*, p. 226.

15. The incident is vivid in my memory. We were at the apartment of Dr. Howard Smith and his wife, Kitty, good friends of my mother's.

16. As I recall, a lieutenant colonel's pay in those days was $500 a month, so the augmentation that Ike had been receiving from the Philippine government of $300 nearly doubled his normal salary.

17. This is according to my memory. The letter is not among Ike's papers. However, the incident occurred before the days when Ike's papers were kept in an orderly fashion by a secretary. If he bothered to keep it, it might have been lost in a footlocker of Ike's papers that disappeared somewhere without a trace.

18. MacArthur is known to have carried a lifelong resentment against what he called the "Chaumont crowd," Pershing's staff officers in the Great War who had little affection for him. MacArthur apparently included Chief of Staff George Marshall among the targets of his wrath.

19. *PDDE*, XI, p. 1393.

20. MacArthur to Eisenhower, 4 Nov. 1950, Hopkins, *ibid.*

21. When he learned that the Canadian government had named a mountain in honor of Ike, MacArthur is reported to have consoled himself. "I understand it is only a little mountain."

22. On the other hand, MacArthur is said to have called Ike "the best clerk I ever had."

CHAPTER 3: A GENERAL IN THE WINGS

1. Major Edwin B. Howard to his wife, Janie, fall of 1940.

2. One day Blizzard came up to me and said, "I brought you a lil ol' snake." I accepted the gift somewhat dubiously and later became alarmed when it escaped from the glass jar I kept it in. The idea of its making its way into my mother's bedroom put me in a near panic, since she was afraid of all wild creatures, even bugs. In my imagination I could see it reposed in one of her shoes. Fortunately, I eventually found it coiled in one of my own shoes, and I quickly tossed it out into the back yard.

3. Not to be confused with the Works Progress Administration, or WPA.

4. In front of Colonel Ladd's tent was a large stump, cut off about four feet from the ground. The stump was encircled by the ever present whitewashed stones. The spot was dubbed "Civic Center" by the men of the 15th.

5. Luther Giddings, *Sketches of the Campaign in Northern Mexico in Eighteen Hundred Forty-six and Seven* (New York: G. P. Putnam, 1853), pp. 74–75.

6. The division had consisted of four infantry regiments in the First World

War: the 4th, the 7th, the 30th, and the 38th. In the subsequent reorganization into the triangular division, the 4th and the 38th had been incorporated in other divisions and the 15th added.

7. After Ike's departure, the 15th went on to be one of the most distinguished regiments in the Army. Its most famous member, from Ike's old 1st Battalion, was Lieutenant Audie Murphy, the nation's most highly decorated combat veteran of the Second World War.

8. The Seabees, a highly publicized unit, derived its name from the initials of Navy Construction Battalions.

9. Ed Howard stayed in intelligence work, and six years later, in Vienna, he was a brigadier general, G-2, for U.S. Forces, Austria, and my boss.

10. Ike never forgot the line "The paths of glory lead but to the grave."

11. I have in my possession a photograph taken of Joyce and his aide, both standing stiffly together in blouse and pink riding breeches, the right hands bare, the gloved left hands holding the yellow right gloves in a picture-book manner.

12. When the West Point course of instruction was reduced to three years during World War II, the Class of 1945 became the Class of 1944.

13. In October 1940, while I was away at Millard's, the United States instituted its first peacetime draft. Both the new draftees and the newly federalized National Guardsmen were just being assimilated into service by spring of 1941.

14. I once heard Ike say that he had experienced difficulty, later, in getting General Marshall to warm up to Truscott. Truscott's raspy voice did not add to the first impression he gave.

Chapter 4: Ike and Patton

1. Eisenhower to Patton, 17 Sept. 1940, Martin Blumenson, *The Patton Papers, 1940–1945* (Boston: Houghton Mifflin, 1974), II, p. 14.

2. Patton to Eisenhower, 1 Oct. 1940, ibid., p. 15.

3. Patton to Eisenhower, 22 Feb. 1942, ibid., pp. 55–56.

4. *PDDE*, I, p. 142.

5. Ibid., I, p. 227.

6. Dwight D. Eisenhower, *Crusade in Europe* (Garden City: Doubleday, 1948), pp. 40–41. The date of this incident is not clear. The episode is not substantiated in either the *Eisenhower Papers* or the *Patton Papers*. It probably occurred before the crisis of June 21, 1942, when the fall of

Tobruk to German General Erwin Rommel brought the dispatch of an armored division under consideration. Eisenhower professed that he was "astonished" that his recommendation of Patton was "flatly opposed by a considerable portion of the staff."

7. *Patton Papers*, II, p. 70.
8. Ike always gave much credit for this decision to Admiral Ernest King, Chief of Naval Operations, with whom he had developed a relationship of mutual respect during Ike's months on Marshall's staff. See *At Ease*, p. 252.
9. *PDDE*, I, pp. 426, 427. To be commander of the American force, the other three names in nomination were Robert Eichelberger, Omar N. Bradley, and Alvin C. Gillem, Jr. For the armored corps the other names were Gillem, Geoffrey Keyes, and Orlando Ward.
10. See *Allies*, pp. 122–24.
11. *Crusade in Europe*, p. 82. Forrest Pogue, *George C. Marshall: Ordeal and Hope, 1939–1942* (New York: Viking, 1965), p. 604, says that it is "moot" whether Marshall or Eisenhower first proposed Patton for that critical position.
12. These arguments are covered in detail in *Allies*, Chapter 9.
13. *Patton Papers*, II, pp. 81–82.
14. Eisenhower to Marshall, 17 Aug. 1942, *PDDE*, I, p. 478.
15. *Patton Papers*, II, p. 82, and D'Este, *Patton*, p. 420.
16. *Patton Papers*, II, p. 83.
17. D'Este, *Patton*, p. 533.
18. Ibid., pp. 533–34.
19. Letter, Patton to his wife, 28 Sept. 1918, *Patton Papers*, I, p. 616.
20. *Patton Papers*, II, p. 108.
21. Harry C. Butcher, *My Three Years with Eisenhower* (New York: Simon & Schuster, 1946), pp. 390, 393.
22. *Patton Papers*, II, p. 332.
23. *Crusade in Europe*, p. 181.
24. Eisenhower to Marshall, 24 Nov. 1943, *Crusade in Europe*, p. 181.
25. *Patton Papers*, II, pp. 332–33.
26. Ibid., II, p. 334.
27. Patton diary, September 2, 1943: "Flew to Algiers . . . Ike sent for me . . . and lectured me . . . I realized that I had acted precipitately and accepted his remarks . . . I feel that he likes me. Of course he should. He told me

that . . . Brad was to go to England and form a new Army and plan [the cross-Channel attack]." *Patton Papers,* II, p. 345.

28. Long after the war, Ike was astonished to learn from General Erwin Rommel's chief of staff, Hans Speidel, that their intelligence credited the Allies with sixty-five divisions in the U.K., in contrast to the thirty-five they actually had.

29. Butcher, *My Three Years with Eisenhower,* p. 531.

30. *Crusade in Europe,* p. 225.

31. Patton disapproved. In his diary he called Ike's style that "of an office seeker rather than that of a soldier." Noting that movie and press photographers recorded the scene for the benefit of the men's hometown newspapers, he conceded that this aspect at least had "a good effect." *Patton Papers,* II, p. 468. Ike agreed with Patton's thesis that "a man cannot command and be on the same level [as the men]," but his own position, being so far removed from actual battle command, justified his methods.

32. Eisenhower to Marshall, 2 Aug. 1944, *PDDE,* IV, p. 2049.

33. The Americans and French had landed near Marseilles on August 15, 1944, and had driven up the Rhone Valley. When Alexander Patch's Seventh Army joined Patton's Third at Dijon, the Allies had attained a solid front facing Germany.

34. The Germans, however, had used it in the War of 1870 and in their spectacular victory over the British and French in 1940.

35. Actually the entire attack had fallen on General Troy Middleton's VIII Corps, part of First Army and solely responsible for the Ardennes front.

36. Present were Ike, Bradley, Patton, Tedder, General Jacob Devers, Strong, and others.

37. In describing this episode I have drawn heavily on my own account, *The Bitter Woods* (New York: Putnam, 1969), pp. 256–57.

38. John S.D. Eisenhower, *Strictly Personal* (New York: Doubleday, 1974).

39. Patton's courtly manners were highly resented by his other guest, comedian Jack Benny, who was intent on describing his own experiences while traveling through Germany.

CHAPTER 5: MARSHALL AND IKE

1. Ike was first mentioned in a *Washington Post* column called "The Washington Merry-Go-Round," written by Drew Pearson and Robert Allen. His name was spelled "Ersenbein."

2. The War Department had moved from the State-War-Navy Building down to the Munitions Building across Constitution Avenue from the Federal Reserve Building on the Mall. It occupied one of the temporary buildings that had been constructed for the First World War but had never gone out of use. During the Second World War the set of buildings was expanded so that one hallway stretched across the reflecting pool in front of the Lincoln Memorial. The Pentagon was completed in late 1943, and the War Department, but not the Navy, moved into that building immediately. All the temporary buildings have long since disappeared.

3. *Crusade in Europe*, pp. 16, 17, 482.

4. Ibid., pp. 21, 22.

5. Ibid., p. 22.

6. Ibid., p. 30.

7. In a burst of enthusiasm, Churchill described the prospective Anglo-American operation as two nations, "marching shoulder to shoulder, in a noble brotherhood of arms."

8. Winston S. Churchill, *The Second World War*, Vol. IV: *The Hinge of Fate* (Boston: Houghton Mifflin, 1950), p. 342.

9. *Crusade in Europe*, p. 50.

10. Ibid., p. 50.

11. John S.D. Eisenhower, *Allies* (New York: Doubleday, 1988), p. 106.

12. Ibid., p. 107.

13. Ike gave Admiral King much of the credit. In *At Ease*, p. 252, he wrote, "I later learned that Admiral Ernest King, the American naval officer at the conference table, who had a reputation for being a tough, blunt man, remarked: 'Well you've got him right here. Why not put it under Eisenhower?'"

14. Perhaps General Sir John Dill, the British representative on the CCS, might have filled the role, but that would have been more awkward than an arrangement between two men who already understood each other.

15. John S.D. Eisenhower, *Allies*, p. 231.

16. While conversing with Roosevelt at Casablanca, Ike predicted the date that the Tunisian campaign would be successfully completed as May 15, 1943. His prediction was off by only two days. *Crusade in Europe*, p. 137.

17. Churchill's references to a "soft underbelly" may have concealed other motives. The Alps do not make an inviting approach to Germany.

18. Alan Brooke later wrote, "When arguing with Marshall I could never get him to appreciate the very close connection that existed between the various German fronts. For him they might have been separate wars, a Russian war on one side, a Mediterranean war on another, and a cross-Channel one to be started as soon as possible. I must confess, however, that Winston [Churchill] was no great help. Marshall had a holy fear of Winston's Balkan and Dardanelles ventures, and was always guarding against these dangers even when they did not exist." Arthur Bryant, *The Turn of the Tide* (New York: Doubleday, 1957), pp. 559–60.

19. When Ike came to London to organize OVERLORD, those two officers were the first to go. Their role in this episode was probably not a factor; they were simply not "his men."

20. *PDDE*, II, p. 1339. The mission in question was a bombardment of the Ploesti oil fields in Romania. The raid had been a failure, but the four bomber groups were still on hand at Tripoli.

21. Hermann Göring and 15th Panzer Grenadier Divisions, and the 29th Panzer Division among them.

22. Eisenhower to CCS, 15 Sep 43, *PDDE*, III, p. 1424.

23. Ibid., p. 1425.

24. Butcher, *My Three Years with Eisenhower*, p. 423.

25. *PDDE*, III, p. 1454.

26. Ibid.

27. Butcher, *My Three Years*, p. 431.

28. *Crusade in Europe*, p. 196.

29. Ibid., p. 197.

30. Interview, Forrest Pogue with General Marshall, 15 Nov. 1956, in Pogue, *George C. Marshall: Organizer of Victory, 1943–1945* (New York: Viking, 1973), p. 321.

31. Reproduced in *Crusade in Europe*, p. 208.

32. Pogue, *George C. Marshall: Organizer of Victory*, p. 324.

33. Ibid., p. 326.

34. "Strictly speaking, my commanders were the Combined Chiefs of Staff but, realizing General Marshall's earnestness in the matter, I quickly cleared the point with the British side of the house and made ready to leave for the United States. After a week I planned to return briefly to Africa. . . . All this would consume time, the most precious element of all." *Crusade in Europe*, p. 216.

35. Eisenhower to the Combined Chiefs of Staff, 23 Jan. 1944, *PDDE*, III, p. 1673.
36. John S.D. Eisenhower, *The Bitter Woods*, p. 33.
37. *PDDE*, IV, p. 2696.
38. The incident occurred when Marshall and Churchill visited Algiers in the summer of 1943. Marshall had been admonishing Ike to taper off on his work schedule, and Ike had responded that everyone had to operate in his own individual manner. That evoked the remarks, "You haven't done so bad thus far."
39. GCM to DDE, 8 May 1945, *PDDE*, VI, pp. 14–15.
40. Ibid., p. 14.
41. Frank McCarthy's formal title was Secretary of the General Staff, but Marshall disliked aides in general, and refused to have one—formally. McCarthy performed all of an aide's services without the title. This attitude on Marshall's part is puzzling, considering the long periods of time he served as aide to General John J. Pershing just after World War I.
42. Marshall was sent to China to try to salvage some of America's interests in the final days of Chiang Kai-shek's tottering regime.
43. Marshall was sixty-five years old and had practically burnt himself out in organizing the World War II Army. During the last days of the war, Ike said to me, "General Marshall is tired. He is said to go home at 3:00 P.M. every day. He says that nobody ever had an original thought after that time of day." I have often wondered if the death of his stepson, Allen Tupper Brown, killed on June 4, the last day of the Anzio campaign, contributed to Marshall's fatigue.
44. *PDDE*, XIII, pp. 1277–78.
45. Dwight D. Eisenhower, *The White House Years: Mandate for Change* (Garden City: Doubleday, 1963), p. 318. That statement incurred the wrath of McCarthy's supporters, of whom there were many. George Creel, Woodrow Wilson's masterful propagandist in World War I, wrote a letter of complaint to Richard Nixon, Ike's running mate. While conceding that Ike was right to defend his patron, Creel declared that he was "incredibly wrong in plunging ahead with a 100% endorsement of General Marshall's entire official record."
46. Wilton Persons, Arthur Summerfield, Senator William Knowland, and Sherman Adams.
47. Speaking before the Annual Convention of Jewish War Veterans on

August 22, 1969, Marshall's close friend and aide, Frank McCarthy, said, "General Marshall was a soldier, a statesman, and a very practical man. Out of [his keen insight into politics] arose a complete understanding of the elimination of that one paragraph in Wisconsin that caused such a furor." John S.D. Eisenhower, *Strictly Personal*, p. 401.

48. Marshall interview with Rose Page Wilson, quoted by Dr. Mark Stoler at Gettysburg, October 27, 2001. Mrs. Marshall, for a time, was not so understanding.

49. *Mandate for Change*, p. 318.

CHAPTER 6: MONTY

1. Bernard Law Montgomery, *The Memoirs of Field-Marshal the Viscount Montgomery of Alamein, K.G.* (New York: World, 1958), p. 484.

2. In my observation, however, Monty was the only subordinate who ever took advantage of this license.

3. In the North African desert, he looked even stranger, from the photos I have seen. Like the rest of his army he wore shorts, but he also sported an oversized campaign hat, one side up, Aussie style, full of insignia, and which looked larger than the rest of his body. I understand that the Aussies did not appreciate this gesture, however, and he soon discontinued it.

4. In *Crusade in Europe*, p. 223, Ike says, "For control of ground forces no special appointment was contemplated." He goes on to explain that the initial Normandy landing was to be made on such a narrow front that only one army group would direct tactical coordination. But he continues, "Plans called for the early establishment of separate British and American army groups on the Continent."

5. Walter Bedell Smith, *Eisenhower's Six Great Decisions: Europe, 1944–1945* (New York: Longman, Green, 1956), p. 73.

6. The theory was that when his identity became known, the impact on the public would be dramatic because of the suspense. In fact, it turned out that way.

7. Actually, the problem was nothing new. A year earlier, during the Sicilian campaign, Ike had vainly complained to Churchill about the distorted news broadcasts emanating from the British Broadcasting Corporation. In an era before satellite communications, the BBC provided the only source of current information to everyone in the European Theater, including the Americans.

8. A term popularized by Cornelius Ryan's excellent book *A Bridge Too Far*.

9. Major General John Whiteley, interview with the author, London, October 1966.

10. Ike was crippled with an injured left knee, which he had wrenched while pulling his light aircraft off a beach three days before. The forced landing had been a close call.

11. General Omar Bradley, no friend of Monty's, made this concession: "Had the pious teetotalling Montgomery wobbled into SHAEF with a hangover, I could not have been more astonished than I was by the daring adventure he proposed. For in contrast to the conservative tactics Montgomery ordinarily chose, the Arnhem attack was to be made over a 60-mile carpet of airborne troops. Although I never reconciled myself to the venture, I nevertheless freely concede that Monty's plan for Arnhem was one of the most imaginative of the war." Omar N. Bradley, *A Soldier's Story* (New York: Henry Holt, 1951), p. 416.

12. Ambrose, *Eisenhower,* I, p. 350.

13. *Crusade in Europe,* pp. 306–7.

14. *PDDE,* IV, p. 2134.

15. Ibid., p. 2135, n5.

16. Forrest Pogue, *The Supreme Command* (Washington: Department of the Army, 1954), p. 312.

17. *PDDE,* IV, p. 2324.

18. Arthur Bryant, *Triumph in the West, 1943–1946* (London: Collins, 1959), p. 341.

19. See John S.D. Eisenhower, *The Bitter Woods,* pp. 90–99, from which I have gotten most of this.

20. Most of Monty's staff agreed that the First Army staff was tired and dispirited, but Major General Francis de Guingand, his chief of staff, thought that, though tired, they "remained cheerful and seemed to have the situation in hand." De Guingand, *Operation Victory* (New York: Charles Scribner and Sons, 1947), p. 429. See also David W. Hogan, Jr., *A Command Post at War: First Army Headquarters in Europe, 1943–45* (Washington: Center of Military History, 2000), pp. 219–20.

21. David Hogan admits that the British system for keeping track of subordinate units was better developed than that of the Americans.

22. "The change in command drew a protest from Bradley, but the 12th Army Group did not have much of a case. While his staff technically

had never lost contact with its northern armies, the communications network . . . involved in command and control of the armies was tenuous at best. It would soon break down irreparably. . . . Bradley, in Luxembourg, was in a poor position to provide the personal presence necessary in the crisis. . . . Bradley probably had such confidence in Hodges and Kean and was so slow to grasp the true dimensions of the German offensive that he believed they could handle the situation on their own, but to some on Hodges' beleaguered staff, the 12th Army Group headquarters appeared remote, even uncaring." Hogan, *A Command Post at War,* pp. 218–19.

23. Ibid., p. 229.
24. John S.D. Eisenhower, *The Bitter Woods,* pp. 381–82.
25. This version of events comes from de Guingand's *Generals at War* (London: Hodder & Stoughton, 1964), pp. 109–11. I have no reason to doubt its essential accuracy.
26. John S.D. Eisenhower, *The Bitter Woods,* p. 387.
27. *London Daily Mirror,* 8 Jan. 1945; cited in ibid., pp. 388–89.
28. Eisenhower to Marshall, 12 Jan. 1945, *PDDE,* IV, p. 2422.
29. Eisenhower to Brooke, 16 Feb. 1945, ibid., p. 2480.
30. Bryant, *Triumph in the West,* p. 417.
31. *Crusade in Europe,* pp. 415–16.
32. Ike's SHAPE command included both Europe and the Mediterranean.
33. Interview, General Andrew J. Goodpaster, 23 May 2002.
34. Montgomery, *Memoirs,* p. 484.
35. Ibid., p. 256.

CHAPTER 7: IKE AND DE GAULLE

1. David Schoenbrun, *The Three Lives of Charles de Gaulle* (New York: Atheneum, 1966), p. 5.
2. The fact that Khrushchev had said nothing about previous American flights may be explained by his desire to maintain his new friendship. He could pull off that balancing act while the fact of American flights was kept from public knowledge in the Soviet Union. Now, however, the American activity could no longer be ignored.
3. Dwight D. Eisenhower, *The White House Years: Waging Peace* (Garden City: Doubleday, 1965), p. 555.
4. Ibid., p. 556.

5. Phillipe Masson, *De Gaulle* (New York: Ballantine, 1972), p. 13.

6. On December 16, 1942, de Gaulle wrote to Admiral Stark, USN, "When leaders fail, new leaders are projected upward out of the spirit of eternal France: from Charlemagne to Joan of Arc to Napoleon, Poincaré, and Clemenceau. Perhaps this time I am one of those thrust into leadership by the failure of others." Schoenbrun, *The Three Lives of Charles de Gaulle*, p. 3.

7. Winston S. Churchill, *The Second World War*, Vol. II: *Their Finest Hour* (Boston: Houghton Mifflin, 1949), p. 218.

8. Ibid., p. 226.

9. Schoenbrun, *The Three Lives of Charles de Gaulle*, p. 4.

10. Masson, *De Gaulle*, p. 38.

11. *Crusade in Europe*, p. 83.

12. *PDDE*, I, pp. 522–23.

13. John S.D. Eisenhower, *Allies*, p. 312.

14. Jean Monnet, future "Father of the Common Market," was supposedly a member of the FCNL in Giraud's camp. He described Giraud thus: "When the general looks at you with those eyes of a porcelain cat, he comprehends nothing." Robert B. Murphy, *Diplomat Among Warriors* (Garden City: Doubleday, 1964), p. 180.

15. Charles de Gaulle, *The Complete War Memoirs of Charles de Gaulle* (New York: Simon & Schuster, 1972), p. 433.

16. Eisenhower to Marshall, 19 June 1943, *PDDE*, II, pp. 1200–1201; de Gaulle, *Memoirs*, pp. 433–35.

17. De Gaulle, *Memoirs*, p. 545.

18. John S.D. Eisenhower, *Allies*, p. 457.

19. Eisenhower to Marshall for CCS, 19 Jan. 1944, *PDDE*, III, p. 1667.

20. John S.D. Eisenhower, *Allies*, p. 458.

21. De Gaulle, *Memoirs*, p. 556.

22. Ibid., pp. 556–57. It should be noted that this was de Gaulle's opinion, which I consider almost outlandish.

23. Ibid., p. 558.

24. Arthur Layton Funk, *Charles de Gaulle: The Crucial Years, 1943–1944* (Norman: University of Oklahoma Press, 1959), p. 258.

25. De Gaulle, *Memoirs*, p. 559 and passim.

26. Ibid., p. 560.

27. After having visited Montgomery in his headquarters, de Gaulle

described his reception in Bayeux thus: "When I reached the gates of the city, [François] Coulet was there with Mayor Dodeman and his municipal council. We proceeded on foot, from street to street. At the sight of General de Gaulle, the inhabitants stood in a kind of daze, then burst into bravos or else into tears. Rushing out of their houses, they followed after me, all in the grip of extraordinary emotion. The children surrounded me. The women smiled and sobbed. The men shook my hands. We walked on together, all overwhelmed by comradeship, feeling national joy, pride and hope rise again from the depth of the abyss. De Gaulle, *Memoirs*, p. 564.

28. Ike was naturally saddened, on July 24, to learn that Lieutenant General Leslie J. McNair had been killed while watching the bombing near St. Lô. Ike's sorrow at losing a fine officer and friend was somewhat tempered, however, by his anger that McNair had come to the ETO unbeknownst to him and had proceeded directly to the front lines without attaining Ike's permission. Ike would have at least discouraged McNair's daring.

29. It is interesting that the Ardennes has been considered so "impassable." The Prussians used it in the Franco-Prussian War of 1870 and again in the campaign of 1940, both times crushing the French. Only in the First World War, generally following the so-called Schlieffen Plan, did they make their main attack across the North German Plain north of the Ardennes, through Belgium.

30. Pogue, *The Supreme Command*, p. 400.

31. *Crusade in Europe*, p. 363.

32. Pogue, *The Supreme Command*, p. 401.

33. Ibid., pp. 459–61. Oddly, Ike recollected the outcome differently. According to his version, "I warned the French commander that under the circumstances it was necessary for me to inform the Combined Chiefs of Staff that I could no longer count with certainty on the operational use of any French forces they might be contemplating equipping in the future. The threat of possible curtailment of equipment for the French forces proved effective, and the French finally complied." *Crusade in Europe*, p. 413.

34. Ike had instructed the State Department to inform Koslov, at the steps of the airplane as he left the United States, that he would invite Khrushchev to visit the United States in September, *provided that sufficient*

progress was evident in the current foreign ministers conference. But nothing had come of the foreign ministers conference, so Ike presumed the invitation to be dead. He was astonished, therefore, that two top State Department officials, Robert Murphy and Douglas Dillon, had issued the invitation to Khrushchev without condition.

35. Harold Macmillan, *The Blast of War, 1939–1945* (New York: Harper & Row, 1967), p. 324, describes the occasion in which he told de Gaulle, previously left in the dark, about the Italian surrender. Explaining the need for security in such matters, Macmillan "ventured to observe that, as a soldier, he would understand the need for secrecy. To this de Gaulle replied, 'I am not a soldier.' I was tempted to ask why he dressed himself up in a peculiar and rather obsolete costume which surely no one would choose to wear unless it was imposed on him by military necessity."

36. Ike had retired early as Chief of Staff of the U.S. Army, because he had little taste for the process of demobilization. He had, however, put his uniform back on about two and a half years later in order to help establish NATO as its first Supreme Allied Commander.

37. John S.D. Eisenhower, *Strictly Personal*, p. 251.

38. Presidential trips have since become commonplace and are hardly memorable. The Eleven-Nation Trip, however, was a novelty at the time, made possible by the arrival of the Boeing 707 passenger liners. Ike and his advisers were a little less than candid when claiming that he was in close touch with the United States at all times, especially while in India.

39. De Gaulle was always very cordial with me, probably because he had a son, Philippe, of my age. Philippe de Gaulle, whom I met in 1990, is a consummate gentleman. He had the good sense to spend a career in the French navy, in the light of his father's army career.

CHAPTER 8: IKE AND WINSTON CHURCHILL

1. *Mandate for Change*, pp. 530–31.

2. The name of Franklin D. Roosevelt is conspicuously missing. However, Ike's direct dealings with Roosevelt were minimal. All his official communications with Roosevelt went through Marshall.

3. Churchill before Congress, December 26, 1941. Cited in John S.D. Eisenhower, *Allies*, p. 27. Oddly, Churchill's reproduction of the speech on pp. 671–72 of *The Grand Alliance* makes no mention of referring to his mother's being American.

4. *The Times* (London), November 11, 1942; quoted in John S.D. Eisenhower, *Allies*, pp. 195–96.

5. It was not Churchill's lack of determination but the forces of history that defeated him in the retention of India. Fortunately for him, that event occurred under the stewardship of Clement Attlee.

6. One general impression that Ike, in later years, tried to dispel was Churchill's reputation as an excessively heavy drinker, which Churchill, somewhat humorously, made a hobby of promoting. Ike observed that during serious discussions, the Prime Minister would order a strong scotch and then keep pouring soda into the same glass throughout the evening.

7. The British had also been blockading French North African seaports.

8. John S.D. Eisenhower, *Allies*, p. 124.

9. Ibid., p. 136.

10. Attlee, General Alan Brooke, Lord Louis Mountbatten, Admiral Sir Dudley Pound, and Foreign Secretary Anthony Eden.

11. John S.D. Eisenhower, *Allies*, pp. 137–38.

12. Robert Sherwood, *Roosevelt and Hopkins: An Intimate History* (New York: Harper & Brothers, 1948), p. 550.

13. Macmillan, *The Blast of War*, p. 165.

14. Ike predicted the end with remarkable accuracy: May 15 of 1943.

15. In the early stages of the Anglo-American alliance it was tacitly assumed, particularly by the British, that the British were the senior partners in the relationship. Geography had much to do with that; operations would have to be based on their home territory. But they also claimed superior experience, having been fighting Hitler since September 1939. The Americans tended to sniff at British "experience," which, the Yanks said, had consisted of a series of lost battles. But the British staffs were better prepared than the Americans when it came time for bilateral debate. When a point of contention arose, the British chiefs had at their disposal volumes of facts and figures to which the Americans had no answer. As a result, a good many of the bilateral decisions went to the better prepared partner.

16. Winston S. Churchill, *The Second World War*, Vol. V: *Closing the Ring* (Boston: Houghton Mifflin, 1951), p. 204.

17. Pogue, *George C. Marshall: Organizer of Victory*, p. 251.

18. Churchill, *Closing the Ring*, p. 150.

19. *PDDE,* II, pp. 1460–61.

20. Churchill, *Closing the Ring,* p. 208.

21. In late November, when Churchill again brought up the subject of an attack at Rhodes in the meeting at Cairo, General Marshall burst out, "God forbid if I should try to dictate, but not one American soldier is going to die on that goddamned beach." Pogue, *George C. Marshall: Organizer of Victory,* p. 307.

22. Churchill, *Closing the Ring,* pp. 211–12.

23. Ibid., p. 213.

24. Eisenhower to the Combined Chiefs of Staff, 9 Oct. 1943, *PDDE,* III, p. 1497.

25. Churchill *Closing the Ring,* p. 223.

26. Ibid., p. 224.

27. Dwight D. Eisenhower, unpublished manuscript, 24 Aug. 1976, pp. 41–44, in John S.D. Eisenhower, *Allies,* p. 389.

28. He made a short visit to the United States, it will be recalled.

29. *Crusade in Europe,* p. 220.

30. For some days the fate of the American invasion hung in the balance, and it was Tedder, not Marshall, who saved the day, finally wheedling some heavy bombers from British sources. See Marshall chapter.

31. Such was Ike's threat. I have always wondered what would have happened if he decided to go through with it.

32. *Crusade in Europe,* p. 243.

33. See John S.D. Eisenhower, *Allies,* p. 441.

34. Dwight D. Eisenhower, "Churchill & Marshall," Eisenhower Post-Presidential Papers, Dwight D. Eisenhower Library; cited in John S.D. Eisenhower, *The Bitter Woods,* p. 59.

35. *Crusade in Europe,* pp. 282–83.

36. John S.D. Eisenhower, *The Bitter Woods,* p. 77.

37. Churchill, *The Second World War,* Vol. VI: *Triumph and Tragedy* (Boston: Houghton Mifflin, 1953), p. 270.

38. On April 11, Eisenhower wrote Marshall: "I regard it as militarily unsound at this stage of the proceedings to make Berlin a major objective, particularly in view of the fact that it is only 35 miles from the Russian lines. I am the first to admit that a war is waged in pursuit of political aims, and if the Combined Chiefs of Staff should decide that the Allied effort to take Berlin outweighs purely military considerations

in this theater, I would cheerfully readjust my plans and my thinking so as to carry out such an operation." No such guidance ever came. President Roosevelt died almost as Ike was writing this message.

39. Churchill, *Triumph and Tragedy*, p. 468.
40. Butcher, *My Three Years with Eisenhower*, p. 864.
41. *PDDE*, VI, pp. 531–32.
42. Eisenhower to Churchill, 18 Dec. 1945, *PDDE*, VII, p. 651.
43. Eisenhower to Churchill, 16 Feb. 1949, *PDDE*, X, p. 495.
44. Eisenhower to Churchill, 21 Sept. 1950, *PDDE*, XI, p. 1330.
45. Ibid.
46. I do not believe I was included in the dinner given by General Ismay. If so, I have no recollection of it.
47. The late Queen Mother Elizabeth, or "Queen Mum" to the British.
48. Eisenhower Speech at English-Speaking Union, July 3, 1951. Courtesy of Eisenhower Library, Abilene, Kansas.
49. *PDDE*, XII, p. 415, n1.
50. Ibid., XII, pp. 414–15.
51. *Mandate for Change*, pp. 346–47. This proposal later led to the formation of the Southeast Asia Treaty Organization, or SEATO.
52. Cynics in the United States government always insisted that the British should never be given a veto power over American actions. Nehru, Prime Minister of India, had a mysterious hold over the British, and Mao Tse-tung, dictator of Communist China, had great influence with Nehru. Any claim that this sequence threatened a veto by Mao over the United States was far-fetched. However, it is undeniable that American policy toward Mao was much more hawkish than that of the British.
53. James Nelson, *General Eisenhower on the Military Churchill* (New York: Norton, 1970), p. 86.

EPILOGUE

1. See *Mandate for Change* (1963), *Waging Peace* (1966), and *At Ease* (1967). My memoir, *Strictly Personal* (1974), gives my own views of those years.
2. *Crusade in Europe*, p. 225.
3. *PDDE*, IV, p. 2696.
4. Marshall to Eisenhower, 8 May 1945, *PDDE*, VI, pp. 14–15.

BIBLIOGRAPHY

Ambrose, Stephen E. *Eisenhower,* Vol. I: *Soldier, General of the Army, President-Elect, 1890–1952.* New York: Simon & Schuster, 1983.

Blumenson, Martin, ed. *The Patton Papers, 1885–1940.* Boston: Houghton Mifflin, 1972.

————. *The Patton Papers, 1940–1945.* Boston: Houghton Mifflin, 1974.

Bradley, Omar N. *A Soldier's Story.* New York: Henry Holt, 1951.

Bryant, Arthur. *Triumph in the West, 1943–1946. Based on the Diaries and Autobiographical Notes of Field Marshal the Viscount Alanbrooke.* London: Collins, 1959.

————. *The Turn of the Tide. Based on the Diaries and Autobiographical Notes of Field Marshal the Viscount Alanbrooke.* New York: Doubleday, 1957.

Butcher, Harry C. *My Three Years with Eisenhower.* New York: Simon & Schuster, 1946.

Churchill, Winston S. *The Second World War,* Vol. II: *Their Finest Hour.* Boston: Houghton Mifflin, 1949.

————. *The Second World War,* Vol. III: *The Grand Alliance.* Boston: Houghton Mifflin, 1950.

————. *The Second World War,* Vol. IV: *The Hinge of Fate.* Boston: Houghton Mifflin, 1950.

————. *The Second World War,* Vol. V: *Closing the Ring.* Boston: Houghton Mifflin, 1951.

————. *The Second World War,* Vol. VI: *Triumph and Tragedy,* Boston: Houghton Mifflin, 1953.

Conner, Virginia. *What Father Forbade.* Garden City: Doubleday, 1951.

D'Este, Carlo. *Patton: A Genius for War.* New York: HarperCollins, 1995.

De Gaulle, Charles. *The Complete War Memoirs of Charles de Gaulle.* New York:

Simon & Schuster, 1972.

De Guingand, Francis. *Generals at War.* London: Hodder & Stoughton, 1964.

———. *Operation Victory.* New York: Charles Scribner and Sons, 1947.

Eisenhower, Dwight D. *At Ease: Stories I Tell to Friends.* Garden City: Double-day, 1967.

———. *Crusade in Europe.* Garden City: Doubleday, 1948.

———. *Eisenhower at War.* New York: Random House, 1987.

———. *Letters to Mamie.* John S.D. Eisenhower, ed. Garden City: Doubleday, 1978.

———. *The Papers of Dwight David Eisenhower* (21 Volumes). Baltimore: Johns Hopkins University Press, 1970–2001.

———. *The White House Years: Mandate for Change.* Garden City: Doubleday, 1963.

———. *The White House Years: Waging Peace.* Garden City: Doubleday, 1965.

Eisenhower, John S.D. *Allies.* New York: Doubleday, 1982.

———. *The Bitter Woods.* New York: Putnam, 1969.

———. *Strictly Personal.* New York: Doubleday, 1974.

Ewald, William Bragg. *Who Killed Joe McCarthy?* New York: Simon & Schuster, 1984.

Funk, Arthur Layton. *Charles de Gaulle: The Crucial Years, 1943–1944.* Norman: University of Oklahoma Press, 1959.

Giddings, Luther. *Sketches of the Campaign in Northern Mexico in Eighteen Hundred Forty-six and Seven.* New York: G. P. Putnam, 1853.

Hogan, David W., Jr. *A Command Post at War: First Army Headquarters in Europe, 1943–45.* Washington: Center of Military History, 2000.

Holt, Daniel D., and James W. Leyerzapf, eds. *Eisenhower: The Prewar Diaries and Selected Papers, 1905–1941.* Baltimore: Johns Hopkins University Press, 1998.

Macmillan, Harold. *The Blast of War, 1939–1945,* New York: Harper & Row, 1967.

Manchester, William. *American Caesar: Douglas MacArthur, 1880–1964.* Boston: Little, Brown, 1978.

Masson, Philippe. *De Gaulle.* New York: Ballantine, 1972.

Montgomery, Bernard Law. *The Memoirs of Field-Marshal the Viscount Montgomery of Alamein, K.G.* New York: World, 1958.

Murphy, Robert B. *Diplomat Among Warriors.* Garden City: Doubleday, 1964.

Nelson, James. *General Eisenhower on the Military Churchill.* New York: Norton,

1970.

O'Connor, Richard. *Black Jack Pershing.* New York: Doubleday, 1961.

Pogue, Forrest C. *George C. Marshall: Ordeal and Hope, 1939–1942.* New York: Viking, 1965.

———. *George C. Marshall: Organizer of Victory, 1943–1945.* New York: Viking, 1973.

———. *The Supreme Command.* Washington: Department of the Army, 1954.

Schoenbrun, David. *The Three Lives of Charles de Gaulle.* New York: Atheneum, 1966.

Sherwood, Robert. *Roosevelt and Hopkins: An Intimate History.* New York: Harper & Brothers, 1948.

Smith, Walter Bedell. *Eisenhower's Six Great Decisions: Europe, 1944–1945.* New York: Longman, Green, 1956.

Tedder, Arthur (Lord). *With Prejudice.* London: Cassel, 1966.

Truenfels, Rudolph L. *Eisenhower Speaks.* New York, Farrar & Straus, 1948.

ACKNOWLEDGMENTS

Any set of reminiscences written by a son about his father must needs be a one-man job. Nevertheless, in writing this short book I found myself turning once more to the three people who have helped so much on my last several books, my wife, Joanne, Professor Louis D. Rubin, Jr., and Mrs. Dorothy "Dodie" Yentz.

Joanne set aside her own prospective book on President Woodrow Wilson and British Prime Minister Herbert Asquith to assist with her usual editorial help and conceptual advice. She was invaluable in procuring difficult photos. Using her legal background, she acted as my agent. We have now been a team for five books.

Once more Louis Rubin has taken the time to go over the entire manuscript in its early stages, calling attention to any assertions of mine that might be questionable—often to my astonishment. But his greatest contribution has been to give encouragement when I entertained doubts as to whether this whole project was even worthwhile.

Dodie Yentz has, as always, been a tower of strength and stability. With her remarkable knowledge of grammar, rhetoric, and computers—not to mention a filing system I will never understand—she has always kept the "manuscript of record."

Kate Flaherty, of the Photo Section of the National Archives, went all out to make the difficult and vital task of photo procurement easy.

I am also indebted to McPherson Conner, grandson of General Fox Conner, for so quickly providing me with informal photos of the general.

David W. Hogan, Jr., of the Center of Military History, author of *A Command Post at War: First Army Headquarters in Europe, 1943–1945,* has provided perspectives on First Army Headquarters and their relations with Field Marshal Bernard L. Montgomery.

Robert T. Horvath and the staff of the Talbot County Free Library, Easton, Maryland, found books that have all but disappeared from the scene.

Jade Newman, of the Association of Graduates, West Point, helped in tracking down relatives of graduates.

Friends and especially family have offered help, encouragement, and offers to assist in such matters as publicity. These include my children, David, Anne, Susan, and Mary; my daughter-in-law Julie Nixon Eisenhower; General Andrew J. Goodpaster; Admiral William L. Read; General John H. Cushman; Colonel Charles M. Tyson; Louise Arnold-Friend; Daniel D. Holt and Stacy Menli of the Eisenhower Library, Abilene; and Mitchell Yockelson, of the National Archives. Special thanks go to Joe Davis and Rose Palombo.

Jim Enos, photographer, of Carlisle, Pennsylvania, is always ready to go out of his way to be of help.

Chris Robinson, cartographer, of Laurel, Maryland, did the same great job as he did on *Yanks.* A thoroughgoing professional, Chris is able to take a concept and make it appear vividly on paper. He is a pleasure to work with.

INDEX

Index

ABOUT THE AUTHOR

A graduate of West Point and retired Brigadier General in the Army Reserve, John S.D. Eisenhower has served on the U.S. Army General Staff, on the White House Staff, and as U.S. Ambassador to Belgium. He is the author of the *New York Times* bestseller *The Bitter Woods,* an account of the Battle of the Bulge, as well as *Allies: Pearl Harbor to D-Day* and, most recently, *Yanks: The Epic Story of the American Army in World War I.*